Grace and Peace

Grace and Peace

Essays in Memory of David Worley

EDITED BY
THOMAS H. OLBRICHT AND STAN REID

WIPF & STOCK · Eugene, Oregon

GRACE AND PEACE
Essays in Memory of David Worley

Copyright © 2017 Wipf and Stock Publishers. All rights reserved. Except for brief quotations in critical publications or reviews, no part of this book may be reproduced in any manner without prior written permission from the publisher. Write: Permissions, Wipf and Stock Publishers, 199 W. 8th Ave., Suite 3, Eugene, OR 97401.

Wipf & Stock
An Imprint of Wipf and Stock Publishers
199 W. 8th Ave., Suite 3
Eugene, OR 97401

www.wipfandstock.com

PAPERBACK ISBN: 978-1-5326-3547-2
HARDCOVER ISBN: 978-1-5326-3549-6
EBOOK ISBN: 978-1-5326-3548-9

Manufactured in the U.S.A.   SEPTEMBER 8, 2017

Contents

List of Contributors | *vii*

Acknowledgments | *xi*

1 David Worley as Husband and Father | 1
   —Melinda Worley

2 His Hands | 18
   —Heatherly Worley McDaniel

3 David Worley as Mentor | 20
   —Stan Reid

4 David Worley as Student | 34
   —Carl and Donna Holladay

5 David Worley as Entrepreneur | 50
   —Bob King

6 Memories of a Father | 63
   —Elena Worley Coggin

7 A Shepherd in Word and Administration | 68
   —Allan J. McNicol

8 David Worley as Churchman | 79
   —Charles K. Johanson

9   Living to the Praise of God's Glory:
    David Worley, Colleague | 96
        —Jeffrey Peterson

10 David Worley as Missions Promoter | 102
        —Charles Whittle

11 David Worley and the Mission of God | 110
        —Joel Petty

12 David Worley as Lecture and Teaching Planner | 128
        —Thomas H. Olbricht

13 David Worley as Worship Planner | 144
        —R. Mark Shipp

14 My Own Experience as a Friend | 156
        —Igor Egirev

15 David Worley as Teacher | 171
        —M. Todd Hall

16 David Worley as Fundraiser | 183
        —Royce Money

17 David Worley as Philanthropist | 191
        —Judy Siburt

18 The Center for Heritage and Renewal in Spirituality (CHARIS)
    at Abilene Christian University | 199
        —John B. Weaver

Images | 209

List of Contributors

Elena (Worley) Coggin is the youngest daughter of David and Melinda. She graduated in 2008 from ACU with a Bachelor of Science in international studies. She loves to create beautiful things whether it be sewing, painting, or music writing. She lives in Austin with her husband, Chris, and their three children.

Igor Egirev is a servant leader of the Neva Church of Christ, St. Petersburg, Russia, and president of the Christian Resource Center in Russia, which focuses on training leaders for Russian churches and spreading the gospel in Russia. He has received a certificate from the Institute of Theology and Christian Ministry, and an Master of Arts from St. Petersburg State University.

M. Todd Hall is assistant professor and director of the David Worley Library at Austin Graduate School of Theology in Austin, Texas.

Carl R. Holladay is Charles Howard Candler Professor of New Testament at Emory University's Candler School of Theology in Atlanta. He recently published *Acts: A Commentary* in the New Testament Library Series of Westminster John Knox Press.

Donna Holladay is retired from Greater Atlanta Christian Schools, where she began in 1980 as a first-grade teacher and then served successively as a counselor in the lower school, middle school, high school, and finally as director of counseling.

Charles K. Johanson is Minister of the Word and Adult Education at the Brentwood Oaks Church of Christ in Austin, Texas, where David Worley served as an elder beginning in 1998.

Bob King, member of Brentwood Oaks Church of Christ, former board member at Brentwood Christian School, former Bible Chair student leader, former "BBQ Pit Master" for the Friends of the Institute and Austin Grad, blessed by the friendship of the Worleys.

Heatherly (Worley) McDaniel, eldest daughter of David and Melinda Worley, graduated from ACU with a Bachelor of Science in home economics and a minor in early childhood. She owns Heatherly Hope Design, an interior consulting company. She resides in Austin, Texas, with her husband, Les McDaniel (CMO Commercial), and their four children.

Allan J. McNicol is emeritus professor of New Testament, Austin Graduate School of Theology, Austin, Texas. He was a faculty member during the tenure of David Worley.

Royce Money is chancellor and former president of Abilene Christian University. He is also on the faculty of the Graduate School of Theology at ACU, where he teaches in the areas of leadership and church history.

Thomas H. Olbricht is Distinguished Professor Emeritus of Religion, Pepperdine University. He served on the Foundation for Biblical Studies board in regard to the work in Russia. He was also a dean and professor at Abilene Christian. He has authored or helped edit twenty-five books.

Jeffrey Peterson is the Jack C. and Ruth Wright Professor of New Testament at Austin Graduate School of Theology in Austin, Texas. He was educated at Abilene Christian University, Princeton Theological Seminary, and Yale University. His published work concerns principally the letters of Paul and the Synoptic Gospels.

Joel Petty holds a Master of Arts in theological studies from Austin Graduate School of Theology. He has served in missions with Churches of Christ in Russia full-time since 1997. Joel partnered with David in several mission efforts in St. Petersburg, Russia.

Stan Reid is president of Austin Graduate School of Theology in Austin, Texas. He was blessed to be a student, friend, and colleague of David Worley.

R. Mark Shipp is the Pat E. Harrell Professor of Old Testament at Austin Graduate School of Theology in Austin, Texas. He is the editor of *Timeless: Ancient Psalms for the Church Today* and is the author of books on Isaiah and the Akkadian language.

Judy Siburt lives in Abilene, Texas. She is a retired high school counselor and for many years served in ministry to couples in crisis on the staff of the ACU Minister's Support Network. She is a longtime friend of David and Melinda Worley.

John B. Weaver is the Dean of Library Services and Educational Technology at Abilene Christian University, Abilene, Texas. A biblical scholar, he has published books both on the Acts of the Apostles and religious practices of reading for faith and learning.

Charles Whittle served as a missionary in Russia for fifteen years. He was a co-founder of World Christian Broadcasting Corporation (USA), the Christian Resource Center (Russia), and Vita International (Russia). He has published a book on his years in Russia, *The Chaotic Road to Russian Redemption*.

Melinda Ann Worley received a Bachelor of Science in elementary education from ACU and a Master of Arts in religion from Yale Divinity School. She has taught at ACU Campus Elementary School, Austin Graduate School of Theology, Brentwood Christian High School, and Brentwood Oaks Church of Christ. She was married to David R. Worley for forty-five years. They have three married daughters and eleven grandchildren.

Acknowledgments

DAVID WORLEY WAS AN important presence in the lives of many persons. He was mentor, teacher, administrator, shepherd, and supporter when needed. We are honored that David's family gave us permission to publish this volume of essays in his memory, and submitted essays themselves. David impacted our lives as he did all who wrote essays for this book. We are grateful for the time and effort expended by these authors. Many others would have gladly contributed. All of us will cherish memories of David into the distant future. We invite you to participate, through these essays, in the life of an uncommon man. David would never have commissioned a volume like this. He preferred that his skills and characteristics remain quietly in the background. But he himself insisted that we don't need to toot our own horn; God himself will lift us up. We assume therefore that David must approve the way in which, in this case by these essays, God has administered his accolades.

We express our heartfelt thanks to those who supported the publication of this volume with their gifts. These benefactors have blessed myriads of contemporaries and anticipated the impact of these words on coming generations. Farewell faithful friend and mentor—David Worley. We salute you for your work's sake.

Thomas H. Olbricht and Stan Reid

1

David Worley as Husband and Father

Melinda Worley

My family and I would like to thank Tom Olbricht, Stan Reid, and the other friends and colleagues who have written in this book; it will be a treasure to our family. David, however, would not have agreed to this book since it is about him, his commitments, and his way of life; he would not have enjoyed the attention on himself. I believe, though, that he would have appreciated the opportunity readers of this book might have to see the grace of God at work in one person's life and to praise the name of our Father above for it.

I've been asked to tell something of the man David Worley as I have known him for fifty-two of his sixty-seven years. He would have wanted me to say that what follows here is not what David accomplished but what God, by his grace, accomplished through David.

In that regard, I hope you will see here the beginnings of a life of faith, amidst false steps and imperfections. I believe I can look back at David's life and see how God prepared him, nurtured him, and equipped him to take advantage of the opportunities he was to be given to participate in the coming of the Kingdom. Indeed, I believe I could see some of it happening as it was lived.

As I tell this story, I will include some statements from family members and friends that help to illustrate David's character. I will focus on aspects that seem to have had the greatest impact on the people around him.

If I were to write a lionized version of David's life, he would have rolled his eyes at me and moved on to something else he found more interesting. So, I will say on his behalf that he was not perfect. For one thing, his communication style was based on the assumption that less is more, as anyone who has received one of his terse emails will testify. He often recited his grandmother's old adage from his childhood, "If you don't have anything important to say, then say nothing." Those of us who lived and worked with him would have preferred she'd kept that little gem of wisdom to herself.

David had strong, well-conceived convictions about most things he thought to be important and could articulate these convictions with enormous skill, particularly in written form and classroom lecture. In our family when our girls were young, these convictions largely went unchallenged. As the girls grew up, married, and had families of their own, they and their husbands each had to balance their own perspectives with David's, tempered by their love and respect for him. It was not easy to do with a father who is beloved, articulate, and has such a commanding presence, but each managed it successfully in his or her own way.

Also, David was fearless. When he began traveling to Russia in 1990, in that era of bread lines and unrest among her people, I was terrified. He called me from the hinterlands of one of Russia's eleven time zones; the phone connection was often very poor and characterized by odd clicking noises that, in my imagination, sounded surely like KGB wire taps, gathering information for his arrest and imprisonment in Siberia. But he couldn't understand that kind of fear. Our middle daughter, Christiana Peterson, remembers that her dad sometimes made light of such fears.

> There is a photo of my dad and me from the late 70s. I was a baby, perhaps just within reach of walking. My dad, his signature beard a little shaggier and a lot darker than it was in later years, holds out a mask for me to look at. I'm looking away from him with a smile but his hand gently placed on the back of my head indicates that he's trying to get me to face this strange carved creature that he's holding. This photo is innocuous on its own, but knowing what I know about my dad, I have always looked at that picture with a combination of irritation and amusement.
>
> I am quite sure that he would've been amused in the moment that photo was taken. I'm sure of this because I knew what he was trying to do: he wanted to see my reaction to a creepy troll-ish mask that some family member had brought back on one of his travels. Perhaps the mask was a relic of Scandinavian folklore . . . aimed at naughty children and intended to scare them into being good.

> I was mostly a well-behaved child, but I was quite fearful. I was desperately afraid of what crept about my room at night and in the grains of wood on my closet door in the dark, a fact that wasn't helped by my dad's amused introductions to me of scary images and stories.
>
> But I don't believe my dad was trying to scare me into being good. I don't know that he was trying to scare me at all. I think he was actually amused and a little baffled by my fears. He didn't understand why I was so afraid. So, his response was to show me what was behind the curtain, to amuse me out of my fear.
>
> I am not sure his tactics worked. I still struggled with fears well into adulthood. But I do wonder if his periodic insistence on showing me frightening things actually gave me the courage to face some of my own fears: fears like traveling the world and moving overseas as a single woman, knowing absolutely no one. I watched him do the same for years, and I knew there was something to be gained by stepping out into the unknown, even if it frightened me.[1]

Not only was I unnerved by David's travels to a place I once regarded as dangerous, I also worried about David's frequent absences and how that would affect our daughters and their relationship with him, and frankly I was mad at him about it for the first few years of his travels. After all, every parenting seminar I attended or book I read emphasized how important a daily relationship is between a father and his daughter. And I think each of our three girls struggled in her own way with this. But this brings me to another aspect of David's character. He almost never did anything, including parenting, the way other people thought it should be done. And, by God's grace, his unorthodox choices could sometimes be redemptive. Christiana wrote the following about traveling in this supposedly dangerous place with David and her older sister, Heatherly. Being in St. Petersburg and meeting the people her dad left home to see helped to shape her view of the world and the relationships people have with each other.

"What My Dad Didn't Teach Me"

Olga seemed old at the time, hobbled over by years of labor and sorrow. But it might be that I was just young, thirteen at the time, and everyone seemed old to me. I remember the darkness of her apartment on the outskirts of St. Petersburg, Russia:

---

1. Christiana Peterson holds a PhD in creative writing from St. Andrews University in Scotland. Her forthcoming book *Mystics and Misfits* will be published by Herald Press in 2018. She and her husband, Matthew, have four children..

the natural light streaming through the gaps in the curtains, the dusty red walls, the simple decor, and the table full of food.

When she got up to check the hot water on the stove, my sister and I noticed the flies buzzing around the food: cakes and treats, her best baking. I ate it anyway, not because of any mature understanding of hospitality but because I was hungry enough to eat.

My father had been traveling to Russia since the Soviet Union fell; starting the first Christian radio program in Russia since the collapse. He wanted his daughters to see where he'd been traveling, and to meet the people who had moved him so much.

Through a translator, Olga told us about her life. How her father had been stolen away in the night when she was a girl, then her husband too had disappeared, then her son killed in war. The secret police had stolen so many of the family members of people we'd met. There were tales of the famous horror of the Russian breadlines that stretched out for miles down the sidewalk, when food was scarce.

I don't remember my dad talking much to us afterwards about the high rises we visited on the outskirts of town or the Russian children's hospital where kids with broken bones were forced to spend months in a room they shared with dozens of other children, only because their parents couldn't afford to cart them back and forth to the doctor or care for them at home.

At Olga's house and in the other places we visited, I learned that suffering was a common experience that didn't deplete one's ability to offer the best of what they had. My dad visited Russia several months out of the year, becoming more and more comfortable blending into the culture he'd fallen in love with, befriending and learning from the people he met. But he never offered us an "us and them" narrative, or told us how blessed we were compared to them and weren't we wonderful for helping them? I could tell that his Russian friends didn't need him because he was wealthy; they loved him because he spent time with them and wanted to share his faith with them. Even though we missed him when he left, I also knew from an early age that it was our father who needed to be with the Russian people.

In Russia, I learned that we all need each other.[2]

---

2. This piece originally appeared on my blog christiananpeterson.com on February 7, 2017, two days before my dad's death. I sent it to him the morning that he died. I will never know if he got a chance to read it.

Though I had reservations at first about David's absences in faraway places, his sharing these experiences on occasion with his family and bringing people from those places into our home gave us all opportunity to see the world in exceptional ways. David's approach to life was unique, and his careful and creative use of words was no exception. He believed that words shaped character and clarified thinking. Christiana writes that her father's approach to words was life changing for her.

> My dad was very careful with words. He used phrases that became part of our family lexicon like "Sweet sleep" instead of "Good night." A word spoken to him in anger or frustration was met with the response: "Remember to give thanks to the Father above."
>
> He began church services and ended his emails with: "Grace and peace."
>
> And he infuriated hospital and hospice nurses near the end of his life when they asked, "What is your pain level today, Mr. Worley?" because he would reply the way he always did to a question about how he was doing: "I'm very blessed."
>
> My dad's language could sound strange, atypical, slightly off-kilter when you first heard it. His words were certainly apt to make you pause, reconsider, and wonder. And truthfully, I think that was his purpose.
>
> My dad loved words, but he was also a man of few words. As his daughter, and especially as a teenager, I found that his lack of words could be annoying; his cryptic one sentence or one-word email responses just weren't satisfying. I just wanted him to communicate like a normal person.
>
> But eventually, as I matured, I began to realize that what had frustrated me as a teenager was something that became a cherished part of who I was: Dad passed his love of words onto me. But I think I've come to the conclusion that my Dad didn't use words in the same way that I do, that most of us do: he didn't use them primarily to communicate a shared experience.
>
> Instead, he believed that using the most biblical language, the truest language, pushed him and the rest of us forward toward the Kingdom.
>
> My dad used words sparingly and very specifically because he believed that every word counted. Every word had meaning. Every word spoken had the capacity to reveal our true spirits and also change our hearts. And for those of us who knew him, his consistent use of Kingdom language revealed a gentle, generous, and unique man of God.
>
> I feel very blessed to be his daughter.[3]

3. Christiana delivered this piece at David's memorial service, February 18, 2017.

IN CHRIST TWENTY-FOUR HOURS A DAY

I met David Worley on his first day of high school choir at Eastern Hills High School in Fort Worth, Texas. It was our junior year, 1965. He was fifteen. We did not begin dating until the end of that year, but I remember vividly on the day I met him that he wore a plaid button-down shirt, a dark cardigan, and khaki-colored corduroy jeans that were a trifle too short. He had dark curly hair, beautiful green eyes, and tan skin. He was quiet in a crowd and smart, but had a ready laugh. I especially remember his low, resonant radio voice that I would later come to understand he had inherited from his father.

David's father had died unexpectedly a year earlier. That loss and the McKay melancholy inherited from his mother's side of the family would help to form his character, and give him both direction and challenges as he matured.

His family had assumed he would go to Texas Tech University as both his parents had. Then, they assumed, he would earn a degree in business and join his mother, Iva Lea, overseeing their radio stations in Austin, Lubbock, and Lovington, New Mexico. But David, newly baptized, was beginning to take a new direction. He often said in those high school years, "I just want to know what God's will is." He carried his black Bible with him when we went to church, and I could tell by looking at it and hearing him speak about what he read that he was reading it often. So, as a freshman at Abilene Christian College in 1967, he took one business course but began his work toward a BA in biblical Greek. He labored to understand what Scripture in its original language really said and what it meant in his life. We stayed on at ACC another year after we were married in 1971 so he could earn a master's in Old Testament under Dr. John Willis.

A year later, when we were living in New Haven, Connecticut, and David had begun an MDiv at Yale Divinity School, he started to ask a different question. He had come to believe that God's will for each of us is that we live faithfully, whatever our line of work. He often came to bed late at night, having spent ten to twelve hours on his studies. I would have gotten our little ones in bed and would be just about to fall asleep when he came to bed. He would lie back, look up at the ceiling in the dark, and ask, "What's worth pursuing in life?" Then, as he always could, he would fall asleep five minutes after his head hit the pillow. I felt compelled to lie awake in the dark and ponder the question for a little while, but David had been asking himself that question throughout the day. He had inherited his father's focus, intelligence, and ambition; he was trying to point these inclinations in a direction that would honor God.

By the time he had finished his PhD in New Testament at Yale eight years later, David had decided that the full-time academic life he had thought to pursue was not for him. David and I moved to Austin in July 1980, along with our two daughters, Heatherly, age five, and Christiana, age two. By December of that year he finished his dissertation on God's promises and oaths in Hebrews. He began then, after all, to learn the radio business alongside his mother, the station manager, Jim Ray, and his staff.

KOKE AM/FM called itself Sterling Country and was part of an Austin environment in which such notables as Willie Nelson began to make themselves known. The format had been in place years before David arrived. Over the next months, though, as he constantly listened to the format and that of the station's competitors, he became concerned about the lyrics of many country songs. He later said that the "I gotta get drunk" lifestyle suggested in the lyrics was inappropriate for his young daughters to listen to with him in the car, and he felt a responsibility for the lifestyle he was fostering in his listeners. He had begun to see that entertainment was a powerful shaper of character. Consequently, over time, he persuaded his mother to agree to change the format to adult contemporary, with carefully selected lyrics.

Naturally, the on-air people were unhappy with the change, and many of them left. It took a while for the station's ratings and sales to recover from the move. But David wasn't surprised there was a price to pay for the judgment he had made. It was an initial answer to the recurring questions in his early life about the will of God and the worthiness of daily pursuits.

While David sought answers to these questions in business, he also pursued them in academics and church life. Sometime in the 1980s, David asked me if I would like to work with him to develop a short lecture series he had entitled "In Christ Twenty-Four Hours a Day." He wanted us to think carefully about daily living and try to articulate what life in Christ would look like in the mundane tasks of the day. My assignment was to think about my own tasks this way, so I spent time considering, for example, how my managing the chaos of our busy, messy household could be illuminated by the fact that God tamed the chaos in creation and Jesus stilled the storm. It was a fresh perspective on such things and I enjoyed it very much. David found some wonderful Celtic Christian prayers for me to use that women had been praying for centuries as they lit the cook fire in the morning or swept the doorstep. This was one of many examples of the ways David frequently served as my spiritual and academic mentor. His encouragement was often life changing for me, beginning with his insistence that I apply to Yale Divinity School for an MAR while he was in his MDiv program there. I watched him in his role as a master teacher and tried to model my own teaching after his. I always tried to be present when he was teaching anywhere, in church or other settings, because I learned so much from him about the understanding and practice of the gospel as a seamless whole in one's everyday life.

It wasn't only in the mundane that David tried to live faithfully, but also in the more profound moments of life. Our son-in-law Matthew Peterson writes about the first discussion he had with David about just such an important matter.

> I had known David less than 24 hours when I asked for his blessing to marry his middle daughter, Christiana. I was living in Washington, DC, at the time and had flown down to Austin for a few days to attend the wedding of his youngest daughter, Elena. Not knowing when I would see him in person again and knowing that I wanted to ask Christiana to marry me soon, I decided that morning to speak with him.
>
> As we enjoyed the spicy food we both love at a Thai restaurant where he took me, I nervously asked him for his blessing to marry his daughter. David didn't seem concerned, as other fathers might have been, about the fact that I had only met his daughter in person a few months prior to our lunch. Nor did he give me a perfunctory blessing. Rather, David's primary concern and condition for marrying his daughter was rooted in something much more profound, the very things which anchored his own life: Scripture, Christ, the church, and sacrifice. "I will give you my blessing," he said, " . . . on the condition that you meditate on Ephesians 5:25 and what it means to love your wife as Christ loved the church."
>
> Through the months that followed, my initial meditation on Ephesians 5:25 gave me an understanding that a marriage should involve service and sacrifice to my wife, something I think David was certainly asking of me. But over time, as I have returned to this passage on various occasions, I have come to see that Paul, and likely David, was saying that marriage is about more than just two people. Marriage gives us a glimpse, a physical manifestation, of the mysterious union between Christ and the love he has for his bride, the church, the "great mystery" Paul mentions in verse 32 of this passage.
>
> David often answered my questions in ways I didn't expect, but ways that deeply affected and continue to affect my life and faith. Paul writes in Romans 12:2, "Do not be conformed to this world but be transformed by the renewing of your minds." I believe the reason David so rarely answered our questions the way we wanted, whether related to the mundane or something as consequential as marriage, was because David's thinking was

conformed less to the world around him and more to Scripture, which had both saturated and renewed his own mind.[4]

GENEROSITY

One evening while David and I were in high school, he came by my house to pick me up for a date. He and my mother were just finishing a conversation in the den when I joined them before he and I left. A day or two later, my mother told me that she and David had been discussing his feelings about his upcoming inheritance. He would receive a portion of his father's estate when he turned twenty-one. My mother was struck with how deeply David felt the responsibility of it and how great a burden it seemed to him. She said he had told her that he wished he could refuse it.

David's inheritance was certainly more than the average twenty-one-year-old young man would have to begin his life, profession, and family. His thirteen-year education would be paid for, from a bachelor's degree to a doctorate, as would my own master's. In addition, we were able to buy a house near the end of that time and start a family before some of our peers were able to. He made lots of mistakes in those early years. He learned to only play the stock market with money he was prepared to lose. He learned the hard way never to lend money to friends or family if the money was to pay off bad debt. He came to believe that it was best to gift the money, if a friend really needed it and if giving it would not enable bad habits or poor judgment. And he learned that, in spite of careful consideration, his trust in others could sometimes be misplaced. Our son-in-law Chris Coggin recalls such a situation.

> I began my career in business as a bookkeeper for many of David's businesses. Although I was twenty-three years old with almost no accounting experience, I knew something was strange about the way one of the managers was recording payments. David did not seem to share my concerns but told me to keep looking and call the manager with any questions. In my first call, I got a jargon-filled explanation. Over lunch later, I told David the manager had probably said something that explained the problem, but I wasn't sure what it was. This was one of the many times my conversations with David began with business and ended in laughter.

---

4. Matthew Peterson graduated from Abilene Christian with a Bachelor of Arts in international studies. He spent two years in Benin, Africa, with the Peace Corps. He is pursuing a Master of Ministry degree in a Mennonite seminary and is the pastor at a Mennonite church in the Midwest..

I called the manager every week for two months and asked him more questions but got no real answers. I finally told him I didn't believe what he was saying, and I needed a clear answer in writing.

The following day, the manager unexpectedly dropped by my office and sat down across from me. He put his head down and began weeping. After a few minutes, he took a breath and admitted to stealing thousands of dollars over multiple years. After he was done, he asked what I was going to do. I told him I had no clue, but I would call him the following day.

I had been gathering evidence of this theft for months and felt enormous validation and pride and was excited to tell David I was right about everything. So, before I called him, I researched every legal action we could take. He listened intently to the story with only an occasional "hmm." I talked through all the legal actions I found that would result in recouping every dime and ending the manager's career, until I finally ran out of breath.

I waited anxiously for David to shower me with gratitude for my great work, but there was only silence. I looked at my phone to make sure he was still there. I then heard him quietly say, "Always lean on the side of grace and mercy," and he hung up the phone. That moment was the first time of many that David elevated my understanding of how Christians should behave. To him, 1 Corinthians 6 was not a suggestion.[5]

David had come to believe that when he was taken advantage of by an employee he should forgive, because Christ had made his own forgiveness possible. In his paper "Occupations and Preoccupations," which David delivered for a conference on Christians in business, he wrote, "What is unique for the Christian employer . . . is the persistent effect on employee relations of remembering a heavenly Lord who forgave in Christ and remembering a Christ who loved and gave himself up" (Eph 4:32—5:2).

Another thing David learned was to recognize good causes addressed by good people in a prudent way. A year or so after we moved to Austin in 1980 and enrolled our oldest daughter, Heatherly, in kindergarten at Brentwood Christian School, David was asked to serve on the school's board. Under the extraordinary leadership of Marquita Moss, BCS was formulating a vision of Christian education that went well beyond the usual Christian school formula of offering regular academic classes but beginning each class with a prayer and having daily chapel. They were beginning to structure an

---

5. Christopher Coggin is married to Elena, the youngest Worley daughter. He holds a BBA and MBA. He teaches in the Acton School of Business, Austin, and is the president of Thelese Management.

education that was steeped in a Christian perspective through which the children could learn to view the world and all their experiences. This vision was similar to David's drive to live life faithfully in work, family, entertainment, and neighborhood. He became a contributor to the school and served several years as the chair of the BCS board.

In addition to his contributions to Brentwood Christian School, David also supported and encouraged other entities over the years, such as Austin Graduate School of Theology, where he served as president and later as chancellor, Abilene Christian University, and Eastern European Missions.

In 1990, David was invited to join Wesley Jones and others involved with World Christian Broadcasting (WCB) on a tour of Russia to meet long-time listeners to WCB's short-wave Christian programming broadcast across the Soviet Union. David had been a supporter of this work and was excited to meet those who had been touched by this ministry. In passing, David suggested they also schedule meetings with broadcasters in the cities they would visit, to get a feel of what opportunities might be available for further programming, since Russia was beginning to welcome foreign influence under their president, Mikail Gorbachev. What followed from this initial Russian trip was a new focus for David. His resources and his energies would subsequently be divided primarily among the work in Russia, his teaching and leadership at Austin Graduate School of Theology, and his eldership role at the Brentwood Oaks Church of Christ.

As David began to travel back and forth to Russia on a regular basis, another blessing was given to our family. At the death of David's father back in 1963, David's mother, Iva Lea, pulled him aside to tell him some shocking news. She said that Dave, his father, had been married before and had a daughter, Janet, a few years older than David. She told him this news because she knew that in the estate probate process Janet's name would come up. David didn't meet his half-sister at that time and knew almost nothing else about her.

Later, in the 1990s, as David had become active in Russia, one of the airline in-flight magazine staffers had contacted David for an interview about his initial broadcasting success on national Radio Russia. A small article about him appeared in the magazine. One afternoon, David received an odd phone call. The caller asked if he was speaking to the David Worley who traveled extensively in Russia. David said he was. The caller then said, "My name is Dick Drake, and I'm pretty sure I'm married to your sister." Dick had read the article and recognized David in the story. He took the article home to Houston, showing it to his wife, Janet, and encouraging her to call, but she was reluctant to do so. Dick offered to make the call for her. Subsequently, David flew through Houston on his next Russian trip to meet

Janet and her family. There were further visits now and again through the years: a wedding, a birthday celebration, and the like. But it wasn't until David's oncology visits to the Houston MD Anderson Cancer Center in 2015–2017 that the two began to spend time together, comparing memories about their dad, piecing together the way their lives were often parallel. David was grateful to have had the privilege of knowing this lovely, joyful, resilient woman, and to call her Sister.

Though David had begun to find an outlet for his resources, he had also learned to see all he'd been given as a gift from God and that, like all of God's gifts, it was to be enjoyed with gratitude. On his many travels he enjoyed exotic food, art, and music, the theatre (especially musicals); and dance. He was always generous with his family, giving gifts and planning family trips. He took me to Italy, for example, in April of 2015, scheduling private tour guides for the two of us as we toured the ruins of Rome, Herculaneum, Naples, and other locations, because he knew how much I love ancient archaeology. It was the best trip we ever took as a couple, and the last trip, as it turned out. He was diagnosed with cancer a month later.

"WEIRD WORLEY"

My family had just moved to Fort Worth before my sophomore year in high school, so I was still a new kid in school when David and I started dating. David, though, had gone to late elementary and junior high with many of the students we went to high school with and had quite a few good friends among them. As I got to know some of them, I realized that most of these people recognized that David was different from his peers but didn't seem to dislike him for it, as kids are sometimes inclined to do. Instead, his closest friends admired him for it. One of his best friends, Bill Stevens, sometimes teasingly called David "Weird Worley," but this epithet was always uttered with great affection and often with Bill's hand on David's shoulder.

During David's work on his master's degree at Yale Divinity School, he wrote a paper for a psychology of religion class entitled "Little Adults." These were people, as he described in his paper, who as children were always more comfortable with adults than with peers, and who would be chosen for special tasks in school, like crosswalk guards or hall monitors. They were the ones teachers would call on for answers in class and choose to be the line leader in elementary school. David was consciously describing himself.

In David's maternal extended family, there were his mother's two sisters and one brother, each married but with no children. His grandmother was a farm widow—bright, personable, and industrious—who greatly valued education. His own mother was a loving disciplinarian; his father a model of hard work and creative ambition in his profession. Among all these nine adults, David was the only child. He grew up as the center of attention, love, and admiration; but rather than being weakened or coddled by these circumstances, he became self-assured, even bold, and he absorbed the enormous expectations placed on him by these adults.

After David's mother, Iva Lea, died at age ninety-three, only nine months before his own death, our daughters and I found hundreds of pictures Iva Lea had saved. Among these were packets of Christmas pictures taken each year in front of the tree. They show a bright, growing boy, surrounded by unwrapped presents of puppetry, science, art, dance, music, books, and toys of all kinds. There were always family dogs to be seen and there were photos of five-year-old David in a cowboy costume on his grandmother's front porch and ten-year-old David in one of several costumes his mother had lovingly created for his dance recitals. There were pictures of the family taken at Uncle Raymond's lake house, where twelve-year-old David was allowed to drive the family Jeep up and down the dirt roads of the property. And there were photos of him playing in the snow with his parents in front of the various houses they lived in as his father pursued his broadcasting career. David seems to have lived the quintessential American postwar childhood.

But as David grew up in this loving extended family, there was also growing within him a solitary nature. He always had lots of friends and fun, but by the time I knew him as a teenager David had developed a separateness from his peers, an inclination to see life from a broader perspective, a wisdom and seriousness beyond his years, an openness to people who were usually overlooked, and an expectation that all might not turn out in life as one might hope. Since his father had died of a brain aneurysm at age forty-two, David assumed he too would be unlikely to live beyond that age. All of his maternal blood relatives for three generations developed some form of cancer, and David himself had witnessed their suffering—with the exception of his grandfather, who died before David was born. He died of the same form of cancer David would eventually succumb to. He grew to believe that life on earth is tenuous, to be enjoyed with gratitude but used to fullness in purposeful pursuits, ever to the praise of God's glory. These convictions defined his life and what he chose to pursue.

Though David was singularly different from those around him, people were often drawn to him. There was something in the way he related to people that made them connect with him. He told me once he had decided that people would much rather talk about themselves, especially when they are troubled, than hear what the other person in the conversation wanted to say. So, he began to listen more carefully. I teased him that he had missed his true profession; that he'd have made an excellent journalist because his questions were gentle but so probing. And he managed to have these exchanges almost always without revealing much about himself. My brother Bill recently told me that he would anticipate a conversation with David with the intention of focusing on David and what he was up to, but he always looked back on the exchange with the realization that David had kept him talking about himself. This practice on David's part reflected his understanding of people and their needs. It also was a way to protect his great sense of privacy, the solitary person that he was.

When David was appointed an elder at Brentwood Oaks Church of Christ, he accepted the role with some hesitancy. He said that a shepherd in a church was to be held responsible for the spiritual well-being of all its members. In our congregation of six to seven hundred people, he did not see how it would be possible to know each person's joys and struggles well enough to shepherd each; however, after David's death in February of 2017 several people from Brentwood Oaks stopped me or members of our family to say what a great friend David had been to them by meeting for coffee, by emailing or calling to ask after their health, or by stopping them in the hallway to ask about a struggling child or parent. Quietly, persistently, he pursued his responsibility to know and listen to those whom he was to shepherd.

When David was diagnosed with cancer in 2015, I knew our church, our friends, and our family would pray for us and support us for as long as we were in need. What I did not expect was the degree of grief that so many of these people seemed to feel at his illness. To put it another way, I knew we were cared for, but I didn't know how beloved David was to all these people. All of the coffee visits, emails, calls, and listening he had been doing through the years was something he had rarely talked about. I had no idea he had developed all these relationships with people who needed him. As all this became clearer to me through his illness, I began to marvel that, by God's grace, he had behaved so directly against his solitary nature, out of his love for the church and her people. This realization was a great blessing to me as David's illness progressed and people continued in daily, fervent prayers.

David's listening and guiding was not limited to church members or colleagues. Randy Boggs, a casual acquaintance who had become a friend, wrote the following message to our family just after David's death.

> I was never a student in one of David's classes, or a member at a church he shepherded. I didn't attend a seminar or conference at which he spoke. I am just a random guy that he met briefly at a business meeting. He had such a generous heart and wise

countenance that I continued to seek him out many times over the course of 25+ years. He helped guide me through both painful and victorious moments (counseling me in the aftermath of my father's murder, persuading me to forgive the murderer, assisting me in leading colleagues to faith, teaching me to pray through the day making the routine sacred). On behalf of all the "random guys" like myself that had brief but spiritually renovating encounters with this great man, I offer my sincerest thanks to Melinda and all the rest of your treasured family.[6]

YOUR WILL BE DONE

During our senior year in high school, David was a leader in his youth group, overseen by Dale and Carolyn Wilson at Meadowbrook Church of Christ. Some of the adults in the church recognized David's seriousness about his faith and encouraged him in speaking, leading devotionals, and praying in assemblies. Maggie Warren, his fifth-grade Sunday school teacher, told him several times over the years that she prayed for him every day. Meadowbrook was a good beginning for him as a young Christian. Later, when we were at Abilene Christian College and then at Yale, David made and kept a promise that he would never skip church for his studies. The promise was part of his developing commitment to love the church. This commitment deepened over time.

At Minter Lane in Abilene and later at the Hamden Church of Christ in Connecticut, David actively led and planned the Sunday morning assemblies and taught classes. He continued these activities in Austin at the Brentwood Oaks Church of Christ, where he eventually became an elder, teacher, and a frequent assembly planner. He worked with a committee of elders and ministers to develop the Bible study curriculum for adults and teens, creating a four-year cycle in which it was intended that all the books of the Bible were to be studied by at least some members in the various services and Bible studies of the church. Many Brentwood members have said that, over time, this focused scriptural study profoundly nurtured their maturity in faith.

Though David had decided against a full-time academic life of teaching and writing in biblical studies, his training in the field had shaped him profoundly. His deepening understanding of the story of God's love, and particularly of Paul and his letters, were central themes of his teaching in the church as well as in the academic classes he taught from time to time

---

6. Used by permission.

at Abilene Christian University, Pepperdine University, and Austin Graduate School of Theology. Recovering the use of the Psalms in the church's worship was a passion he shared with Mark Shipp, Mel Witcher, and other colleagues, musicians, and singers, which culminated in the Timeless Project he supported—collections of original compositions of the Psalms, printed and recorded for use in church assembly. Weeks before his death, he and another colleague and friend, Woody Woodrow, published "Learning to Love God," a collection of scripts David originally wrote to be read to Russian Radio audiences in the 1990s. These are brief commentaries on each book of the Bible, written for those who had never read the Bible nor heard its stories.

But one particular passage that he returned to frequently, both in his teaching and in his own practice of faith, was the Lord's Prayer. He believed that our heart's desires are shaped by the prayers we earnestly pray. In a sermon he delivered in 2013 about the Lord's Prayer, he said, "Saying the Lord's Prayer daily in our closet reinforces our orientation toward God's Kingdom and His righteousness."

David was first diagnosed with gastric cancer in June of 2015. When we told our children about the diagnosis, our youngest daughter, Elena, asked David what he wanted us all to pray. "Pray that God's Kingdom will come in this, as in all things," he said. I'm sure he was thinking about that phrase in the prayer, "Thy Kingdom come." As he said in that sermon, when we pray those words, "We are asking the Father to indeed let His rule be fully realized and felt everywhere in every way . . . even in our future plans."

But there are also these other words: "Your will be done." Again, in the sermon, connecting this phrase to Gethsemane, he said, " . . . as His children, the Father so wants us to learn to accept His purposes in creation, which in becoming like him . . . entails suffering." And suffer David did—ferociously, and, in the beginning, not always patiently. But in his directing the members of our family to pray this prayer for him, amid all our other prayers, he led us to see his illness, suffering, and death in a different light: in the light of the cross to which we are each called. In praying it for himself, he seemed to have found a way to endure it with grace. And he led us to a deeper understanding of God the Father, who is the provider of water and manna in the desert.

As I think of David now, as I remember our life together, it's hard to think about him and his influence on me without thinking about the powerful impact his Christian life had on my own. He is inseparable in my mind from that faith. As a married couple, we certainly had our struggles through the years. But, in spite of these struggles, and sometimes during them, God spoke to me often and eloquently through David.

There was a time many years ago when David was speaking about the Lord's Prayer to our congregation, particularly about Jesus' instruction to pray, "Forgive us our debts as we forgive our debtors." As he continued to speak, I began thinking about anyone whom I had not yet forgiven. I suddenly realized that the person in my life I needed to forgive was David. There was no great injustice that had happened between us. It was just the resentment that can accumulate in a marriage over differences and perceived slights. I never told him about that moment, but it was a turning point for me in our married life. I came to understand that the normal struggle in marriage for Christians is a spiritual struggle, a laying aside of what we want for ourselves in preference for what is best for the other. And it is in forgiveness that we are healed in order to lay aside what we must.

So, by God's grace, I came, over time, to see our marriage and David's choices from a broader picture; to see that the Father above had gifted him in unique ways to travel, often over great distances, to speak boldly so that God's Kingdom could grow. David's solitary nature, his bold and unconventional choices, his resources, his training, his vision, and his faith all contributed to his usefulness for the task. And I grew to rejoice in that.

Now that David is gone, I miss him, of course, for many reasons. But I feel his loss the most when I need his words of grace and peace. It is perhaps an unusual arrangement in a marriage, but it was true in ours. I will ever be grateful for it.

2

His Hands[1]

Heatherly Worley McDaniel

Holding mine

Lifting in prayer and praise to the Father, cupping the two toward heaven

Wrapping each of our hands, walking us down the aisle and handing us off to another

Holding each of his grandchildren's tiny hands with joy

Pulling a rolling bag through many airports, airplanes, countries, cities, hotels, and homes around the world

Pushing each of us forward when we didn't move quickly enough

Driving us for many hours in jeeps in the mountains, cars in the rolling hills in Scotland and Ireland, rain forests in New Zealand, and biblical sites in Greece

Rolling his wedding ring around his finger

Clasping his tiny grey-blue Greek Bible to and from church

Putting on and pulling off one of three glasses frames that he had chosen to wear

Sharing a plate of food in countless restaurants

Teasing his grandchildren when pretending to remove his thumb in disbelief of the magic trick

Holding a book to add to his collection

---

1. Delivered at David's memorial service, February 18, 2017

- Typing on his computer letters of encouragement, love and support, business plans, and travel plans
- Opening the door to his office, signaling to us by the way it creaked at its hinges he was gracing us with his presence
- Chasing his grandchildren as to grab and tickle them
- Picking up and dropping donuts off on our front porch just because it's Saturday
- Placing three presents in a bag for his three daughters to fight over for Christmas
- Eating three tacos with habanero peppers fully loaded and then going back for seconds
- Picking up an extra-large cup of black coffee at a new local coffee shop
- Lifting an extra-large glass of iced tea to his mouth every evening that mom had prepared
- Putting his hand on my sisters growing belly to say a prayer
- Grabbing the hand of Carla his hospice nurse to say thank you
- Touching and holding my mother's hand as she sat next to his bed
- Then
- His hands
- Cold to the touch with purple fading at the fingertips
- Released hands to sleep and spirit to rest

3

David Worley as Mentor

Stan Reid

Like many others, I was drawn to David Worley the first time I met him. He was personable, intelligent, and articulate. While exuding confidence and authority, David also displayed genuine interest in people. I vividly recall my initial encounter with David. It was during the first term of summer school at Abilene Christian University in 1978. David, a doctoral candidate in New Testament at Yale University, had been invited to teach a graduate-level New Testament seminar. The course was "Exegetical Seminar in the Epistles." I was one of a half-dozen or so graduate students eagerly waiting to meet this "bright and promising young scholar." That is how our professors had described David.

The class began with the perfunctory personal introductions. As the students introduced themselves, David engaged each one with general questions. When it was my turn, David surprised me with a specific question that caught me off guard. It was not the last time that he would surprise me with an incisive question.

When I mentioned that I had graduated from high school in Lovington, New Mexico, David asked me if I knew Hoyt Caldwell. I was stunned that he knew anything about my small hometown in southeastern New Mexico, much less that he would know who the station manager was of the local radio station, KLEA.

After collecting myself, I replied, "How in the world do you know Hoyt Caldwell?" With his signature smile, David replied in his mild voice, "Let's talk after class." With that gentle deflection of my question and by postponing the conversation until after the class was dismissed, I immediately grew to appreciate the social awareness with which this "bright and promising young scholar" handled himself. In delaying our conversation until a more private moment, David demonstrated that all students would be on equal footing with him. Whatever common ground that he and I had because of connections to Lovington would not affect any of the other relationships in the classroom. David showed much social grace in that he protected himself and me from any appearance of special interest or partiality. In the classroom, he was the professor and all of us were the students.

In the private conversation after class, David told me that his family was in the communications business. It was my first encounter with David's aversion to pretension and how he was always careful when speaking about himself. During the conversation, David never mentioned that his late father had been the principal in founding a number of radio stations across Texas and New Mexico.

A special bond did develop out of our first private conversation. In some ways, that was surprising. David and I had grown up in different worlds. Through his father and mother's business dealings, David had come of age in the presence of powerful entrepreneurs, influential politicians, and famous entertainers. I, on the other hand, had grown up among the farmers, ranchers, and oil field workers of eastern New Mexico. Yet, David treated me as his equal. That is what happens when one's perspective on the world and its people has the cross of Christ as its focal point.

David was not much older than his students. But the opportunities granted to David by his encounters with powerful and influential people during his youth had not been wasted. He immediately took command of the class. His academic acumen enabled David to guide us deep into the nuances of the Greek text of Paul's Letter to the Ephesians, its historical circumstances, and its theology.

However, within the first few days it became clear that this class would be more than an academic exercise. Thirty-nine years later, I still remember how David's interpretation of Ephesians 1:3–14 during that first week of class was not only exegetically intense and intellectually stimulating, but also a worship experience. He showed us how those verses were fundamentally a prolonged prayer, with phrase after phrase extolling the glorious grace of God's actions accomplished in the Lord Jesus. In effect, his personal assimilation of Paul's intent in this ancient letter inspired David to lead his students into the very presence of God. He guided us into a sense of the praise and gratitude that should be stimulated by careful Bible study. The bland concrete walls and floors of that classroom became, in a sense, a magnificent chapel for those six weeks in the summer of 1978.

That is not to imply that rigorous scholarship was not at the heart of the class. The sessions were demanding, as an exegetical seminar should be. All of the assignments were challenging. I remember how I struggled with the topic David assigned me for my seminar paper. Since it would be read before him and my peers, I was anxious. David knew that and came alongside me. He gave me specific guidance in my efforts to write responsibly and accurately. In the end, I left the course refreshed, inspired, and encouraged.

David made himself available outside of the classroom as well. All of his students were given access. Many of us seized the opportunity for private conversations. These discussions were such a blessing that I did not want to see the term come to an end. I wanted to be around this man more. I didn't know what a mentor was at that time. But, in effect, I wanted David to mentor me. I wanted to spend more time with him in order to absorb his knowledge and drink from the overflow of his unassuming and humble walk with the Lord.

David returned to Yale to finish his doctorate. But I reached out to him and we started a correspondence that would see us through my move to Las Cruces, New Mexico, to become the campus minister at the Church of Christ Bible Chair at New Mexico State University. David would soon move to Austin, Texas, to take over management of his family's radio station, KOKE. He and his wife, Melinda, immersed themselves in the life of the Brentwood Oaks Church of Christ. It proved to be a lifelong commitment.

David and I continued an infrequent correspondence with one another over the next few years. Then in 1983 I became the preaching minister for Northside/Hyde Park Church of Christ in Austin. This allowed me to continue to draw near to David in order to learn from him and to be nurtured by his gentle grace, which seemed to have grown even more. During this time, I never said to David, "I want you to be my mentor." David never said to me, "I want to be your mentor." At that point, our relationship was more like that of a mentor and a protégé, but in time that changed.

Within a few years David began to treat me more as a peer and conversation partner. On my side, it would take a number of years before I ever looked at the relationship from that vantage point. But the knowledge that David loved me like a brother, was interested in my growth as a Christian and minister, and was always willing to invest time in me became a sustaining grace in my life. That is what a mentor does.

I was not alone in experiencing that grace. There are dozens, if not hundreds more, who can tell stories similar to mine. David's family gave me access to the emails that began flowing in upon the announcement of his passing. I read account after account about how others were drawn to David as I had been. They saw something in him that made them want to spend time with him, hoping that they might be able to think, act, and live like he did. In other words, they wanted to be mentored by David. The stories revealed how he had quietly and confidentially advised, encouraged, or corrected them much as he had me.

A few comments about mentoring would be in order. In the last half of the twentieth century, *mentoring* became a buzzword in business management. Mentoring occurs when a relationship is established between a person with knowledge and skills in a particular field (mentor) and another person who needs or wants to grow in knowledge and skills in that field (protégé). The key word in the process is *relationship*.

Of course, family members, and especially parents, have considerable impact on whom we become. This can be for both good and bad. But most of us have other people who came into our lives and had a profound effect on us. We might choose them, or they might choose us. The mentor knows what we need and intentionally chooses to nurture a relationship that aims to encourage and guide us so that we grow and change.

The relationship can be formal or informal. It is usually done through face-to-face conversations and hands-on experience. For example, Dwight Eisenhower has been quoted as saying that he watched closely to discover the smartest, most efficient, and competent officer on every military base where he was assigned. He then took every opportunity he could to be near that officer in order to watch, listen, and learn.

A key component of a successful mentorship is for the mentor to listen as much as speak. David had incisive listening skills. It was not unusual for him to spend more time listening than talking. In our conversations, he always asked provocative and probing questions. His careful listening enabled him to process information quickly and precisely.

I remember a back-to-school party my wife, Laynne, and I hosted at our house. David took up residence on a stool at the kitchen counter where the refreshments were being served. Students, faculty, and staff were regularly coming through the kitchen. Laynne stayed in the kitchen as the host. But she also got to see firsthand how David would draw a person he did not know into conversation. Some might call it buttonholing, but it was not. David was not trying to influence the person to do something he wanted. Rather he was focused on the other person, trying to learn as much about the person as he could. It was genuine interest.

That interest intensified when he could have time with a person over coffee. David always had a new coffee house at which to meet. I remember many of those conversations over coffee. Some were initiated by him. I instigated others. David typically took the lead. There was rarely much small talk. However, David was always interested in how I, my family, and my colleagues at the school were doing. Even those aspects of the conversation were seasoned by provocative and probing questions. David always led me to think more deeply about an idea, relationship, or practice. The conversation would lend itself to matters of the spirit and faith without becoming sanctimonious or arcane.

I am convinced that David's ability to listen intuitively was the strongest aspect of his mentoring work. In addition, he could direct the conversation in non-threatening ways so that the person would have an opportunity to grow. But I also believe that David wanted to test his ideas and convictions. The best mentors do not look to gain followers, but aim to develop leaders. If a protégé had knowledge or insights that David did not, David was willing to become the learner. It was like iron sharpening iron.

As I write, I sense David looking over my shoulder. If he were here to give me direction in what should be written about him as a mentor, I'm not sure that David would want to be described as a mentor. One of David's most admirable characteristics—some might say that it was a quirk—was his careful attention to the use of words. For example, David quickly and firmly, but gently corrected me the first time he heard me say that I was *fortunate* to have something. For him, using that word would be to ascribe, if not succumb, to the pagan belief of being controlled by the fortunes of fate. For David, Christians are never fortunate or lucky, but rather blessed and graced by the Creator and Sustainer of the universe, who revealed himself as our Father through the incarnation of Jesus.

Therefore, I expect that David would have preferred some word other than mentor as the descriptor of his efforts to nurture and shape people. I would add that David certainly did not want to be addressed as "Doctor Worley." He could have worn that title with pride. A PhD from one of the most prestigious universities in the world granted him "all the rights, privileges, and immunities there unto appertaining."

However, David intentionally refused to presume on those rights, privileges, and immunities granted to one who earned a doctor of philosophy degree. He never used that title to identify himself in conversation or correspondence. In a conversation with him about advanced academic degrees and titles, David once expressed his dismay about how academic accomplishments led some to pride and pretension. That awareness led him to be on guard against falling into that trap and to be concerned for those who did. He was genuinely humble about his accomplishments. For him, all the glory was given to the Father above.

I expect that David may have chosen another word instead of *mentor* to describe his work with people. His speech was always intentionally seasoned with biblical terminology. I think the word David may have chosen would be *shepherd*. The shepherd metaphor is used widely in the Bible. David often used the term to describe the essence of his person and his work. His shepherding instinct began with his family first. It then extended to his church family and narrowed to the individuals he mentored.

For me, the word shepherd is certainly descriptive of David's approach to mentoring. A shepherd leads a flock. The sheep are led to nourishing food, good water, and safe shelter. The shepherd also disciplines wayward and stubborn sheep. Lost ones are sought and brought back to the fold, and injured ones are carefully attended. As a mentor, David exemplified all of those qualities of vigilant and tender care for those under his leadership.

Although David might have preferred a term other than mentor for the reasons given above, I will proceed with the theme of David as mentor. The Apostle Paul stands as a fine example of a Christian mentor. Mentoring was at the heart of Paul's ministry. The essence of Paul's approach is expressed in 2 Timothy 2:2: "And what you have heard from me through many witnesses entrust to faithful people who will be able to teach others as well" (NRSV).

The context of that passage is that Timothy was working with churches that were beset by teaching that was deviating from the basic principles of the apostolic gospel that Paul had carefully handed down to the churches. Just as the Lord had entrusted Paul with the gospel, Paul was entrusting it to faithful people like Timothy. In turn, Timothy was to seek out faithful people and entrust the gospel to them so that they could pass it on to others.

It was a difficult setting in which Timothy was to accomplish his assignment. Personal spiritual strength gained from God's empowering (see 2 Tim 1:7) was needed in order to face the challenges. It was also of utmost importance that Timothy remembered and adhered to the particulars as well as the core of message he had received from Paul. It was critical for the church's present health and future well-being. Timothy and others mentored by Paul needed to correctly handle the gospel message while communicating it courageously and faithfully.

David was one of the successors in this line of authentic apostolic succession as described by Paul. The nature of apostolic succession is often debated. But this passage favors the view that the gospel message itself is the succession more so than those who teach it. Apostolic succession is the handing down of the apostles' doctrine intact and undiluted from generation to generation, like a baton being handed from one runner to another in a relay race. David was one of those sought out by one from a preceding generation to take the baton.

More than once David told me how Professor J. W. Roberts led him to change his major in college from business to New Testament Greek. Although a declared business major, his interest in the Bible and spiritual things led David to approach Roberts with the request to enroll in his introductory Greek course. Roberts not only welcomed David into the class, but also pressed him into majoring in Greek. The rest is history. Just as Roberts had pressed David into changing his major, David would become someone who was not timid about asking others to change plans or direction in order to better serve in God's Kingdom.

David would have several other mentors through the years, including another beloved professor. In a number of our conversations, David spoke fondly of Nils Dahl, who directed David's dissertation at Yale. David was one of Dahl's last students. Dahl concluded his teaching career at Yale in 1980. He soon returned home to Norway. However, David continued to visit his teacher and mentor in Norway for the next twenty years. Dahl died in 2001. More than a decade later, David would still mention that he missed his conversations with his beloved mentor.

What David had received from faithful Christian teachers and mentors, he strove to faithfully pass on to others, especially those in the coming generations. Just as Professor Roberts had pressed him into the study of Greek, David pressed many others into Christian service. I remember in that first class in 1978 that David urged his students to use their biblical scholarship in service to the church. He pressed us to write in such a way that it could be published in one of the periodicals written for preachers and church members. In other words, he urged us to write not for academic specialists but for people in the pew and those preaching and teaching people in the pew.

With the message of 2 Timothy 2:2 in mind, I think that David comes as close to emulating the Apostle Paul as any Christian I have known. He, like Paul, was passionate about serving God. The love of Christ compelled him (see 2 Cor 5:14). Observing David closely for nearly four decades allowed me to discern that everything he did was done in the name of Jesus, through the power of the Holy Spirit, and to the glory of God. That meant that David strove to fulfill the first commandment, to "love God with all your heart, and with all your soul, and with all your mind." David's efforts were also driven by what Jesus identified as the second commandment, to "love your neighbor as yourself" (see Matt 22:36–40).

That dual focus also shaped David's tenure as president of Austin Graduate School of Theology. The school's mission statement was written while David served as its president. I expect that David had a part in shaping our school's stated mission "to promote the knowledge, understanding, and practice of the Christian faith by equipping Christians and churches for service in the Kingdom of God." This institutional mission statement reflects David's personal mission focus.

As a mentor, David stressed and modeled Paul's passion for mission. David was compelled to promote, support, and participate in local and global mission efforts. Those efforts are addressed in other essays in this volume. He, like Paul, was a vocational missionary. David's financial support was generous and his encouragement was constant. Like Paul, he carried a daily concern for all the churches he nurtured around the world (see 2 Cor 11:28).

Paul said, "Be imitators of me, as I am of Christ" (1 Cor 11:1; cf. 4:16; 2 Thes 3:9; Heb 6:12; 13:7). I never heard David say, "Imitate me, as I imitate Christ." However, the silent example of his life was stronger than words (see 1 Pet 3:1). The context of Paul's appeal lies in the circumstances surrounding First Corinthians. Paul challenged a rampant spiritual conceit among some of the church members by holding up the cross of Christ and the self-abasement and humility it demands. The cross stood in stark contrast to the proud attitudes and boastful speech of those challenging him and his message. Paul was stressing that the cruciform nature of the Christian life is worked out practically when the common good of the Christian community and the welfare of each fellow believer are given precedence over one's self-interest.

David worked hard to embody the cruciform life in every aspect of his daily existence. Once again, without ever saying a word to draw attention to himself, David's personal example cried out, "Be imitators of me, as I am of Christ." Such is expected of a Christian mentor. David was alert to discover the next generation of Christian leaders. When he found one who showed promise, David might press or even cajole them, in the sense of gentle urging, into service. The pressing and cajoling was for a much greater purpose and service. It was so that the apostolic gospel would be passed to succeeding generations. David had reaped the blessings and benefits of a life given in service to the Lord Jesus. He had tasted that the Lord is good and wanted those blessings and benefits to be enjoyed by others (see 1 Pet 2:3; cf. Psa 34:8). So David's pressing and cajoling put him in the line of succession for the practice of Christian mentoring used by Paul, but begun with the Lord Jesus.

David's imitation of Jesus sustained him and carried him to the doorstep of death. As I have implied, the trajectory of my relationship with David moved from that of student, to protégé, to friend, and finally to colleague. But with David's illness and death, I moved back into the role of protégé. David once again became my mentor, teaching me the meaning of preparing for a good death.

When David informed me of his cancer diagnosis, I was stunned. Like all who knew and loved David, I began praying for his healing. But I also knew that David would have preferences for what we prayed. I asked him what he would have me pray. His reply was, "Consecrated be His name . . . be done His will on Earth as it is in heaven . . . " Once again, David's words were shaped by biblical language. David's prayer was his own translation of the prayer Jesus taught his disciples to pray (see Matt 6:9–13; Luke 11:2–4). His death, like his life, would be a conscious attempt at complete submission to God.

Thus, David was saintly. He was a saint in the New Testament sense of the word. All Christians are called saints. A saint is one who is called to be separated from sinful and selfish thinking and behavior, and separated for self-sacrificial thinking and behavior. Christians cannot accomplish this transformation on their own. It requires the power of God that raised Jesus from the dead. David, like the rest of us, was powerless to transform himself. Like the rest of us, he continued the daily struggle to be transformed into the image of Christ (Rom 8:29). However, I've never known anyone who wanted to become like Jesus more than David did.

The last time David and I sat down for a face-to-face visit was on November 3, 2016. Neither of us knew that it would be the last time we would be in each other's company. There were emails and text messages after this, but this last visit was special.

I took charge of the conversation at the beginning. I said to David, "I know that you don't like to talk about yourself, but today we are. I want to know how you are doing." David then said, "Actually, I am not opposed to talking about myself or my situation." For several minutes, he spoke about the current state of his health—that the chances for him to be included in a medical trial were not looking positive, and that without such treatment the cancer would continue to have free reign in his body. He spoke with clinical precision about how his life would likely end. Some would have probably heard this as the words of a Stoic. But I knew they were coming from a man whose heart and mind was so immersed in Christ Jesus that he knew the peace of God that passes understanding (see Phil 4:7).

David lived and died in the Christian hope of the resurrection. The announcement of his death read in part, "David Worley Jr. fell into sweet sleep in the LORD Jesus on February 9th" and was "buried in a private family service to await the resurrection of the body. A memorial will be held on Saturday, February 18th at Brentwood Oaks Church of Christ."

I believe that the memorial service for David also lends insight to why and how David mentored. He left an outline and brief instructions for the memorial service. David titled the memorial service "Sabbath Worship, Buried, Awaiting the Resurrection." The instructions called for two brief exhortations to be given during the service. It is clear that the exhortations arose from the Great Commandment given by Jesus and the second one like it. First, we are called to love God with our entire being. Second, we should love our neighbor as we do ourselves. I believe that David wanted the memorial service to serve as his personal faith statement and to stand as a last will and testament as he once again led us into worship. He was mentoring to the end.

At the beginning of the service, David directed that the words of Christian greeting "Grace and peace from God the Father and our Lord Jesus Christ" be spoken to the congregation. Because of David's influence, those words of Christian greeting have been spoken at the beginning of every chapel service and event held at Austin Grad for decades. This was consistent with David's insistence that worship should have a vertical focus.

David was not indifferent toward the horizontal dimension of worship. However, he recognized a danger (i.e., when a horizontal focus dominates we are likely worshiping the creature rather than the Creator). In connection with that conviction, David left instructions that his "autobiography" was not to be read during service. The obituary written by David was again marked by humility and grace. All the glory belonged to God.

The vertical focus was continued when the following words were read immediately after the Christian greeting:

> We are gathered here because of one man; a man known personally to many of us, known only by reputation to even more; a man loved by many, questioned by others; a man known for great controversy and for great compassion.
>
> That man, of course, is Jesus of Nazareth. It is he whom we proclaim: Jesus Christ, Son of the Father, born of the virgin Mary, crucified, buried, risen, seated at the right hand of the Father. It is because of his life, death, and resurrection, that "we do not mourn as those who have no hope," but in confidence we commend David Worley to the mercy of God.

Politically astute readers might recognize this as being very similar to the opening remarks given by Paul Scalia in the eulogy for his father, Justice Antonin Scalia. David evidently filed away the quote and then chose to have it included in his memorial service. When Melinda invited me to review the order of worship with her and I began reading the lines quoted above, I thought to myself, "This is so unlike David." Then I found a smile forming when I read the line, "That man, of course, is Jesus of Nazareth." I then thought, "This is so like David, and he got me—again!"

The first exhortation in the memorial, per David's instructions, was under the simple heading "Love God." He wanted the second exhortation to be "Love the Brethren." Under each heading David listed three ways in which he had been blessed to serve God and the church. David was keenly aware that he was a blessed man. He also believed that those blessings were a trust and that he was to use them in service to God and others.

David instructed that the first exhortation was to be based on Deuteronomy 6:4–9. In his notes for this section, David outlined three ways that he sought to love God in his daily life. First, he wrote in his notes, "David was blessed to wrestle with daily living in Christ and the entertainment culture." David had inherited a family business centered on entertainment. He knew the idolatrous and seductive nature of the business. As a Christian thinker and scholar, he worked to bring a corrective and redemptive voice into that culture. His voice was not always welcome, but he was courageous in taking a stand based on his Christian convictions. In that, David became a credible witness when he urged those he mentored to do the same.

The second way he stated his effort to "Love God" was that "David was blessed to plan [worship] assemblies to God's glory." Although David worked with a committee to plan the worship assemblies at his church, David's mind, heart, and hands were all over the content, structure, and flow of those assemblies. My analysis of those assemblies is that David was also concerned that worship itself could become idolatrous if the horizontal or human dimension was given precedence over the vertical or divine dimension. Those mentored by David often heard his convictions about how the church should approach God in worship.

The third emphasis in his desire to "Love God" was that "David was blessed to encourage Psalm singing for today." Those mentored by David heard him speak about the importance of recovering the practice of singing the Psalms together. Mark Shipp, in his essay in this volume, gives some detail about how this was important to David.

The second exhortation in the memorial service, per David's instructions, was "Love the Brethren." He wanted it to be focused on John 13:34 and 15:12–17. The congregation was to be reminded that loving God inherently has a horizontal dimension. In his directions, David listed three ways that he strove to love the church. The first way was that "David was blessed to be a teacher/supervisor in the local congregation and in schools." That is why David believed in, preformed, and promoted rigorous biblical scholarship in service to the church. That is why he did the arduous work to earn a PhD in New Testament. That is why David taught at various Christian universities. That is why he envisioned and established the Institute for Christian Theology and Ministry in St. Petersburg, Russia (see Tom Olbricht's essay in this volume).

Secondly, "David was blessed to serve brethren in Russia." When the doors to Russia opened in the 1990s, as a Christian entrepreneur and as a

Christian evangelist, David took his knowledge of the radio business and put it to work as a means to introduce the Russian people to the Christian gospel. As president of Austin Graduate School of Theology, David led the faculty to write a basic introduction to the Christian faith. It was titled *Things That Matter: A Guide to Christian Faith*.[1] It was translated into Russian and began to be disseminated among the people. David maintained a deep love for the brothers and sisters in Russia for the remainder of his life.

Thirdly, "David was blessed to provide living space for many brethren." Only David knows how many people he helped in this way. David's benefaction was always anonymous. He gave to many causes and people whom he trusted or for whom he had compassion. But as one blessed by God, he wanted his beneficence to be for God's glory only.

Those mentored by David would know that David wanted them to love the church as he did because he strove to love the church as Jesus did. I remember two or three occasions when I became critical of the church. I expressed my thoughts with what I thought was articulate detail. I thought, "How could David argue with such an astute and well-defined case?" He didn't choose to argue with it. I received an email from David after each diatribe. Each email read, "Love the church."

David's email messages were known for brevity. In fact, they could be exasperating on occasion. A two- or three-word message with an ellipsis was fairly standard. Sometimes there was no punctuation and the thought was left open-ended. On this occasion, he punctuated the sentence with a period. I believe he was making his point even stronger. He said, "Love the church." Period. There was no ellipsis, nor an exclamation point. The point was not left open-ended with no punctuation mark. It ended with a period. His point was made. Without putting it into words, I think David's message to me was, "Stan, you need to love the church as I do because I'm trying to love the church as Jesus does." That's the sign of a good mentor—one who corrects wrong thoughts and practices as well as praises good thinking and behavior.

When I first learned that David left instructions for me to give the second exhortation at the memorial service, I was humbled but also fearful. The fear intensified when I saw that I had been assigned the topic of "Love the Brethren." I wondered if David was using this as one last opportunity to remind me to love the church. Period. After the memorial service, I learned that a number of others had also received the same admonition from David when they criticized the church. I was still humbled, but also thankful that he had entrusted me with the task of reminding us to love the church.

---

1. Edited by Michael R. Weed and Jeffrey Peterson (3rd ed.; Austin: Christian Studies, 2000).

In conclusion, my thoughts about David as a mentor have been largely anecdotal because they arise mostly from personal experience. The key factor in mentoring is being in relationship. My earthly relationship with David was one year shy of four decades. The trajectory of our relationship changed over time. It started with my being his student and protégé, then changed to that of friend, and finally colleague.

However, in those thirty-nine years the trajectory shifted back and forth. When David stepped down as president of Austin Graduate School of Theology, he was appointed chancellor. On the organizational chart, the chancellor serves the president. The role is primarily to serve as an advisor to and be available for assignments from the president. In 2003, I accepted the invitation to become president of Austin Graduate School of Theology. My predecessor, Carson Stephens, who had succeeded David, arranged for the three of us to have coffee together soon after I began my work. It was in that meeting that I witnessed how David would work as my chancellor. I remember us sitting on the patio of a Starbucks in downtown Austin on a warm October morning. I recall one thing from that meeting. We were discussing the challenges he and Carson knew that I'd be facing in the new role. At one point in the conversation David said, "Stan, I'll tell you the same thing that I told Carson. Be quick to listen, slow to speak, and slow to become angry" (see Jas 1:19). Once again, David showed much wisdom. It was wisdom he had gleaned from Scripture. Scriptural wisdom saturated his life. He trusted it as the very revelation of God that was ultimately embodied in the Word that became flesh, Jesus Christ.

As my teacher, David taught me that the careful and close reading of the Bible can and should lead to worship. As my mentor, David believed in me and entrusted me with assignments that I would have never accepted without his encouragement and guidance. As my friend, David loved me unconditionally, as an older brother should. As a colleague, David used our conversations to test his ideas and thoughts against mine and as a time to try to convince me to join him in his way of thinking.

We often agreed about our understanding and practice of the Christian faith, but not always. I remember the first time that I disagreed with David on a matter. I also remember the first time I said "No!" to something that he wanted me to do. In both instances, I feared that it would adversely affect our relationship in some way. But it did not. There was still mutual love and respect. That is another sign of a good mentor. David was not seeking followers, but wanted to raise up leaders.

While planning the memorial, Melinda said to me—and I paraphrase— "David's name will not be long remembered—two or three generations by the family. I know that we are but vapor. But I believe that what David did will be eternal. I'm content with that." So am I.

Royce Money, president emeritus and now chancellor of Abilene Christian University, said to me after the memorial service, "David left a large footprint." We both agreed that will be hard to fill. I have no idea how many people David mentored formally and informally through the years. But that is one of the important ways he left his footprint. Those of us who were nurtured by him will always be thankful.

Finally, I recall Paul's words to Timothy, " . . . and what you have heard from me through many witnesses entrust to faithful people who will be able to teach others as well" (2 Tim 2:2 NRSV). David's participation in the succession of the faith from generation to generation will have a lasting effect. It is eternal because it is held by the One who holds eternity in his hands.

4

David Worley as Student

Carl and Donna Holladay

We have been asked to reflect on David's life as a student at Yale. When we arrived in New Haven in the summer of 1975, David and Melinda were already there. We probably met them at the Whitney Avenue Church of Christ in North Haven, in which both were active members. We moved to New Haven because Carl had been appointed as Assistant Professor of New Testament at Yale Divinity School, and we lived there until 1980, when we moved to Atlanta, where Carl had accepted a position as Associate Professor of New Testament at Emory University's Candler School of Theology. During our time at Yale, David was mostly preoccupied with his doctoral program, which he had begun in 1975.

I knew that David was working on a dissertation on Hebrews and that his doctoral supervisor was Nils Dahl, an eminent New Testament scholar from Norway, who had moved to Yale in 1965, and who had brought great distinction to the New Testament doctoral program and to New Testament studies more generally at Yale Divinity School. The other senior New Testament faculty members were Abe Malherbe, whose institutional home was Yale Divinity School, and Wayne Meeks, whose primary appointment was located in Yale's Department of Religious Studies, which served primarily undergraduate students.

At some point I learned that David's dissertation topic focused on promissory language in the Letter to the Hebrews, and I can remember discussing aspects of his research. But, as a newly appointed junior professor, I was mainly concerned with teaching my Divinity School courses and trying to get my dissertation published. Since all my courses were new preparations, most of my time was devoted to preparing lectures, grading papers, and the usual committee responsibilities that fall to junior professors.

Because David and I spent most of our working hours during the week doing our respective academic work, which did not require the two of us to interact directly, the times when we met and spent time together were mostly related to church. We were active members of the Whitney Avenue church, as were David and Melinda, and some of our most vivid memories relate to these common interests. As is the case with many Churches of Christ located near major universities and seminaries, this church included a number of students in various programs, who complemented the faithful contingent of local members drawn from New Haven, North Haven, Hamden, and the surrounding area. Overall, the church probably numbered about fifty to seventy-five on Sunday morning, and there was a complete Sunday school program with classes in which both David and Melinda taught. At the time, Allan Eldridge served as the minister, along with his wife, Donna, whose lives were kept busy raising their two daughters.

David frequently led the singing, but more than this, he had a major role in planning the worship services. Given his interest in worship and liturgy, David naturally took the initiative in leading this aspect of the church's life. The services were well planned and thoughtfully coordinated, usually around a specific theme. He worked closely with Allan in planning the service to ensure that the theme of the hymns dovetailed with that of Allan's sermon. We used *Great Songs of the Church*[1] as our hymnal, and David's taste in songs gravitated toward the more sophisticated hymns rather than revival songs. Convinced that liturgical innovation was a good thing, he occasionally tried to introduce new elements or themes into the worship. On one Mother's Day he called out the hymn number of "Faith of Our Fathers," but suggested that, given the occasion, we would alter the lyrics to "Faith of Our Mothers." Eventually the congregation adjusted to David's suggestion, although initially it took some of us by surprise.

David and Melinda also participated in the church's teaching program—Melinda in the children's classes and David in the youth and young adult classes. For a while David functioned as the de facto youth minister of the Whitney Avenue Church. But David and Melinda also extended their teaching ministry into their home by arranging and conducting Bible studies, to which they invited students from Yale and other colleges and universities from the area. I remember that David took these home Bible studies seriously and made a concerted effort to reach out to students, especially

---

1. Compiled by E. L. Jorgenson (Louisville: Great Songs Press, 1937).

those from Churches of Christ, but also those from other religious traditions. Aware of the intellectual and spiritual challenges often experienced by students enrolled in high-profile research universities, David took special pains to relate to the needs of these students. At one level, he and Melinda provided critically important emotional support, but they also consistently sought to articulate and interpret the tradition of faith in ways that made sense in students' new academic setting, especially given their own church background. Among the students who participated in these home Bible studies was Jim Browning, a Yale undergraduate at the time, who also played football for Yale, and later attended University of Virginia School of Law and subsequently practiced corporate law in Albuquerque, New Mexico, before being appointed as United States District Judge in the District of New Mexico. This interpretive role required special sensitivities, which David and Melinda possessed in abundance. It was also an opportunity for them to practice Christian hospitality, an ideal prominent in the Letter to the Hebrews (13:1).

This was only one way in which the Worley residence functioned as an extension of the church. David and Melinda were fortunate to live in a nice home, well-furnished throughout, but they shared their Hamden home freely, hosting Christmas parties and other festive events there. Typical was their hosting of a baby shower for one of John and Karol Fitzgerald's daughters. Even before they moved to Hamden, they practiced hospitality. One of the most memorable parties occurred during their first year at YDS when David invited the legendary professor of church history Roland Bainton for dinner. On such occasions the usual barriers between town and gown, students and professors, faded away as the entire group enjoyed each other's company.

Another memory I have of this house is David's study. He converted one of the upstairs bedrooms into his study, which, as one might expect, had walls lined with bookcases and the usual accoutrements of scholarly work. But rather than the usual desk and chair, there was a table that David had had constructed (or possibly constructed himself) that basically dominated the center of the room. It was as though the room had been built around the table rather than the table for the room. But it was the envy of every other student (and faculty member)—this spacious square of finely polished wood on which books and papers could be stacked with abandon. Nothing on the floor—it was all on the table. At least that's my memory. What this signaled, of course, was that David's research was a high priority and that this work space had acquired a sacred quality. Whether the table followed him to Texas, once he left New Haven, I have no way of knowing.

DAVID'S YALE DISSERTATION

I do not know how David came to choose a theme from the Letter to the Hebrews as a topic for his dissertation, although I suspect it may have arisen out of coursework or conversations with Rowan Greer, who taught patristics at Yale Divinity School and had a special interest in Hebrews. In 1973 he published *The Captain of Our Salvation: A Study in the Patristic Exegesis of Hebrews*.[2] David may well have been influenced by the work of James Thompson, who had preceded him at Abilene Christian College and who published a commentary on Hebrews.[3] Thompson's exegetical work on Hebrews drew on his dissertation research at Vanderbilt, which was published as *The Beginnings of Christian Philosophy: The Epistle to the Hebrews*.[4] The sources of David's interest in Hebrews may be much deeper, considering how influential Hebrews had been in the Stone-Campbell tradition. Robert Milligan's *Scheme of Redemption*,[5] although purportedly covering the entirety of the Holy Scriptures, heavily relies on Hebrews for its construal of God's plan of salvation.

Regardless of the originating sources or influences, David's dissertation, "God's Faithfulness to Promise: The Hortatory Use of Commissive Language in Hebrews," was completed in 1981. Since it was presented to the faculty of the Graduate School of Yale University, it should be remembered as work that he did in Yale's Graduate School rather than Yale Divinity School, which is a professional school within Yale University some of whose faculty also served on the Graduate School faculty.

As one might expect, in the Acknowledgements David pays tribute to those who encouraged and mentored him throughout his doctoral work. Informative at so many levels, it is worth quoting in full:

> Melinda, my loving companion, grace and peace be to you. The breadth of your understanding and the depth of your support have known no limits.
>
> Nils Dahl, my graduate advisor, the fullness of your knowledge and your common sense have made my study with you a rich experience. I appreciate most your expressions of confidence in me when my own self confidence was faltering.

---

2. Tübingen: Mohr/Siebeck, 1973.

3. *The Letter to the Hebrews* (Living Word Commentary 15; Austin: R. B. Sweet, 1971).

4. Washington, DC: Catholic Biblical Association of America, 1982.

5. *An Exposition and Defense of the Scheme of Redemption: As It Is Revealed and Taught in the Holy Scriptures* (rev. ed.; St. Louis: Christian Pub. Co., 1894).

Abraham Malherbe, my mentor in method, your care has no doubt made me a more careful person. You have been a friend, though never a flatterer.

Brevard Childs, my exemplar in approach, your resolute effort to 'degnostify' scholarship has encouraged my interpretation of the Bible as the scripture of the church.

Rowan Greer and Wayne Meeks, for your initial encouragement and advice at the genesis of this project.

I have known what it means to be nurtured and equipped for ministry through the body of Christ. Blessed be the Father for the churches of Christ in Meadowbrook, on Minter Lane and on Whitney Avenue. I must thank these special friends in Christ who have given support to my family these past eight years: Reuben and Nita Slone, Fred Barton, Roger and Camille Dean, Steve and Barbara Hays, Allan and Donna Eldridge, Tom and Dorothy Olbricht, Charlie and Judy Siburt, Ken and Sue Frazier, LaVerne and Gene Barrett, Opal and Dick Cozby, and Maggie Warren.

Finally, Iva Lea Worley Barton, without you faithful guardianship as mother and as steward of possessions my academic quests for knowledge would have been impossible.

Given the critical role that spouses typically play in helping students get through a rigorous doctoral program and complete their dissertation, David's dedication is also worth reporting:

To Melinda Ann Worley

> never flagging in zeal
> aglow with the Spirit
> loving as Christ loved
> faithful woman
> loving companion
> patient mother.

In many ways it was a propitious time for David to be at Yale. Abe Malherbe had arrived at Yale in 1970, having taught the previous year at Dartmouth, and prior to that for five years at Abilene Christian College. At that time it was unusual for a biblical scholar in the Churches of Christ to have achieved such a highly visible professorial appointment in one of the leading Protestant seminaries in North America. While numerous aspiring scholars from colleges and universities associated with the Churches of Christ had over the previous decades attended and gotten degrees from prestigious schools such as Harvard, Yale, Chicago, and Johns Hopkins, Abe nevertheless began attracting students to Yale shortly after he arrived. They would often be admitted to the Master of Divinity program or perhaps the Master of Arts in Religion program at Yale Divinity School, from which they would apply to the doctoral program at Yale or elsewhere. This was certainly the case with David, along with several other students from the Stone-Campbell tradition, including John Fitzgerald and Michael White. Stanley Stowers did a master's at Princeton Theological Seminary (1974) and then came to Yale for his doctorate. Fitzgerald and Stowers completed their doctorates under Malherbe's supervision, while White had Wayne Meeks as his advisor.

Just as they had done at Harvard, Abe and Phyllis Malherbe took an active role in the Whitney Avenue church, which several of the Yale students from Churches of Christ attended. The Malherbes' commitment to congregational life—which included teaching Bible classes and preaching, serving on church committees, participating in periodic work days, and supervising and teaching at Ganderbrook, a summer church camp in Maine—modeled a form of discipleship that was also attractive to David and Melinda. They may have chosen Yale for their master's and doctoral level work had Abe not been there, but his presence at Yale was certainly a major incentive.

Nils Dahl's reputation as an international scholar was certainly a drawing card, and his willingness to direct David's dissertation is noteworthy. Dahl had already attracted a string of New Testament doctoral students at Yale and had exercised significant formative influence of such prominent scholars as Wayne Meeks, Paul Sampley, Roger Aus, and David Adams, to mention only a few. A scholar of vast erudition who had wide-ranging grasp of Jewish texts and traditions from the Second Temple Period, Dahl also had strong ecclesial sensibilities that were shaped by his commitments to the Lutheran tradition. His published dissertation, *Das Volk Gottes: Eine Untersuchungung zum Kirchenbewusstsein des Urchistentums*,[6] had influenced scholarly discussions about ecclesiology, as evidenced by its use as a resource for the Second Vatican Council. During David's time at Yale, Dahl had also emphasized God as the "neglected topic" in New Testament theology, which tended to emphasize Christology. David's interest in God's faithfulness was congruent with Dahl's call for investigating how the New Testament spoke about God. It would have been difficult to find a New Testament scholar in North America more finely attuned to the major theological currents, especially in Europe, than Nils Dahl.

By the time David came to Yale, Brevard Childs had established himself as a major voice in Old Testament studies internationally. His early

---

6. Norske videnskaps-akademi, 1941; reprint by Wissenschaftliche Buchgesellschaft, 1963.

book *Biblical Theology in Crisis*[7] had signaled some of the major shifts in Old Testament studies. His commentary on Exodus in the Old Testament Library series bore the subtitle, "A Critical, Theological Commentary."[8] Childs had begun to argue for what he called a canonical approach to Scripture, in which he pushed for an alternative to narrowly construed historical-critical exegesis that embraced Scripture's theological claims and took seriously Scripture as a collection of writings shaped by the church's desire to have a normative, canonical text that informed the life of faith. This way of reading Scripture was already being worked out in his Exodus commentary but especially came to full flower in his *Introduction to the Old Testament as Scripture* and *The New Testament as Canon: An Introduction*.[9] David warmed to Childs's hermeneutical approach, as clearly indicated in his words of acknowledgement. I can remember conversations with David in which he expressed worry about the ways in which biblical exegesis was being taught and practiced. He operated with the strong conviction that Scripture is the church's book and that appropriate methods of interpretation have to be used in order to grasp its distinctive revelatory dimensions.

It is no surprise that David would be attracted to Rowan Greer, an Episcopalian priest who embodied high Anglican liturgical sensibilities and also exemplified a form of piety that connected with the deepest springs of the Anglican tradition. Although Greer's primary field was patristics, he had conspicuous interests and impressive expertise in New Testament exegesis. He could also be contrarian in his own way, for example, in the way he saw patristics scholars ignoring some of the strong theological dimensions of the church fathers and concentrating instead on a variety of historical and literary issues. This became evident in a paper he presented at a conference on Gnosticism coordinated by Bentley Layton, in which he gave a critique of some of the major trends of Gnostic studies.

Wayne Meeks, whose professorial appointment was in Yale College and whose teaching duties focused mainly on Yale undergraduates, also shared Malherbe's interests in the social world of early Christianity. His *The First Urban Christians: The Social World of the Apostle Paul*,[10] a field-defining work that exercised enormous influence in the 1980s and 1990s and still remains influential in Pauline studies, drew upon renewed interest in the social sciences and ethnographical studies. Much of the spade work for *First Urban Christians* was done in doctoral seminars in which Meeks

---

7. Philadelphia: Westminster, 1970.
8. Philadelphia: Westminster, 1974.
9. Philadelphia: Fortress, 1979 and 1985, respectively.
10. New Haven, CT: Yale University Press, 1983.

required his students to read the work of such scholars as Peter Berger and Mary Douglas, along with New Testament scholars such as Gerd Theissen, who were trying to ascertain the social status of the earliest Christians and understand the social dynamics at work as these small Christian communities or *collegia* were relating to their broader social culture.

Having access to this rather remarkable constellation of Yale scholars, each of whom was doing pioneering research in his own way, offered David a broad interpretive framework within which he could work out his own hermeneutical approach to Scripture, while sharpening his own ecclesial and spiritual sensibilities. Other settings might have been less congenial to David's thoughtfully considered theological-ecclesial hermeneutic, which shared some of Childs's and Greer's suspicion of historical-critical exegesis as practiced within the mainstream of North American and European biblical scholarship. It was never quite clear to me whether David thought that historical-critical exegesis was in principle inimical to the life of faith or that theological education as practiced in most Protestant seminaries somehow alienated ministers and professors from church practice.

Rather than trying to summarize the argument of David's dissertation, it is simpler to report the abstract that David himself drafted:

> This study is an attempt to account for the extensive use of "promise" and promising in Hebrews by an approach to the commissive vocabulary in Hebrews which proceeds from a heightened awareness of the phenomenon of promising. To this end, the work of J. L. Austin has been seminal for this study in the formation of certain basic categories for isolating the distinctive features of commissive language and for interpreting their use in Hebrews. The more traditional question of "what is the author *saying* with promises" has been broadened in our work to "what is the author *doing* with commissive language" in his letter.
>
> The first chapter introduces the basic categories for talking about commissive language: the words denoting promise, the components of promise, the felicities of promising, the forces of commissive utterances. The latter category is elaborated through a classification of the sorts of things people in the ancient world tried to accomplish by promising and using past "promises." Since our primary concern is with promises in a literary whole, we also raise in this chapter the question of "what our author is doing with his letter." Against a background of ancient hortatory literature, we isolate certain features of Hebrews which lead us to regard the letter as an Exhortation. This generic conception is reinforced by a reconstruction of the readers' situation.

Chapter 2 is an investigation first of the degree to which the stories of Abraham and the heirs in Heb 11:8–22 are depictions of *felicitous promising*. What the author has done with these depictions in his letter is then pursued by considering the functions of Abraham's story within the anaphora of faith and within the listing of the exemplars of faithful endurance in Hebrews 11. Next, the particular impact these depictions may have had on the readers is gauged by comparing the story of the ancient heirs with the situation of the readers in order to see if Abraham has been made into the image of the readers.

The interest in the *forces of promising* leads us in chapter 3 to interpret God's solemn oath in 6:12–18 in light of the ancient orator's use of the forensic oath. From this framework of what was done with oaths, it becomes clear that our author has tried to encourage his readers not only by appeal to the integrity of God as oath-taker, but also His faithful guardianship as oath-witness. God's faithfulness to His solemn oath to Jesus is then placed within the hortatory concerns of Heb 4:14—7:28.

Attention to the *linguistic phenomenon of promising*, the way we ordinarily use "promise," makes the use of "promise" by some in their formulations of Jesus' role in Hebrews vis-à-vis God as Promisor sound strange and somewhat awkward. In Chapter 4, we offer alternative formulations of Jesus' relationship to God's promises, as well as a description of what the author has attempted to do to his readers by depicting such a relationship. First, Jesus' possible role as an exemplary promise in 5:5–10 and 11:39—12:3 is examined. Next, particular concern is focused in Hebrews 8–10 on the connection of Jesus' priesthood to the "better promises" of the new covenant. Finally, we raise the possibility that our author's own perceptions may have been formed, at least in part, by a regard for the "Jesus" of the LXX who was sent ahead into the promised Rest.

We conclude that our author's use of commissive language was not prompted by criticisms within the church over a delay in God's promise-keeping; rather that our author seized upon God's commissive activity and the behavior of promisees of Scripture as a way of emboldening a people tempted to withdraw from one another and from God to endure social and financial difficulties and to remain confident in the face of threats to the promise.

David's dissertation should be seen as imaginatively conceived, extensively researched, and exegetically rigorous. The footnotes and bibliography attest to the wide range of sources, both primary and secondary, with which he engages critically in arguing his thesis. There is ample evidence of his careful attention to the relevant literature in English, German, and French, not to mention ancient sources in Greek, Latin, Hebrew, and Aramaic. Signs of innovation are also evident in his use and appropriation of J. L. Austin, White's Professor of Moral Philosophy at the University of Oxford, who specialized in philosophy of language and called attention to the performative dimensions of language. Distinguishing between what people accomplish *in* utterances (illocutionary acts) and *by* utterances (perlocutionary acts), Austin explore how ordinary human beings use language to communicate knowledge, but also how in the act of communication certain things are also accomplished that transcend what is said. He drew an important distinction between what we *say* with our words and what we *do* with them. Drawing on Austin's work, David insists on seeing the language in Hebrews as both communicative and performative, and when this distinction is applied to the commissive language in Hebrews, it enables him to analyze God's promises as perlocutionary acts, as language that not only states the content of what is being promised but also in its utterance assists in accomplishing the promise.

Signs of influence by his teachers are also apparent, as would be expected in a doctoral dissertation. David had been introduced to the literature on moral exhortation in Greek and Roman philosophers in Malherbe's graduate seminar titled Hellenistic Moral Philosophers. In that seminar David wrote a paper on the *peristasis* (tribulation) catalogs, a topic John Fitzgerald later pursued in his dissertation. In that seminar students also translated the texts that became Malherbe's *The Cynic Epistles: A Study Edition*.[11] In that volume David is acknowledged as the translator of the Epistles of Heraclitus (185–215). Abe was furious when the students' names were not included on the title page when *Cynic Epistles* was first published in 1977 (since he had included the students' names on the manuscript he submitted), but that was corrected in the 2006 reprint, in which David's name appears on both the title page and on the first page of the Heraclitus section. It is also worth noting that in the second edition of *The Society of Biblical Literature Handbook of Style* David's translation is used as one of its examples.[12]

David's immersion in the Hellenistic moralist literature enabled him to see, among other things, that much of the commissive language in Hebrews is closely aligned with the well-established hortatory tradition. Just as Malherbe had done and had taught him to do, David read extensively in the

---

11. Atlanta: Scholars, 1977; reprint, Atlanta: Society of Biblical Literature, 2006.

12. Pp. 100–101. Edited by Patrick H. Alexander et al. (Peabody, MA: Hendrickson, 1999).

ancient moral philosophers such as Dio Chrysostom and Plutarch, and adduced relevant passages from their work to illuminate aspects of his analysis of the language of Hebrews. His discussion of formal aspects of the language in Hebrews includes attention to numerous features of ancient rhetoric and literary style, such as philophronesis and syncrisis, along with other features of ancient traditions of *paideia*. At places in the discussion, David moves beyond Malherbe by finding additional comparative texts from these authors and by pushing further the implications of seeing exhortation as an inescapable dimension of commissive language in Hebrews. David's penchant for insisting upon nuanced distinctions is seen in his discussion of "word of exhortation" (*logos tēs paraklēseōs*, 13:22), in which he objects to translating the phrase as "sermon," as a number of scholars had done. "The problem," he writes, "in too readily associating *logos tēs paraklēseōs* with 'sermon' is that it tends to narrow the field for understanding how exhortation works" (53). He adduces pertinent parallel references from the Maccabean writings to reinforce his point (see 1 Macc 10:24; 2 Macc 15:11).

David's indebtedness to Nils Dahl is also evident not only in his close exegetical attention to the theme of promise in Hebrews but also to a selected set of texts in which the theme is prominent. Wide reading in Philo of Alexandria and Josephus has informed his exegetical analysis, but beyond that David also cites less well-known Jewish authors, such as Eupolemus and Artapanus, along with a broad range of so-called intertestamental or pseudepigraphical Jewish writings, and rabbinical texts. Beyond this, he also examines papyrological evidence, as, for example, when he explores the ways in which *hypostasis* can be used to designate "property," a sense roughly equivalent to *hyparxis* (89). His use of Egyptian papyri is quite extensive and consistently careful and illuminating. David's discussion of the use of "oath" in Hebrews and the social function of oaths in the ancient world is especially rich (124–30), and, here again, he adduces dozens of well-chosen comparative texts to amplify his point. Noting, for example, the many and varied contexts in which oaths functioned in the ancient world, David cites a string of pagan texts to illustrate the use of oaths in various public and private agreements, in reporting finances, and in diplomacy (127 n. 22).

His treatment of the frequently discussed question of why the writer of Hebrews would assert that God actually made promises under oath is even handed, squarely confronting the theological difficulties posed by this claim: If God cannot lie, why should he take an oath? But David concludes, "The author sees nothing contradictory or illogical in both speaking of God's faithfulness to promise and discussing God's oath-taking in the same letter" (162). Insisting that the author's intentions are hortatory, David writes, "Because [the author] desires to encourage his readers to endurance, he finds in God's solemn oath an opportunity to reaffirm God's unchanging intention to keep His promises to His people; not only to reaffirm, but also, by magnifying God's oath-taking and oath-witnessing, to assure his readers that their promised inheritance is safe and secure" (162). So central is this problem in Hebrews and in David's analysis that it is the focus of his concluding paragraph:

> Finally, it is one of the ironies of Hebrews, yet at the same time one of its most telling points, that the author can be so concerned about God's faithfulness to *promise* and in the same breath, without any sense of contradiction, be equally concerned about God's faithfulness to *oath*. It is ironic because the presence of oath-taking in human society is a way of compensating for false witnesses and unreliable promisors. That our author would unabashedly use the divine oath is but one more indication that what our author is doing is not responding to criticisms of the promises but rather taking the initiative to place before his readers' eyes a God who has obligated Himself, even with the most solemn oath, to bring about a relationship with the seed of Abraham which will endure forever.

It is regrettable that David's dissertation was never published. It is a superb piece of scholarship. I do not know whether David ever submitted it for publication or even whether he thought about publishing it. By the time he finished his doctoral work, he had moved back to Austin, having already begun to shift his attention toward his businesses. Perhaps he decided that it was time to move on to other ventures rather than to fret over revisions or refinements of the argument that would make it suitable for a monograph series.

The copy of David's dissertation that I have been using for this paper is an authorized facsimile from University Microfilms International that was obtained by Emory's Pitts Theology Library in the early 1980s. In this copy, which still contains the small slips in the back of the book indicating "Date Due," the earliest due date recorded is October 12, 1983. The first "Date Due" page is full of stamped dates in two columns, and another page has been glued on top of the first one. It is clear that David's dissertation was read continuously by Emory faculty and students from 1983 until 2004, the last stamped date, and probably the time when Pitts Theology Library began to shift to an electronic catalog. It is not clear from these sheets who checked out David's dissertation, but I suspect it may have been Fred Craddock, who taught seminars on Hebrews, lectured widely on it, and wrote the commentary on Hebrews for the *New Interpreter's Bible*.[13] Another user may have been Thomas L. Blackstone, who wrote a dissertation at Emory titled "The Hermeneutics of Recontextualization in the Epistle to the Hebrews" (1995).

Two documented users at Emory are Patrick Gray (*Godly Fear: The Epistle to Hebrews and Greco-Roman Critiques of Superstition*), who cites David in his modern authors index;[14] and Bryan J. Whitfield (*Joshua Traditions and the Argument of Hebrews 3 and 4*), who acknowledges David as one of his sources.[15] David's claim that the author of Hebrews, in his portrait of Jesus, may have been influenced by the "Jesus" (Joshua) of the LXX, who was sent ahead to the promised land, anticipates one of the key arguments in Whitfield's book—hence his book title. Beyond Emory, in his Anchor Bible commentary on Hebrews Craig R. Koester also cites David, but rather than his dissertation it is his article "Fleeing to Two Immutable Things, God's Oath-Taking and Oath-Witnessing: The Use of Litigant Oath in Hebrews 6:12–20."[16]

Without attempting to compile a complete citation index pertaining to David's dissertation, these scattered indications suggest that his work has been read and taken seriously by scholars working on Hebrews. This is also evident from the Pitts Theology Library copy that I have been using. In defiance of standard library protocols prohibiting the marking and underlining of books, one user, perhaps more, has filled the volume with faint pencil markings in the margins, occasional check marks, and—the bane of all librarians—interlinear underlining, albeit in pencil.

While it is impossible to ascertain what David's dissertation accomplished or the extent of its influence on other Bible readers and scholars, one can detect strong resonance between the topic of God's faithfulness as it relates to divine promises articulated in Hebrews and the contours of David's own life. The dissertation bears all of the earmarks of finely tuned scholarship—numerous lengthy footnotes, extensive bibliography, careful analysis, and numerous proposals, some tentative, some confident. It is not a devotional work in the conventional sense, but it is profoundly devotional in the sense that David understood his scholarly work as an act of devotion to God. It is theologically rich because David had developed ways of doing exegesis that, to use the image of Leander Keck, not only "listened to" the text but also "listened for" the Word of God coming through the text. He

---

13. Vol. 12 (Nashville: Abingdon, 1998).
14. P. 257 (Atlanta: Society of Biblical Literature, 2003).
15. P. 314 (Berlin: De Gruyter, 2013).
16. In *Restoration Quarterly* 36 (1994) 223–36.

had developed a way of reading and listening that took seriously the complexities of the biblical text and dealt with them using the standard array of tools and resources available to biblical scholars—concordances, lexica, commentaries, ancient comparative texts, modern scholarly articles, monographs, and commentaries. But, while respecting these exegetical details, David sought to see (and to hear) the theological message embedded within the text and to articulate it in ways that were faithful to the text or to the ancient author, in this case the author of Hebrews, but also understandable and even compelling to his modern readers.

TWO MEMORABLE STORIES

In drafting these remarks, we talked with John Fitzgerald and Ann Eichelberger Page, who were at Yale with David and Melinda. John and David entered the MDiv program at the same time. In fact, John related that when he and David were at Abilene Christian College, after both of them had been admitted to the MDiv programs at Harvard, Yale, Union (New York), and Princeton, they made a shopping tour to visit these schools in spring of 1972. At Harvard they heard George MacRae lecture and also had dinner with Paul Hanson, an Old Testament scholar and a specialist in Jewish apocalyptic literature. As John recalls, they probably stayed with Abe and Phyllis in New Haven when they visited Yale. Eventually they decided on Yale and both were in the MDiv program at the same time and were admitted to the doctoral program in successive years: David in 1975, John in 1976 after spending the 1975–1976 academic year in Germany on a Rotary fellowship.

Recalling David's days as the functional youth minister at the Whitney Avenue church, John remembered several teenagers who were quite a challenge to any Bible school teacher. On one occasion, Carey Gifford, who also assisted David in teaching the teenagers, was trying to explain the Trinity to his unruly charges, noting that it was a difficult concept over which theologians had labored for centuries. But one teenager objected, explaining that it was not all that complicated. The difference between the Father and the Son was simply that the Father was older!

Another story John recalled was an incident in which someone attempted to steal the tires off David's car while it was parked in the vicinity of the Divinity School. probably along the street near the student housing where David and Melinda were living. Somehow the thief was seen and reported, and the police showed up, along with John and some other friends of David, including some other students. The officer explained to David what the thief was trying to do and what actions might be taken. But in the midst of all the confusion, David began talking with the perpetrator and learned that he was stealing the tires because he needed them for his car. Moved by the man's story, David decided to give him the tires and not press charges. It is a poignant modern parable illustrating that when others tend to be accusatory and quick to judgment, there are those rare individuals, who, shaped by the contours of the Christian story, incline toward forgiveness even when the circumstances call for punishment. David well understood the Pauline imperative: "If your enemy is hungry, feed him" (Rom 12:20).

POSTSCRIPT

Although we were asked to focus on David's days as a student at Yale, we are taking the liberty of engaging in recent reminiscence. About two years ago, the Eastern European Liaison Committee, which works under the auspices of the international Society for New Testament Studies, received an invitation to hold its International East-West Conference for New Testament scholars in Moscow. This invitation came from Metropolitan Hilarion, a highly placed Russian Orthodox cleric currently serving as chairman of the Department of External Relations. The meeting was to be held in September 2016. Having never visited Russia, we decided to spend the week prior to the conference in St. Petersburg.

Although I knew David had been diagnosed with cancer in 2015, I emailed him to let him know we were planning to visit St. Petersburg. And as one might expect, this ignited his interest immediately. He put us in touch with Igor Egirev, the minister of the church in St. Petersburg, who responded immediately, offering his help in arranging accommodations and tours. David also introduced us to Joel Petty, who has been involved in the Russian work for several years. Through numerous emails David explained how he had become interested in Russia and what had been accomplished over the years. At the time, there was major concern about an action taken by the Russian Duma that appeared to limit the freedom of religious groups in Russia. We discussed the implications of this legislative action, and I agreed to make further inquiries in Moscow if I found an appropriate occasion to do so.

In St. Petersburg we were accompanied by Frank and Ursula Kolb, longtime friends of ours from Tübingen. The four of us attended the Sunday morning church services on the day after we arrived in St. Petersburg. We thoroughly enjoyed the lively, uplifting service, and were struck by the power and quality of the choral singing. We accepted the invitation to stay for the fellowship meal afterward, and this gave us a chance to meet some of the church members. Throughout the week Joel and Igor were attentive to our needs. Among other things, Igor arranged for us to attend an opera one evening, a Russian ballet performance another evening, and a performance by the St. Petersburg City Choir another evening. Joel also accompanied us one day, which gave us an opportunity to hear his perspectives on Russia and Russian-American relations.

One of the initiatives of the Eastern European Liaison Committee in the early 1990s was to identify two libraries in Eastern Europe that we could build and strengthen, since many of the theological facilities and libraries had deteriorated or been destroyed during the Communist period. One of these libraries is located at St. Petersburg State University, and David played a crucial role in stabilizing that library. The details of his participation in this venture are explained elsewhere in these essays. Since I had never seen the library, I was eager to visit it. Once Anatoly Alexeev, who is a member of the philological faculty at St. Petersburg State University and is the librarian of this collection, learned that we were in St. Petersburg, he invited us to visit the library and for me to give a lecture to his students. I gladly complied and Igor joined us; in fact, he drove us to the location. I lectured to about a dozen students, mostly undergraduate and mostly female. The library now numbers about 17,000 volumes and, according to Anatoly, is the best library in Russia for doing advanced research in biblical studies.

Although we were in St. Petersburg only a week, we got a good sense of how pivotal a role David had played in the life of the Russian churches of Christ, and how highly revered he was. Later, in an email to David, I rehearsed our trip to St. Petersburg and how helpful Igor and Joel had been in expediting our trip. I told David that among those folk he had attained sainthood, to which he responded in one of his legendary, cryptic emails: "In Russia the criteria for sainthood are lower!"

Compared with others contributing to this volume, our visit to Russia lasted only a nanosecond. But through it we came to appreciate the substantial role that David played in that missionary initiative over many years; and also his willingness to engage in lively email correspondence at a time when his suffering was acute.

On September 19, 2016, David wrote to us while we were in St. Petersburg:

> How are things going?
> I know the time difference can be challenging at first.
> Remembering you in prayer this morning.
> grace and peace
> david

5

David Worley as Entrepreneur

Bob King

When asked to contribute to this book I started looking for reasons to say no. I certainly didn't think I had twenty pages to write and had no idea what to say. An unstated requirement for being David's friend was to forget what he might say about himself so you didn't accidentally reveal it to anyone else. The thought of writing down my memories of David was like breaking trust with a good friend. David was not comfortable with accolades about his good works or embellishing his status based on what he had accomplished. I hope I can respect his feelings while honoring his life.

THE INTERSECTION OF LIVES WAS A GAME-CHANGER FOR ME

My first introduction to David and Melinda occurred at a progressive dinner hosted by friends from the Brentwood Oaks Church of Christ. I still have a picture of the group seated in the family room of our hosts (Larry and Nancy Fuller). We were waiting to start our first course. There were introductions around the circle and I vividly recall the Worleys being introduced to us. I had heard of them but it was my first sighting of the Worley bird! Looking like a scholarly professor in his plaid sports coat and maybe in need of a trim, my first thought was, what do I have in common with him? He seemed likable but maybe a little distant. I just didn't grasp the significance that David and Melinda would come to have for Linda and me. Our children were close in age and that encouraged our interaction. I was consumed with making my fortune and off-round in other characteristics. Self-discipline, prayer, study of the Scriptures, and Christian parenting were worthy ideas but very low on my list. This was in part because I was clueless about parenting, and not comfortable with prayer or the study of the Bible. The Scriptures seemed likely to make me feel like a failure. David, on the other hand, was all about self-discipline, prayer, study, and teaching God's Word to his family, his church community, and to the world. I perceive our friendship to be by the grace of God.

David had an uncanny knack of sensing and perceiving the areas of my life that needed nurturing and change. He was clearly capable of quoting Scripture and giving scholarly advice. His maturity on both a human and spiritual level was so far beyond me that I struggled with the contrast.

But by God's grace David was gentle and kind, committed to honoring the Lord, and encouraging others on the same path. I recently told Melinda that my visual image of Jesus at the well or in the crowds is of David. There was a piercing but gentle warmth in David's eyes as he listened and encouraged. He used few words to communicate God's teachings. He was astute and loving but, I must say, very stubborn.

It was not always easy to work with him or for him, but I was always confident that he was acting in love and had the best of intentions. David was different in how he perceived others. Over the years it became clear to me that David saw others through the eyes of God. He was able to see beyond our frailties with the knowledge that we are all made in the image of God and therefore worthy of grace and mercy. His assessments weren't always with approval but with tenderness and compassion. In my dealings with David in any business situation, it was clear he could work with anyone and wasn't opportunistic or looking for a weakness in the other person that he could exploit. The story I shared with Christiana at church the week following David's death was about how a deeply spiritual and faithful man could go into the offices of a prospective tenant and patiently listen to the chatter regarding the lessee's accomplishments and the importance of his business. The tenant was in the business of building up the physical body while David was in the business of building up the spiritual body. The tenant was oblivious to the fact that none of the hype was of interest to David. What I learned after the meeting was that David had only needed to look at the artwork hanging from the walls to determine the man's life view. David had such an incredible knowledge of art, literature, and culture that he could quickly assimilate the implications of the person's interest, and how it would influence the business relationship. He wasn't unwilling to engage in business with a nonbeliever. He knew that doing business with a believer might not have any better outcome. I encourage you to read David's writings on believers participating in the marketplace. When I read his comments, I knew I had seen them in action before I read them on paper.

I'm sorry to disappoint those who are expecting a full account of all of David's business affairs. I can only come up with a few people with that knowledge. It isn't me. David was one of those need-to-know types who seldom shared himself or his activities in detail. Maybe if I were an early riser we would have had more opportunities to meet at his favorite coffee shop and visit about the second chapter of his business life. Take a look at the Thelese website and you can read about the diversity and scope of David's enterprises.

THE NAME

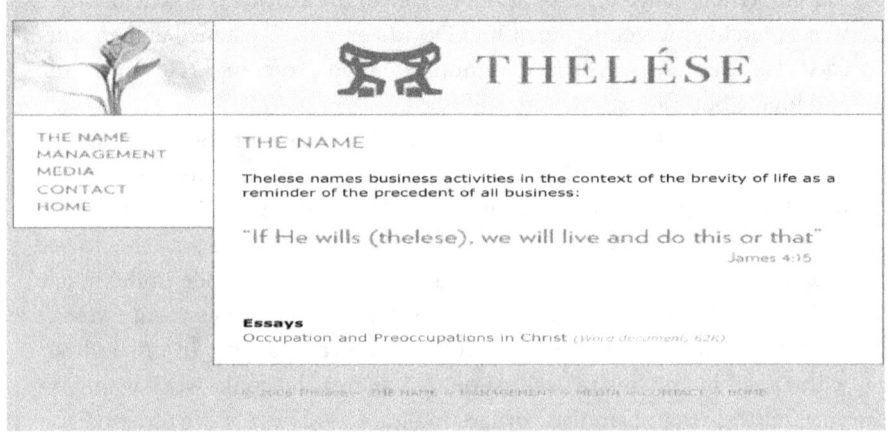

THE ENTERPRISE

Thelese encompasses a family of companies, investments and projects in diverse geographic and economic areas.

Thelese Management provides financial and information technological assistance to its sister companies in communication, the media, the arts and the academy. Thelese Broadcast focuses on projects in radio and the arts. Thelese Investments maintains equity positions in the transportation, oil and health care sectors. Thelese Properties oversees developments in real estate in the US and in Russia.

It was typical of David to make a statement about his core beliefs utilizing one word. Of course, *thelese* is a Greek word—not easy to pronounce and the meaning of which few know. No problem for David. The word had a powerful significance to him and if anyone was interested he was happy to explain the meaning. It was the word he used one afternoon in Aspen. We were driving up one of the mountain roads to look at a property. We had talked on several occasions over the past year about God's will. My world had been turned upside down in 1985 with the collapse of the real estate market and financial institutions in Texas. What to do next was very important to me and I had done a lot of study and reflecting on how to discern God's will for my occupation. David always had a listening ear and the patience to let me share my thoughts. I could trust his wisdom, discretion, and friendship in spite of my often misguided thoughts. I was coming to believe that God's will was more about who I was becoming, not so much what I was doing. I shared my thoughts (probably for about twenty or so minutes) with David as we drove up the mountain. As we arrived at our destination, he told me it was God's will for us to be content in all circumstances. David then used the word *thelese* to describe his understanding of how we should approach our plans and aspirations. "If he wills, we will live and do this and that." As time went along, I saw him handle the ups and downs of the marketplace with that understanding. It allowed him to be focused at a different level. The success or failure of a venture was not defining. It was all temporary and what mattered was living a faithful, purposeful, and serving life with the time available. He lived boldly and without concern of humiliation if he failed or of looking foolish in taking on ventures that seemed to have no hope of success.

An example of his mindset, and also his ability as a businessman, was demonstrated during the period he co-managed KOKE AM/FM Radio 95.5. David and Melinda arrived in Austin after completing his Yale PhD to join his mom, Iva Lea Worley Barton, in the management of their radio stations. KOKE Radio was the most valuable of their radio properties. The station was popular for country music fans, but for David and Melinda there were deep concerns about whether the music was healthy for the listening audience. David once observed that he questioned whether he could support the music programming if he wouldn't allow his children to listen to it. But it wasn't possible to be successful in commercial radio broadcasting in that region without picking a country western or pop/rock format. Neither format provided the audience with a healthy listening experience

His mom, a pioneer in the radio business, had done an incredible job running the business since her husband, David Worley, died in June 1964 when David was fourteen years old.

I don't know actual details, but the programming content was one of David's first priorities. He didn't declare a mandate to the staff and management of the station, but in dialogue and conversation he expressed his concern and elicited their support in changing the format. He offered alternatives but they were not well received. His position was considered naïve or foolish. Austin was a smaller community then and it was not long before word got around about his folly. David was too smart not to recognize how his position would be perceived. I think he knew that success was doubtful.

David loved and respected his mom and it had to be awkward for David to be critical of the business when his mother had worked very hard to maintain and manage it. He didn't want to make her feel like she had not done a good job or was at fault about the music. He knew Iva Lea was a good businesswoman with a strong faith, but she was also slow to change and very loyal to the staff who had contributed to her success. It must have been a very difficult period for them as they navigated David's desire to change things. She had grasped the reins of the business and supported David in all his scholastic endeavors. She was proud of him and respected his perspective. But to contemplate putting the business in such danger of failing must have been daunting.

While that concern was being addressed, David took on the responsibility of locating a site and erecting a new tower, which was essential for keeping their signal strong and more powerful to serve the expanding suburban areas and communities. This task was much like finding a needle in a haystack. The demand for land was soaring. The opportunity to purchase a site in the preferred area for a radio tower was gone. But David wouldn't accept the prospect until he diligently searched for a site that overlooked a property he could make work. I think David became an expert on every parcel in the area suitable for a radio tower. David could have really benefitted from Google Maps or a drone! It would have saved us at least one trip to see a reasonably flat property that was wide enough to work. The site was not as suitable as a hilltop but was doable. This piece of real estate, however, didn't make the cut when it became evident that the tower would be in the line of sight for some homeowners located on a hilltop several ridges over. Eventually David was convicted that he needed to locate the tower in another area of Travis County. This time he located a site on the east of side of town. Engineers and consultants worked on the design and plans for the tower and proceeded to obtain the federal permits required.

The next hurdle was getting the cost of the tower financed. It was a unique type of loan and finding bankers willing to participate was very difficult. I talked to several of my banks about the loan and it drew polite interest but no loan. Trying to use the radio tower as the security for the loan just wasn't flying. The bankers were asking how it would be possible to sell a radio tower if the borrower defaulted. Although the station was making money, the current revenues did not support the cost of the tower. The Worleys needed a source of financing that looked beyond the short term and could be comfortable possessing the tower as collateral. It was a long process but David stuck with it and found a lender.

What a relief and accomplishment!—but only briefly. The contractor made mistakes on the construction and after a serious investigation it was concluded that the completed tower was unsafe. The only solution? Tear it down and build another one! Embarrassing, humiliating, and a hard blow to the business, most persons would think the gods were against them. David knew God had his back. I know he was a master at hiding his feelings, but even in this most difficult time I never heard David complaining about his circumstances or expressing anger at the contractor who caused the near disaster. He wasn't happy about the situation but he was genuinely concerned for the well-being of the contractor. David pressed on to complete the tower and I never saw him waver from his responsibilities and other commitments during this crisis.

Looking back on the events and obstacles that occurred during this period, I would have to say God was closing doors so he could lead David and Iva Lea down new paths of service and work. While the sea was stormy for KOKE operations, the sun was shining on Austin, Texas. Austin gained national attention and was promoted as one of the top cities in the country. Money and investors were actively looking for opportunities to get in on the future of Austin. It was great time for the Worleys to sell the business. Watching the sudden and rapid demise of my real estate development business was the final impetus for David to be persistent in getting Iva Lea's agreement to sell her partnership interest in the business to an outside group.

David continued to juggle the problems at the tower and station operations as he began orchestrating the sale of the station. The Austin economy was spiraling down and station revenues were also declining. They needed a buyer who looked past the short term and would give the station value for its future potential.

It wasn't quick or easy but they made a deal to sell the station. The next hurdle was getting federal approval for the transfer of ownership. David's consultants were top notch, but the process was plagued by special interest groups who made their living objecting to the sale of a media property. The objections slowed the process, added to the cost, and delayed the sale.

Reasonably confident that the sale would occur, David and Melinda began to consider what direction they would take if the station sold. The idea of living in Europe—the Swiss Alps most likely—was a possibility but the focus turned to Aspen. They loved the area and the setting was a good place for David to do some writing. It would be a sabbatical and allow them time to consider other options. Having spent a lot of vacations in the area, they felt comfortable with the local church and looked forward to renewing friendships. But the decision and move was time sensitive. Because of the children's schooling, the Worleys needed to either renew their Brentwood School enrollment or make a financial commitment to schools in Aspen. As deadlines approached the Worleys were in Aspen evaluating their options and having a working vacation. David was monitoring the progress of the sale and both David and Melinda were looking for schools and a home. My family and I met them in Aspen for a short vacation toward the end of their trip. We could tell that David and Melinda were ready to move to Aspen but they weren't going to act until the station sale closed. They left Aspen without an answer. They continued to wait upon the Lord. It was just how they lived their lives; honoring the Lord and waiting for him to set their course in his time. For Aspen, the time ran out. But what good news for Brentwood Oaks Church, Austin Grad, Joel Petty, and countless others, my family included.

The deal was finally consummated and now David and the family had the money to live out their lives in comfort and style. For most people that would be the rest of the story. For David it was the opportunity to do more for his Lord. He gravitated to doing business with people who needed early funding to take their plans to the next level.

It was never the matter of keeping score or striving to be wealthy or for the recognition that money can bring, but about honoring his Father above. This was the time in David's life that he would either walk the talk and live out his convictions, or allow himself to be distracted by his success and new wealth. The theme of business for David now seemed to center on being involved with others.

One of David's first ventures that I know about was with a college friend at ACU, Mel Ristau. Mel was teaching at ACU and he told David about some of his ideas regarding the use of the Internet and how a protocol, designated HTML, would change how everyone interacted with the Web. The other important event was Apple's planned introduction of a CD-ROM drive, which would remedy the limitations of "floppy disks" and media storage. These new developments were of special interest to Mel since his graphic design work needed a lot of storage. Mel had become involved in a conversation on the Internet with some technicians in California who were making plans to employ these changes to create products that were marketable to consumers and businesses. David encouraged Mel to keep in touch and in the loop regarding any business opportunities. For David the opportunity to work with a friend and get involved on the ground floor of new technology was appealing. After more updates from Mel, David decided to schedule a meeting in San Jose involving Mel and the California people. David asked me to go with him so I could give him my take and maybe get me involved in the enterprise. The meeting occurred during an Apple Developers Conference in San Jose. It provided David with the opportunity to hear firsthand what Apple was planning. This meeting led to several months of trips back to San Jose in an attempt to put together a business plan that would work for everyone. After a couple of days and nights of meetings, David pointed out that the California people were entrenched in the Apple culture, and more importantly it was going to be difficult to get a long-range commitment from them. David looked upon the zeal for Apple and its icons as a type of cult. But he continued to fund the effort to work with the group to gain their support and reach an agreement. I advised David on a number of occasions that moving company personnel from Texas to the San Jose area was going to cost a lot of money to compensate for the cost of living. It wasn't making financial sense to me and I worried about wasting his time and money.

David, for whatever reason, was not ready to walk away. But he would never answer my question of how much was he willing to invest.

My greatest complaint when working with David was the lack of parameters for evaluating a venture. He liked to probe and brainstorm but never wanted to share real interest or commitment in a venture. It brought a lot of uncertainty to his business associates and I think distracted them from the objective. The California deal never gelled.

Mel and David continued to consider other options and they did start some ventures together. The most valuable result of that first venture was becoming acquainted with Mel. David and I spent a lot of hours talking with Mel about the venture, and David shared his thoughts about doing business while honoring the Lord. David talked about the name Thelese and what it meant to him. I was fortunate to be with them when Mel gave David a piece of art that conveyed Mel's interpretation of what Thelese is all about. Ultimately that depiction became the logo for David's business enterprise.

David took great care when working through decisions that involved many people. I will relate a story about David's involvement in supporting the addition of middle and high school grades to Brentwood Christian School. It was my first opportunity to see David's kindness and concern for church unity and purpose in action. Because of the limited resources of the school and uncertainty about how quickly each class would fill, the only course of action was to start small, with the goal of adding one class a year. The decision was made during my first year as a board member. David could be exhausting in wanting to identify all the elements of the immediate requirements and, more importantly, the impact of the decision over the long term. He was supportive, encouraging, probing, and attuned to how the expansion would draw on the resources of Brentwood Church. The church was supportive and had been generous in the use of the classrooms and facilities needed, but the shared arrangement of classroom space and church facilities wasn't without difficulties. David was extremely sensitive to how the change might impact the church and possibly increase tensions.

David wanted the addition to proceed as he too had children who would attend the higher grade levels, but he never put his self-interest above the interests of the local church. The school had its share of detractors for a variety of reasons, but David centered on the school's founding vision: creating an educational environment to openly teach God's Word. The school was about more than education; it was an opportunity to share the gospel. It was a mission opportunity for the church. It was that conviction that led him to support and nurture the school then and even today through his estate.

SEEDS OF BROADCASTING IN THE USSR

We were on a flight to San Jose for the Apple Developers Conference when David told me he was interested in broadcasting in the Soviet Union. I was in disbelief and skeptical. What an idea! What a waste of time! Come on, you have got to be kidding! But as we talked it was clear that he had given the idea a lot thought and prayer. A few days later at a business lunch with David's San Francisco attorney, who told David he would be leaving soon to travel to the Soviet Union as part of a trade delegation, I was stunned that we were meeting someone who was going to the Soviet Union. What are the odds? David's response was to tell the attorney that he had been praying about broadcasting in the Soviet Union and would like the attorney to help him get the names of appropriate people with whom to discuss the possibility. How was this happening? Didn't David know that Americans were welcome and, more importantly, those going would likely not be interested in "Christian broadcasting."

The words "grace and peace" were on their way to Soviet radio. There are a lot of stories to be told by others about David's endeavors (spiritual and business) in Russia, but I have to mention that they started with David being a participant in breaking Soviet laws. Getting Bibles to Russian citizens was illegal. What better way to endear oneself to the Soviet officials that David wanted to meet? But David saw it as the opportunity to join a group of Christians planning to meet with seekers and give away Bibles smuggled into their country. Since he was in Russia, why not make calls on the Russian media and make an unannounced visit to the director of Soviet radio? When I heard about this I was fearful and very doubtful it would have a happy ending. In fairness, you have to know I was a child of the Cold War. It is still unbelievable! Never doubting that David felt led to try, I just couldn't imagine having any success. The story could be a modern-day version of God at work in the life of a willing servant—David, a boy from Fort Worth, Texas, who at the age of fourteen committed his life to the Lord. Few if any were better equipped to take the message to the Soviet Union. Biblical scholar, radio station owner, and entrepreneur, David went with boldness and purpose to serve his Lord. It is easy to forget the look you can get by telling someone "no," especially a young child. The word no was an invitation to keep asking. It had to have been God's timing to send David at that crucial moment in history. No one was prepared for how suddenly the barriers to sharing the gospel could fall. That trip was the beginning of David's international business and spiritual endeavors.

Back at home, David continued to invest in people and in businesses that needed capital in order to grow. He was presented with the opportunity to invest in and work with a small medical equipment business whose vision was to become part of the rapidly expanding and changing health field. David spent a lot of time wrestling with the decision to get onboard the train. The train was probably pulling away from the station before David jumped on the first step. It was a very good decision for him. All of his early endeavors supplied insight into this decision.

Wealth was very uncomfortable for David. He never wanted it to define who he was or how his Christian brothers and sisters thought of him. David was possessed with the ability to deny himself if he believed it was for the better good. I know he had always wanted a Land Rover for his personal use. There were very few in Austin but they had a great reputation for off-road travel and endurance. For David it was a perfect fit for traveling in Colorado and other backroads. Coloradans loved four-wheeling over rough mountain passes. But Land Rovers carried an image of status and wealth. He never bought one. He drove an eclectic assortment of cars. One of them was a Buick or Oldsmobile. It was an older model that had belonged to his aunt. For David, the car was reliable and available so why not drive it and use his money somewhere else? At one time he drove a Dodge Ram pickup because, he said, he got a good deal. He did not want a car to separate him from his relationships.

Another example was when Melinda almost didn't get her house. When David started going off the radar and being often out of the country, Melinda and the girls wanted to live closer to Brentwood. He and Melinda asked me to help them find a new home that might give him an open view (remember Aspen) and Melinda and the girls more space and a shorter drive to the Brentwood School. Melinda, Heatherly, and I scheduled a Saturday to look at homes. Knowing David had a love for the hill country, we spent a long morning in the Westlake area. After several hours Heatherly said, "Mom, not any of these homes are closer to Brentwood and we go there at least six days a week. Shouldn't we look at homes closer to Brentwood?"

I tossed out the list of homes I had and suggested lunch at a burger place on Mesa Drive. I didn't have time to come up with another list, so I decided to drive around the area with Melinda to get her input on the style of home she wanted. We had not gone very far and soon came around a bend on Valburn Drive. In the distance Melinda saw a white stone two-story home on our left. She pointed to it, saying it was a style she would enjoy. As we drove closer I was excited to see a For Sale sign in the yard! We were able to get access quickly and went inside. It was perfect for Melinda and Heatherly, much closer to Brentwood, and had space for the three girls and the grandparents when they visited. It even had a room for David's office. What made it even better was the hill country view. Perfect! I prepared an offer and waited for David to return so he could also see the home and sign the papers. I was a little miffed, or maybe really surprised, that he showed little interest and wanted to see other choices. Wow! Melinda and I were both disappointed. But we worked around David's very full schedule to look at about half a dozen additional homes, even at night. I was baffled and worried that the Valburn house would go under contract before David decided. A few days after the first night showing, we met at his office at the Institute (now Austin Grad) to discuss leasing his office building on North Lamar. His assistant, Bridget Casey/West, was at the meeting. I had come to the meeting with another plan in mind but I waited until we were finished with the office building discussion. I told David I had an important matter on which he needed to make a decision. It wasn't like me to be so formal or direct and I could see him going on alert. He didn't have the house on his agenda and I sensed he was being gracious in giving me the time. When I started laying a listing sheet on each home we had considered, he began watching me and paying little attention to the papers in front of him. Having summarized the listing information on each home, I told him I knew of one home that would make Melinda happy and cost less than any of the others. After giving me a piercing look and tossing out a couple of questions, he asked for the contract so he could sign. It is the only time I pressed David to get onboard.

I tell this story because of what Bridget told me later. David did want the house but was hesitating because I had mentioned that Michael Dell was living at the other end of Valburn Drive. I wanted to convey that the neighborhood was solid and used Dell's name to make him more comfortable with the neighborhood. What I didn't consider was David wanting to shun living at an address that might be seen as flaunting his wealth. That attitude was the essence of David. He had no desire for fame and fortune. He would have been content as a teacher who wanted to share his relationship with his Lord. At the age of fourteen he became a partner with his mom in the radio business, but only months before he had become a partner in the gospel with his Lord. That partnership will be everlasting and we are blessed by it.

Words he used to teach us and encourage us are what I consider the most valuable heritage David left for us. Guided by his understanding of Scripture, he took complex subjects and made them have meaning that reached into our hearts and souls. Ending discourses with "grace," or "grace and peace," he was totally comfortable using these words in all his correspondence. Brigette told me once that she had asked David if he really wanted to close his letter to Van Cliburn with "grace and peace." After all, David was soliciting Van Cliburn to contribute some of his music to be used in David's radio broadcasts on Radio 1. David's response was a simple yes. David was David—fearing the Lord and focused on revealing the Word to everyone. David conducted his business exactly like he lived his life. Being aware that he was imperfect, and deeply grateful for God's mercy and grace, David was a good business partner. I will be forever grateful that my life was made fuller, richer, and deeper as a person and as a believer because God saw fit to weave the Worleys into the fabric of my life.

6

Memories of a Father

Elena Worley Coggin

REMARKS AT THE SERMON SEMINAR, AUSTIN GRADUATE SCHOOL OF THEOLOGY

My name is Elena, and I'm David's youngest daughter.

The sun was peeking through the base of the trees. We all gathered in a room in Colorado to hear what news Dad had to share.

He was cryptic, he was calm, he was peaceful: "I have what looks like a tumor in my stomach," he said. We responded, "Well, what can we pray for? Who are your doctors? What's your plan of treatment?" All he said was, "Pray that the Kingdom of God will come out of this."

Uh, no, I thought. I will pray for the cancer to be gone; that we will not suffer through this. An honest, valid response to this news.

Since I can remember, Dad has prepared us girls for this moment. Any time he would leave the country, he laid a clean white envelope atop his desk entitled, "Open at my death." We jokingly called it his "Death Letter." Anytime future plans were discussed, he tagged onto the end, "Lord willing and I live and breathe." And even in 1956, at the age of seven, my dad recorded a pretend commercial at his father's radio station and ended with, "Talk with ya tomorrow, if there is a tomorrow." Classic David Worley.

In the course of the last few years, I prayed my prayers for his healing, as did many of you. But by no fault of our own, Dad was not healed. Dad knew from the beginning that his physical healing was not the end goal. As Dad became sicker and sicker, the words that he told me in the room in

Colorado, surrounded by aspen trees, rested calmly on my heart. What he said about bringing God glory even when we suffer became so clear. Instead of encouraging our despair in the pain that was to come, Dad spoke grace and peace into our hearts and minds.

God has provided fresh water for us to drink through this desert road we have been traveling. Our grief has become the vehicle for seeing God as our Provider, our Sustainer, and our Creator. Our hearts have been softened.

We pray that you can join in our hope for the resurrected life. Grace and peace be to you.

REMARKS AT THE MEMORIAL SERVICE FOR DAVID WORLEY

This piece was much more difficult to write than I had anticipated. But not for the reasons I would've thought. I would've assumed my brain would be in such a state of fog that words wouldn't come. On the contrary, too many words came to mind.

If you have lost someone dear to you, you may relate. Each day of grief brings out a new aspect of the person you've lost. There are days I wake up missing the daddy that held me as a little girl, sharing his iced tea. Then there are days I wake up angry at him for traveling for long periods of time, missing various sport games and performances. But then the next day I remember the day he surprised me in Abilene for freshman follies, cutting his Russia trip short to fly directly to West Texas to see me sing a solo. Grief is, to say the least, a winding drive in the woods that takes you through sunshine, snow, and storms. Yet each turn provides more beauty. In the next few minutes, my prayer is that I will honor my dad in what I have to say, but also that I may offer you a fuller picture of who David Worley, my father, is and was.

I always saw my dad as larger than life. No harm would come to me as long as I was at my daddy's side. He took charge, and people listened. When we traveled, he always had plan B, C, and D. I had almost convinced myself, as well as most of my friends, that he was in the CIA. He was powerful, always thinking, seemed to have friends in odd places, was always more hip than I when it came to restaurants and coffee shops around the world. I admired him in what he accomplished. I wanted to exemplify how precisely he used his words like "blessed," not "lucky." I would stare at his hands during every prayer, palms open and facing upward. I was very comfortable in thinking of my dad as superhuman. But after his diagnosis two years ago, what I characterized my dad by was being quickly stripped away—his traveling, his eldership, his love of drink and food, his love of dry cappuccinos, his strong presence, his drop-offs of his favorite iced sugar cookies, his frequent visits to my kiddos and dog. He could no longer, physically, enjoy these things. What was left of my dad was only his vulnerability.

This was true of my own life.

I was born with a heart that longed to be loved, to be validated, and to please. I was definitely the star child to raise (wink). Since my worst fear was to disappoint, I did whatever it took to avoid that. But, as you can imagine, I reached a point at which I could no longer keep that up. It was around the time of dad's diagnosis when the joy I so easily found in life was being quickly stripped away.

I entered into a state of "Who am I?" and "Who will I be without my daddy?" The symptoms of this new season were anxiety, panic attacks, depression, anger towards the church, and frustration towards my upbringing. When I got to the heart of my anxiety, I realized that I had a mounting fear—a fear that if I followed my own path, not that of my parents, and if Dad disagreed, I would be deemed unlovable. I knew my dad was a wonderful listener. People from all over the world consider my dad as one of the dearest friends, because he sat and listened. But as his daughter I wanted him to do more than just listen. I wanted his wisdom, his encouragement, his heart. It seemed that he gave these freely to most, but I didn't feel like he did as much for me. But soon I mustered the courage to think through a conversation with my dad, about my anger towards everything I knew and what my fears were. As we drove to the restaurant in his tiny blue VW Bug, I began to feel like a nine-year-old girl living in the skin of a thirty-year-old woman. I began to reconsider what I wanted to share with my dad, fearing I would disappoint him. My anxiety built as I followed behind him into the restaurant, not being able to look away from how he now walked like an elderly man, keeping his hands propping his back, mustering the perseverance to continue through his pain caused by the cancer in his bones.

We sat. He ordered his sparkling water with no ice; me, my still water. He asked what the waiter's favorite item was and ordered two. He leaned back, cleared his throat, and began the conversation. "So, baby, tell me about this anxiety you're having." I began to word-vomit all of my symptoms, my triggers, how it was handicapping my life as a mother and wife, how it had all began days after his diagnosis.

His eyes softened. He responded . . .

"I know exactly how you feel. I struggled with claustrophobia after my father's death. It finally stopped after my first trip to Russia. It makes you feel helpless and out of control. I'm sorry you're going through this, but I promise, this is only a season."

My jaw dropped. My eyes swelled with tears. My dad *saw* me. He understood me. He saw and embraced my struggle. The Spirit did its grand finale and he finished by saying, "You know there is nothing you could do that would make me not love you."

Some where along the line, I had forgotten whom I had learned the words "grace" and "peace" from.

Our imperfections, our suffering, our brokenness cannot separate us from the love of God. In the same way, it brings us closer together as well. My dad and I were not only daughter and father, but brother and sister in Christ.

Through dad's stories of struggling with anxiety and claustrophobia, it changed my perspective of this seemingly flawless man. But not the way one would initially think. It was the missing puzzle piece in my childhood. First, that I came by my anxiety honestly: how we would always leave a performance early to avoid the mass exit of people; how he always sat in the very back or very front of an auditorium; the intensity and stillness he exuded on airplanes; his abhorrence of elevators. I went from a little girl seeing her father as flawless to a grown woman seeing her father as just a man—a wonderful one. In that moment I was more proud to be David's daughter than at any other moment in my life. As if I had been holding my breath for thirty years, I took a deep and intentional sigh of relief. My dad saw me, and I saw my dad—imperfect, broken, graced, and deeply loved.

From the moment in Colorado when Dad told us about his cancer diagnosis, our family mantra became, "If we are to suffer, we will suffer well." This may sound strange at first, but let me explain what that actually looked like.

When there was anxiety, we stopped and listened to what our bodies were trying to tell us. When there were no words to pray, we relied on others to carry the prayers for us. When anger or tears came, we let it wash over us, instead of suppressing. We were open about our fears with our children, allowing them to witness how to grieve.

And Daddy, a man who was extremely private and independent, gave up himself and allowed his wife to wholly and completely care take for him. A father who was always outwardly strong and courageous allowed his daughters to come in and partake in the care taking of his feeble, frail, and withering body.

I have never experienced as much of God's grace as I did in those months. I had finally witnessed the joy in suffering that James refers to. I saw my parents' marriage come to an end with grace, beauty, and the most selfless love, which can only come from exemplifying the one who laid down his life for us—Christ Jesus.

In the sharing of his struggles with me, in watching the cancer take over his body, it made my daddy more whole. Not only was it a gift for him to share those struggles, it was a way of leaving a part of himself with me, a part that I will cherish always. A part that is also my story.

In a way, he made it easier to let him go, for now.

In the words of the prayer my five-year-old son says, "Jesus, we miss our Abba, so please, come quickly."

Thank you. May God give you grace and peace as you live to the praise of his glory.

7

A Shepherd in Word and Administration

Allan J. McNicol

I cannot remember when I first met David Worley. However, I do recall when he made an initial impact.

Sometime in the mid-70s of the last century, I was doing some work in my office in the late afternoon. It was a warm Austin day and a friend came by and wondered whether I would be interested in having dinner and then going down to a local radio station afterward. He was interested in the latter excursion because he had heard that Kris Kristofferson and Rita Coolidge were making an appearance there and he thought we might get a chance to see them. This made some kind of sense since I had spent some years in Nashville, where I had come to know some folks with whom they may have had common interests. Hardly enthusiastic, but not being able to think of a plausible way of excusing myself, I agreed to my friend's proposal.

The evening turned out to be much more eventful than I expected. We arrived about the time when Kristofferson and Coolidge were finishing their studio appearance. Shortly afterward they came out to a small side room where my friend and I were seated with a few fans. To my surprise, they were in no hurry to leave and for fifteen or twenty minutes they engaged with us in casual conversations of which I have little recollection.

What struck me was something else that I do remember to this day. The manager of the station was there, and for some reason I chanced to ask about his relationship with the owners. There was a method in this madness.

I was aware that I and the owners were part of the same fellowship. I was curious as to what extent their beliefs had an impact over what took place in an important communication center in a large metropolitan area. The manager was circumspect. But he did say that he was appreciative because he seldom heard from the owners and he could attest that they did not interfere much in day-to-day operations.

Then he spoke one more word that really hit home. "Now that you mention this, there is this odd thing about the management. From time to time one of them will call to query me about the nature of some of the music we play and whether it is helpful and appropriate for a mass audience!"

At that time I knew enough about the family to determine quickly who was making the calls. My knowledge of David was by reputation. But this comment clearly fell within the parameters of everything I had heard about him.

This ring of truth echoes in my mind because it is consistent with what I have known about David ever since. When David first started going to Russia, after the fall of the old Soviet Union, during those chaotic days he somehow invested in a radio station. It once had considerable importance in that formally totally controlled society. Here at last he had major influence in determining the content of programs. I recall several conversations with him at that time where he openly expressed anxiety over some of the programmatic choices he had to make.

Recently, when I began to read his obituary, all of these memories began to flood back into my mind and earlier impressions were validated.

> David had special concerns about how believers listened to the radio (and experienced entertainment) . . .

There was a lot about David Worley that was complicated. But it was not because he was incoherent. In a special sense he sought to tie family, business, daily life, teaching, and church vocation together; and in his own particular way, for the most part, it worked.

This can be illustrated by a longstanding interest David maintained on how the Christian should seek to exercise his or her stewardship across the spectrum of the important aspects of daily life. Benny Tabalujan, a church leader in Melbourne, Australia, had produced a manuscript that had the intriguing title: *God on Monday: Reflections on Christians @ Work*.[1] Somehow David was able to view the manuscript before production and strongly recommended it for publication. His blurb on the back of the book is particularly informative.

---

1. Glen Waverley, Victoria: Klesis Institute, 2005.

> With its pertinent stories from Scripture and the modern business world, the book leaves the reader with concrete ways to both think and act differently at work, at rest and even in unemployment. It is to be recommended.

Within the book there is a chapter on "rest" in which Tabalujan seeks to develop an outline for a "Theology of Sleep." I was struck by this recently and actually made some ungracious remarks to the effect that it was probably pushing theology a bit too far. Imagine my surprise when our school librarian informed me that David worked on the same topic for years and actually had an incomplete manuscript on the subject.

I trust that by now the reader is aware that I have known David and Melinda for a long time (about four decades). In this essay I would like to reflect on two connected topics: the influence of his teachers in theology in preparing him for Christian leadership, and his exercise of that leadership as president and chancellor of Austin Graduate School of Theology, formerly known as the Institute for Christian Studies.

A SCHOLAR ANCHORED IN THE BIBLE

David Worley's theological heritage rests firmly within the borders of the great nineteenth-century American Restoration Movement. His family was anchored in it and he served faithfully all of his life inside its ecclesiological parameters. Among other things, especially among the Churches of Christ, where David worked tirelessly as a shepherd, a crucial watchword was "to follow the faith and normative practices of the early church found in the Scriptures." Consequently, it is no accident that its leaders have made more than their share of contributions in the field of biblical studies and early Christian ecclesiology. David followed directly in that mold.

During his years at Abilene Christian, David improved his knowledge of the Bible and sharpened his skills in biblical interpretation and exposition. As with so many before him, he was especially diligent in the study of Hebrew and Greek. Yet, this was not just preparation for the sake of excelling in the academy. Through his study of Hebrew his lifelong love of the Psalms was deepened. In similar fashion, his work in Greek gave fresh insight into both the Pauline and Catholic epistles in the New Testament.

Nourished by these foundations, in the 70s of the last century David and Melinda set out for New Haven. Arriving there, both engaged in serious theological study in various sections of the Yale theological community. The time that the Worleys spent at Yale was close enough to my time that they shared most of the same teachers with me. Since David's arrival in Austin,

I have had the blessing of having many delightful conversations over the years with him about his formative theological development at that time. Aside from my remembrances of these conversations, if this essay has any lasting value, it will be on my claim that Yale left a strong imprint on David. As is often the case with serous theological study, it prepared and fortified him for success in his work as president and chancellor of a seminary.

A QUARTET OF YALE THEOLOGIANS

Four significant teachers at Yale left lasting impressions upon David. For those who knew them, in his own way, David appropriated many of their insights and utilized them to build the foundation for his later teaching and administrative work. Of course these were not the only figures of lasting importance in David's life from this time, but to this author they seemed especially significant.

Of the four, the first I wish to discuss is Paul Holmer. Aside from a few anecdotes, I seldom heard David talk about Holmer. Indeed, I am not sure whether David ever had Holmer for a class. Nevertheless, Holmer's embrace of Pietism left a deep impression upon many at the school and David was one of them. Holmer's Kierkegaardian insight that Christianity is not dependent on some system of metaphysics for its authenticity appealed to David. The only narrative that Christianity needs is the unfolding of the revelation of the God of Abraham and Jesus to his people. Faith in that God is capable of structuring all aspects of our lives. Faith and the most rigorous demands of the academy can, appropriately balanced together, complement one another. It is a fitting testimonial to the influence of Holmer that David made sure that the library of our school had a full assortment of the Holmerian oeuvre shortly before his death.

David and Abraham Malherbe belonged to the same fellowship and so those ties were enhanced during David's Yale years. My own work with Malherbe was done in Abilene. He influenced me strongly to study the New Testament in the context of an exhaustive study of the Greco-Roman world. Thus, when I went to Yale my first graduate seminar was in Paul Schubert's year-long course titled The Gospels and Hellenism. Unfortunately Schubert died during that year. I immediately urged the Bible faculty to take into consideration Malherbe as his replacement. I am not sure whether my recommendation had any influence, but eventually Yale did appoint him to Schubert's old position. Subsequently Malherbe became a major presence in David's life both academically and ecclesiologically during his years in New Haven.

David seldom said much to me about Malherbe's classroom influence. I tend to think David preferred the Holmerian model of teaching rather than the more classical teaching style of Malherbe. But I do know that David was always very supportive and generous on behalf of the various publishing ventures and symposia that embodied Malherbe's work in subsequent decades. Worley was clearly proud of what Malherbe had achieved. After I would go to a meeting where Malherbe was present, David would always quiz me intensely about any piece of information on what "Abe and Phyllis" were doing. David learned much from Malherbe. Their fraternal bonds in Christ were strong but I was not convinced that he regarded him as his mentor.

When it is all said and done, I do believe that the two most significant teachers at Yale who contributed to David's intellectual and spiritual development were Brevard Childs and Nils Dahl. Respectively, they were the two senior professors of Old and New Testament studies during the time David was doing his doctoral work.

Anyone who was acquainted with Childs will appreciate the impact he had on David. Childs approached the interpretation of the Bible as one who gave a special place to what the church reckoned to be the canonical text. In addition, the Bible was to be understood as one unified consistent work. This coherent text expressed the basic message that God has reclaimed the world in the coming of Jesus Christ. It came to be known as canonical criticism and David was a strong advocate of this theological discrimen. He incorporated this model of thinking into the framework for all of his Bible classes in his later teaching.

Most directly, David stressed in his classes the value of this approach for preaching. As with Childs, so also for David: the canonical text is the unique area where the church hears the Word of God. Thus, whether it involved an analysis of the Psalms or the book of Hebrews, David paid meticulous attention to the literary structure of the particular work studied. Since it is the Word of God, everything depends on whether one understands what the text is saying in the context of the canon. The best way to do this is through a careful literary approach.

The last time I heard David preach was at a chapel service at Austin Graduate School of Theology less than a year before his death. For that semester speakers were assigned passages from the *Megilloth* (books written to be read at particular annual feasts of the Hebrews). On this occasion David took on the Song of Songs (Solomon). It was a grand performance worthy of Origen. He not only discussed what the book was saying about the joys of love and family, but somehow he welded his remarks together with connections to other books of the *Megilloth* to address the church. This was a truly canonical approach.

Speaking of an unlikely source for a text, another chapel sermon of David comes readily to mind. On this occasion he spoke of the significance of the cosmic language in Ephesians for the Pauline vision of salvation. David had taken Nils Dahl's course on Colossians and Ephesians and was thoroughly conversant with the function of this language in the Greco-Roman world. But the question for any teacher of Ephesians is to explain to regular people what the text is saying to us today. I looked around in that assembly on this morning and I saw students completely enthralled by David's explanation. He had not only interpreted clearly God's Word in the text but he also succeeded in making clear the pastoral implications of such difficult passages for today.

Of all his teachers at New Haven, I am convinced that David had the highest regard for Dahl. He looked on him as his mentor. In later years Dahl returned to his native Norway. After the death of his wife, and since his daughter had entered a religious community, Dahl had few immediate family members. David, on his trips to Russia, would come by Oslo and visit his now lonely teacher. David often spoke glowingly to me of these visits. It is hard to know who benefited the most from these times. Although David has not left a long legacy of publications, one of the most substantial that I would like to see made available in a more user-friendly form is his commentary on Ephesians. This is a fitting legacy not only to David but to the influence of his majestic teacher.

DAVID WORLEY THE ADMINISTRATOR

Freshly minted with the rewards of outstanding graduate education, David and Melinda Worley settled in Austin in the early 1980s. David immediately became intensely involved with the life of the Brentwood Oaks Church of Christ as well as managing family business activities. Both David and Melinda began service as adjunct faculty members at the Institute for Christian Studies (later Austin Graduate School of Theology). Although intensely busy, David taught an occasional course at Abilene Christian and Pepperdine. This was the basic pattern of the Worley household for their first decade in Austin.

After James Thompson left Austin in the early 1990s, David shouldered increasing responsibilities with respect to the consolidation of the Institute. He was highly respected by both students and faculty. Administrators loved him because he did not accept a salary for his teaching services. Although there was a faculty replacement for Thompson, the office of the presidency remained vacant. The faculty was becoming deeply concerned about how that important issue would be resolved.

Upon discussion by the faculty, it was decided that its senior members (Allan McNicol and Michael Weed) would invite David to lunch with a view of broaching the possibility that he might submit his name to the board as a candidate for president of the Institute.

I will always remember this meeting. My family, with some degree of regularity, loved to go to the old Granite Café after church for lunch. Close to the University of Texas, we thought it would be an excellent place to have a quiet but extensive conversation. The meeting lasted a couple of hours and covered a whole range of issues about the future of the school. Even though Weed and I were the conveners of the meeting, as it progressed David asked most of the questions. Anyone who has ever been in a meeting with David will appreciate that there are few action matters that arise directly from any discussion. The meeting ended with a promise that he would give the proposal serious consideration. Much to the relief of the faculty, he submitted his name to the Board and in due time he was appointed president.

THE PRESIDENTIAL YEARS

David's tenure as president was from 1993 to 2000. I am arguing in this essay that his presidency was the logical fulfillment of his superb graduate preparation. He had now attained full maturity in mind and in soul. If anyone were prepared to lead this seminary, it had to be David.

I believe it would be helpful to evaluate David's administrative years under the rubric of non-surprises vis-à-vis surprises.

Commencing with the category of non-surprises, I would note that he cultivated a sense of mutual compatibility within our seminary community. This was clearly evident with respect to the direction and operation of the school. Full-time faculty turnover was practically non-existent and support for the administration of the school was very strong throughout his tenure.

David's administrative style was understated and non-intrusive. Despite the fact that he was away from the office regularly and spent an increasing amount of time in Russia, there was no doubt he was completely in charge.

The demands of higher education in the modern era mandate that fundraising is a crucial aspect of the office of president. David pursued faithfully the usual avenues dictated by the office. He had definite views about advertising and developed some unused approaches. His contacts with and knowledge of the business community was especially helpful to the school. With the growing number of startup companies in Austin, David's acquaintance with various entrepreneurs provided some welcome unsolicited gifts to the school.

As an example of David's creativity in fundraising, he put me in contact with a group of young business types who were worried about technical chaos as the year 2000 approached. Not a month passed without a flood of books appearing on this topic. Many had direct religious overtones. David arranged for me to meet the group at a luxurious estate in West Austin. There we discussed the theological implications of these books and the patterns of eschatology that informed them. All of this culminated in a generous honorarium for the school.

What may be more interesting to the reader is the surprises that emerged in David's administration. First, I would note that early in his tenure he implemented a serious update in the school's use of technology. Younger readers may be surprised, but at that time less than a decade had passed since personal computers had become available. Word processing, email, and the subsequent Internet revolution were still being birthed. From the beginning David sensed this was the wave of the future. He abolished the office of faculty secretary and bought personal computers for every full-time faculty member. He introduced a computerized form of interoffice communication. After the shock wore off among the faculty Luddites, most people were grateful to be pushed into the new era.

To me the most surprising feature of David's administration was his unreserved concern to pursue and support mission work. Others in this volume, no doubt, will record and detail his initial support for evangelism in Russia during this era. Along with several leaders of World Radio, David had already found innovative ways to reach massive audiences in the former Soviet Union with the gospel of Christ. He was a major mover and donor behind making Bibles available to Russians in a contemporary readable form of their native languages. He pushed relentlessly to get the faculty to write a small booklet on the basics of the Christian faith called *Things That Matter*. This was immediately translated into Russian. Fifty thousand translated copies were published in the first printing and since then it has been published in many other languages and dialects. Finally, David persuaded several faculty members in Austin and other Christian colleges, at his own expense, to go to St. Petersburg and offer courses to fledging leaders of the Russian churches. Neither before or since has anything like this been seen at what is now Austin Graduate School of Theology. The recruiting was at David's own expense. Some of those who went to teach paid their own way or their own university took care of their monetary needs.

Among all the intensity of this activity, there were other expressions of his great love for mission and evangelism. I especially remember David walking into a routine meeting of the faculty and startling us with what seemed to be an astonishing proposal. He stated that after consideration and prayer he had divided the world into five major areas. Each faculty member would be assigned to take some responsibility in one particular area. The purpose would be to evaluate the status of the church and identify mission opportunities in their assigned region. Although this project languished, the episode made it clear that David was not one to put limits on what could be accomplished in mission.

On the other hand, David was not the type of person who loved the whole world while being indifferent to individual persons. During the years of his presidency he was always teaching and mentoring a variety of people on an individual basis. Most of this activity was done unobtrusively. However, one of these studies did come to my close attention. A middle-aged man from Nepal began to take courses at the school. He was not a Christian and the faculty could think of no reason why he desired to be there, except possibly to improve his English. After several semesters we were all astonished to learn that he and his wife had been baptized. David had quietly taken him aside and led him to faith. But the mentoring did not stop there. David made a trip with the student back to Nepal. There he shared the faith with his extended family.

This is not to say that David's administration accomplished all of his goals. The parking situation in the crowded University of Texas area was becoming more and more difficult and, as always, it was stressful to keep worrying about maintaining the operation of the school on a marginal budget. Perhaps in some frustration, David quietly began to explore an affiliation between the school and a larger Christian college. This was one of his few actions that was met with resistance from the faculty. The overture was quickly tabled. In any day-by-day operation there will always be stress. Yet, in an eventful era David's quiet but authoritative administrative leadership consolidated the school and was deeply respected by all associated with it.

THE YEARS AS CHANCELLOR

After David's presidency, with the full consent of the board, David was appointed chancellor and remained in that position until his death. The landlocked situation of the school during the previous decade continued to be an impediment to its growth and expansion. It would now be the task of successive presidents (Carson Stephens and Stan Reid) to grapple directly with what seemed to be inevitable: the need to find a new location and facilities for the school.

Reaching back to his academic foundation, David was always fond of using the Greek word *thelese*, "in keeping with the will" (of the Lord), to describe the pattern of operation of his life. In this context, his appointment as chancellor could be viewed as a work of divine guidance. It enabled David to free himself from the day-to-day operations of the school and concentrate in assisting in giving direction on major decisions that the administration would be called upon to make.

On the issue of finding a new facility in rapidly growing Austin, David was especially helpful. His association with the business community once again proved valuable and he became the guiding light in discovering the new location for the school. His work included giving additional help both in advice about renovation of existing facilities and in playing a major role in the financial drive to underwrite this important development. Today, after more than two decades of administrative direction as president and chancellor, during some of the most trying times for over a century that seminaries in America have faced, the school is proudly about to celebrate reaching a century with stability of operation. Without question, David Worley was one of the major figures in allowing us to celebrate this accomplishment.

CONCLUSION

David Worley was born and raised in a family of faithful members of the Churches of Christ. His roots were deep within the Southwestern ethos of the American Restoration Movement. Central to his family and church life, he heard the call to express loyalty to Christ by structuring his ecclesiastical practices as close as possible to that of the earliest Christians. If one adds to this a love of sharing the gospel with others, one has a fair understanding of what David stood for and never deviated from throughout his life.

For some people such an ethos could sometimes detour into sectarianism. David would have none of it. His vision was much more expansive and ecumenical. This is especially true as a result of his many connections within higher education. He profited strongly through his time at Abilene Christian University. He had deep family connections with this school. But this essay has sought to bring out another aspect of his journey. I have argued that his time at Yale provided the superb educational preparation that sustained his successful administrative direction of a small but influential seminary in Texas for almost a quarter of a century. Through these associations he became acquainted with two of the major theological figures of the twentieth century—Brevard Childs and Nils Dahl. These were gifts. What is significant is that he put this foundation to the use God intended it. As with the apostle Paul, whom David greatly admired, all of his life was to be lived faithfully in the service of Christ. David wore many hats. But of all of those he seemed to choose the mantle of shepherd. He was God's gracious shepherd and administrator until the end.

8

David Worley as Churchman

Charles K. Johanson

IN THIS ESSAY, I have been asked to share some thoughts and observations about David Worley as a churchman, a topic so broad that one might struggle to find its limits. It remains clear to all who knew David that he was a man intensely committed to prayer and personal devotion to God. One does not speak the language of Scripture as David spoke without retreating often to lonely places to pray and drink deeply of the Word of God. But in thinking of David as churchman, I plan to focus this essay on David's role as a teacher and pastor in the life of the church.

My relationship with David goes back to 2007, when I was hired as a minister of small groups and adult education at the Brentwood Oaks Church of Christ. Even though I had graduated from Austin Graduate School of Theology, I had never met David until my initial interview with the elders. David did not say much during the interview, a trait that I would later find to be typical of him during meetings. However, when it was his turn to ask a question I was immediately struck by the thoughtfulness of his line of questioning. "What are you currently reading and where are you growing in your understanding of Scripture?" These are the questions that should be asked more often among believers, but for David it revealed what he prioritized and valued in the life of a minister. This would not be the last time I received these kinds of questions from him.

This introduction to David serves as the launching pad for a relationship between an elder—David—and minister—me—that spanned almost a decade. Our interactions included serving together on the worship and education committee, which met on average once a month, as well as elders and ministers meetings, which met twice a month. Admittedly, I did not quite know what to think of David in our initial interactions and even the first few years of ministry. It certainly will come as no surprise to those who interacted with David on a regular basis when I describe his communication style as cryptic and even abrupt. I had never corresponded with anyone through one-sentence emails before my interactions with David, and often his wording would leave me scratching my head for days as to its meaning. In those first few years of interactions, I was often frustrated at David's communication and micromanaging style. I remember receiving an email the day after I led my first prayer at Brentwood Oaks in which he informed me that we are not to say "good morning" to the congregation and that we should always use the first-person plural in our prayers instead of the singular. I received several similar instructions in the first few years of ministry, which at the time I often found to be oppressive.

However, as the years went by, these types of emails became less frequent and I began to have a growing admiration and fondness for David. After one meeting around my fourth year at Brentwood, I related to my wife that I had been blessed with a treasure from God in David Worley. Although I cannot recall with clarity the content of our interaction during that specific meeting, the moment marked a turning point in our relationship, at least from my perspective. I began to truly appreciate David's role at Brentwood Oaks as a teacher and pastor.

THE OLD STAG

Those who spent a lot of time interacting with David in spiritual dialogue or sat in his classes were obviously aware of David's fondness for Paul's letter to the Ephesians. In this letter Paul says that Christ

> . . . gave the apostles, the prophets, the evangelists, the shepherds and teachers to equip the saints for the work of ministry, for building up the body of Christ, until we all attain to the unity of the faith and of the knowledge of the Son of God, to mature manhood, to the measure of the stature of the fullness of Christ, so that we may no longer be children, tossed to and fro by the waves and carried about by every wind of doctrine, by human cunning, by craftiness in deceitful schemes. Rather, speaking the truth in love, we are to grow up in every way into him who is the head, into Christ, from whom the whole body, joined and

held together by every joint with which it is equipped, when each part is working properly, makes the body grow so that it builds itself up in love. (Eph 4:11–16 ESV)

David held a radical commitment by the grace of God to the high calling of being a shepherd and teacher. For David, the stakes were incredibly high in the role of protecting and equipping the dedicated ones (saints) for ministry. Although the goal of this essay does not warrant a critical analysis of the above passage, we would be hard-pressed to find a more accurate description of what David Worley as a churchman encompassed.

Perhaps an image is appropriate as we consider Paul's words to the church in Ephesus in relation to David's pastoral role in the life of the church. I recently read Felix Salten's classic, *Bambi: A Life in the Woods*.[1] As I worked through the book I thought of David often, especially in the description of the mysterious stag who watched over the forest. Throughout this essay, stories from this book will be shared as a way of painting a picture of David as a churchman. The parallels between the stag and David as an elder are from my point of view uncanny. Of course, many are familiar with the Walt Disney cartoon based on this classic tale. In both versions, the old stag is revered. In the cartoon, as the movie opens with the forest buzzing with excitement and activity at the birth of the new prince, the camera quickly pans up to the top of a large hill. On the hill stands the great stag with its full set of antlers. The stag stands erect with the posture of a watchmen. He watches over the forest and stands ready to alert the animals under his charge of any danger that he sees from his high vantage point.

I saw David take this very position in our church auditorium on many occasions. Five years into my ministry as a minister of small groups and adult education, I transitioned to pulpit ministry while retaining my role on the worship and education committee. From the pulpit, I would often see David sitting in different places in the congregation. But occasionally, and most memorably, I would look up and see David sitting on the small pew in the very back of the auditorium. Our building is structured, like many church buildings, with a gradual decline in elevation from the back to the front of the auditorium. David was sitting at the highest point in the room, unseen by everyone except the few who faced the congregation. He sat at attention listening for the Word of God, while looking over the congregation. Perhaps David sat in the back in order to take inventory of those in the flock who needed extra attention from the shepherds. It is an image that will always be ingrained in my memory, especially as it relates to David's role in the congregation as teacher and pastor.

1. Translated by Whittaker Chambers (New York: Simon and Schuster, 1928).

Teaching

In Salten's book, Bambi had several run-ins with the old stag, but one encounter in particular speaks to David's role as teacher and pastor at Brentwood Oaks. The encounter happens when Bambi is an adult and has taken a wife, Faline. One morning, Bambi wakes up and notices that Faline is nowhere to be found. After walking around the forest for a short time, Bambi hears the voice of his beloved with the message, "Come, come!" Bambi begins to follow the sound of her voice, but he is soon confronted by the stag, who tells him not to go to her. Bambi does not understand, and he keeps moving in the direction of Faline's voice. The old stag continues to tell him not to go. After some back and forth, the stag finally speaks of Bambi's impending death if he is to continue to follow the voice of his beloved. Bambi finally acquiesces and follows the stag to a secretive place very close to the source of the voice. As it turns out, the voice was not Faline's, but a hunter leaning against a tree using a call to lure his next victim out of the forest.

This is the task of a shepherd as outlined in Ephesians 4:11ff.—a task that David took with the utmost seriousness. The siren calls of idolatry have lured God's people since the garden, and David was keenly aware of the dangers that idolatry still poses for the church today. This awareness and sense of urgency could easily be detected in David's teaching and in personal conversation. David spoke often of the importance of the Shema in the life of Israel and her habitual failure to live out the command to have no other gods before the LORD. Perhaps more effectively than most, David was able to tap into the imaginations of his listeners and take them into the story of Scripture. He understood and communicated that the church has her own wilderness wanderings and trappings that threaten her identity as saints.

Last year, I sent David a preview of a sermon series that I planned to preach based on the Apostle's Creed and asked him for feedback. He sent back the preview in typical David Worley fashion, with at least two sentences in different colors for each one of my sentences. In the sermon on the Shema, David wrote, "You need to be 'direct' about the idols we worship instead of the Jealous One." He issued this admonition on a regular basis in our personal exchanges as well as in the worship and education committee meetings. David would remind us constantly of the last words of John's first letter, where the church is given the imperative to *flee idols*. The greatest command recited by the Lord Jesus to the teacher of the law demands a steady diet of evaluating the idols that so easily slip into the back door of our hearts, competing for our allegiance. From David's perspective, this role of shepherd cannot be understated if the church is to continue to grow in her maturity.

The shepherds of the flock must not only be aware of the idols in their own lives, but they must also stay in tune with the false voices of the wolves in sheep's clothing who would lure the sheep away from the fold. The cruelty of idolatry can be found in its subtlety. A flock that is distracted and weak will chase after the siren songs of the gods of the age if they are not directed and even confronted when necessary. In the years that I knew David, he spent much time and energy on alerting the flock to these false voices of a fallen world. Two especially subtle and potent idols that were important for David to confront were the entertainment and sports industries. One can imagine the resistance he received in pointing out these idols in Austin, Texas, the live music capital of the world and home to University of Texas football. How painful it was for David to watch the flock direct so much of their time, money, and energy to the hours of sports watching as well as mindless entertainment with little to no redeeming value. Make no mistake: David called these idols out in his own gentle and pastoral way. Not only in David's teaching, but also in his worship planning, he challenged the gods of consumerism, entertainment, politics, nationalism, and others who take their place in the modern pantheon.

In his letter to the church at Ephesus, Paul was rightly concerned with *every wind of different doctrine that tossed the people to and fro*. According to Paul, God calls on the shepherds of the church to be diligent in their oversight of the teaching that takes place in the church. We see the havoc that false teaching wreaks in the church from Paul's pastoral letters. David proved to be a strong voice in the worship and education committee in protecting the teaching of Scripture in the church. As someone who was given the task to recruit teachers from the names submitted by the committee, I was often quick to approve a teacher more often for pragmatic reasons and expediency. When the pool of teachers shrinks or time becomes an enemy instead of an ally, one might be tempted to throw up one's hands with an attitude of "beggars can't be choosers" when it comes to teacher selection. David, on the other hand, would not settle for teaching that was suspect when it came to theological soundness. The teaching of God's Word was too important to place in the hands of someone who was less than capable of rightly handling the word of truth. As an overseer, David lived by the mantra that the easy way is not always, or perhaps even seldom, the best way. David was not against efficiency when warranted, but he favored discernment and taking one's time when it came to matters in worship and education. When he was not present in our committee meetings, we tended to move quickly through the agenda, as David had the habit of slowing the pace down to talk through philosophical and theological issues related to the teaching of the Word and worship. Early in our relationship, this style became a source of irritation to me, but, like many aspects of David's life and personality, I grew to admire the wisdom and motivations of his methods.

The episode of Salten's novel mentioned earlier, when the old stag was able to steer Bambi away from the hunter's false call, speaks to the charge given to shepherds to protect the flock, and David dedicated much of his pastoring to this calling. However, in his teaching and careful planning, he also paid much attention to the positive function of the shepherding role, the *equipping of the saints for the work of ministry*. In one chapter of the book, Bambi spends days looking for the elusive stag. Something that the stag had told him in a previous visit bothered him to the point that Bambi wanted answers. After a long search and a little help from an obnoxious screech owl, Bambi was able to locate the stag in a remote area of the forest. And in searching for the Stag, Bambi was being led on purpose to a new part of the forest.

David Worley was very intentional in leading the congregation to deeper and richer parts of the forest. In David's teaching and pastoring, he methodically led the people, along with the other shepherds, to a greater understanding of the story of God and the church's place in that story. Over the last several years, Brentwood Oaks has presented a yearly theme each January. In choosing a theme, David would often ask the question in our committee meetings, "What pasture is God leading the flock to graze in this next year?" We would spend a large amount of time talking about the upcoming books of study in our four-year cycle of working through the canon and how these books, with their particular emphases, would shape the church for the upcoming year. David encouraged pushback whenever the themes would veer outside the boundaries of Scripture. He challenged each of us to think and speak scripturally as a committee and would revise our proposals to more accurately reflect the language and themes of Scripture. Here is a recent example of an email he sent to the committee concerning the theme of joy, which we adopted in 2017:

> Worthy of discussion and discrimination of meaning . . . and effects joy (as understood in NT in Christ)
>
> "my inner being delights in the law of God" Ro 7:22.
>
> "I rejoice as I suffer for you" Col 1:24;
>
> Do we get "joy" by concentrating on it? or do we do other things which effect "joy"?
>
> How are our "affections" changed/transformed/affected "in Christ" so that our emotions, passions, feelings are effected and nurtured in ways different than for those outside of Christ? Does "joy" in NT letters align with what we mean by "joy" (gladness . . .) in our language today?

Although David often kept his cards close to himself in regard to what he was thinking, he was never shy about speaking to the larger goals of education among the elders and ministers at Brentwood Oaks. Perhaps it is best at this point in the essay to hear his thoughts and concerns in his own voice. The following is a lengthy document that David shared with the elders and ministers concerning the aim/vision of teaching. These words, in my mind, provide some keen insight into David's passions as well as his communication style in the context of pastoring the flock. The title of the document is "Aim/Vision Is Love."

> When we as overseers face unhealthy teachings, we can readily understand how young Timothy felt in Ephesus. We need to make sure our compass still points magnetic North with the various interferences. Thankfully, Paul tells Timothy (and us) what is true North in 1 Tim 1:5, "The goal of our instruction is love, out of a pure heart, good conscience and sincere faith."
>
> We must never lose sight of this. While we must sometimes say who we are *not*, we must spend far more time saying *who we are*. What has God in mind for His people at Brentwood Oaks? Why did he create us by His Word? What has He revealed to us about our purpose for being, for thinking, for doing as His chosen people?
>
> We ask these questions now so that in 2016 we might faithfully plan our teaching and our life together as the family of God at Brentwood to please Him who is the father of the Lord Jesus and so our father.
>
> *The Goal of Our Teaching Is Love (1 Tim 1:5)*
>
> Love for whom? We know scripture teaches us that there are at least four loves:
>
> | | |
> |---|---|
> | Love for God | Dt 6:4–9 (our Lord's words also) |
> | Love for neighbor | Lev 19:18 (Lk 10:25ff; Rm 13:8ff; Eph 5:28) |
> | Love for enemy | Matt 5:43ff (Lk 6:27ff; Rm 12:19ff) |
> | Love for the church | John 13:34f; 15:12ff (see below) |
>
> Surely if we "love" truly, we please the Father and are true to His purposes for us (though we may still struggle to understand and say exactly why He has called us as His people!). Surely if we love truly, we do things and effect results we had not anticipated (the law of unintended consequences). How do we as overseers then affect such love through the teaching and activity of the church?

"Consider how to stir one another to love" Heb 10:24. [returning later to attempt some answers to the question of what God has dedicated us to be and do]. To focus it more narrowly: How do we pastor the church to love God and to love one another? How do we provoke one another to love? [I suspect we can love neighbor and love enemy if we can truly love the brethren!] The litmus test for whether we love God is whether we love the brethren (1 John 4:20). This coincides with the stress on philadephia, love the brothers, in all the letters (Rm 12:10; 1 Thes 4:9; Heb 13:12; 2 Pet 1:7). And, it originates in Jesus' own words, in the most difficult command in the Bible, what Jesus calls the new commandment:

I give you a new commandment, that you love one another. Just as I have loved you, you also should love one another. By this everyone will know that you are my students, if you have love for one another. John 13:34f (15:12ff; 1 Jn3:11; 2 Jn 1:5f).

This command of our Lord to the Brentwood church (Jesus' friends) is more difficult than the command to love neighbor. In the latter, we are commanded to love as we love ourselves (as we naturally strive to live, to eat, to breath). Jesus, however, commands us to love as he love us. *No one has greater love than this, to lay down one's life for his friends* (John 15:13). Jesus commands us, not to love as we love ourselves, but rather to love the brethren by *not* loving life itself.

Indeed, Jesus has to command us because we do not want to do this, at least not at first. Love should become "genuine, heartfelt" (1 Pet 1:21f) but it may not be that at first. Do we as the people of God at Brentwood obey Jesus' *new* commandment? Of course, this commandment is finally inseparable from the first commandment (Mk 12:29) and profoundly explains Jesus' new commandment. As fathers over our families and as pastors overseeing God's flock, we are to impress on them (Dt 6:7–9) the first commandment (Dt 6:5). Are we as overseers impressing upon the family of God the *first* commandment and Jesus'*new* commandment? I do not think we are and we must decide each for ourselves if we are obeying.

I come back again to 1 Tim 1:5: *The goal of our instruction is love.* Certainly to remind each other and remember the command to love (God and church) is necessary (with all the challenges to obeying); but equally important is to remind each other, remember and help each other comprehend God's love in sending the son (1 Jn 3:16f; 4:7ff). Such love understood is a compelling surge ("Christ's love compels us" 2 Cor 5:14). The story (the gospel) of God's love and the commandment to love

God (and church) must be told, enacted, recited, sung, prayed, obeyed . . . together, in tandem, in balance . . . continually.

For me and for us, all the above is 101 . . . first things . . . elementary. But . . . somehow, in the miasma of problems and issues and criticisms, at least I forget to come back to the basics . . . as a way of coming to understand why God created us for Himself and . . . what is magnetic North for us. So . . . I believe that I am more likely to obey the command to love God (and church) if I am instructed continually in the story of God's love for His people, for Israel, for the church, for His creation for the nations! . . . and in hearing this, to know not only *what* He did, but to understand also *why* He did it (to the degree He has revealed this to us). I regret I did not, as a father, in my home, with my daughters teach them (as I should have) *what* God did and *why* He did it. I remind my son-in-laws to do this for my grandchildren; I try to do it when I am with them.

For the people of God at Brentwood in 2016, perhaps we could be more intentional, in an OT/NT weekly lectionary readings on Sundays (to replace those we are presently reading), to cover the fundamentals of the story of *what* and *why* God acted as He has in the drama of scripture . . . and perhaps, either in morning or evening assemblies we could be intentional about explaining these (more systematically or sequentially) in the preaching and exhortations. I am presently preparing a proposal for such readings (perhaps for 17 or 26 weeks) which encompass God's ways and purposes from creation, to Abraham, to Israel, to Kingdom (cf Neh 9; Acts 13).

All of this, of course, is for the purpose of continually forming in our hearts and minds an understanding and ever greater love for the only true and living God, the father of our Lord Jesus Christ. I suspect that the telling and wrestling with the story of the Father's love will have the effect of sharpening our understanding (heart and mind) of God in at least four respects (which can be aligned with the Lord's prayer):

Love of God/God's love within Himself
(*our Father in heaven*)

Name of God/God's integrity within Himself
(*hallowed be your name*)

Rule of God/God's communion within Himself
(*your Kingdom come*)

Will of God/God's righteousness within Himself
(*your will be done*)

We could take these four aspects of who God is and elevate them in our teaching. Of course, they are encompassed in our Lord Jesus, the image of the Father, into whose images we are to grow. But to speak of these four aspects is also to draw out from within us, praise, adoration, thanksgiving . . . which should at all times characterize who we indeed are as God's people.

We can't know who we are (or are to be) as God's people if we don't spend most of our time reminding each other, remembering, understanding who God is (in whose image we were formed). It is God's way of making things right (not my way) . . . it is Jesus' faith and faithfulness as son (not mine) . . . which I need to hear, over and over and over again.

Healthy teaching about God the father will shape and reshape the church in ways we can't foresee . . . but I think such engaging teaching about God' love might help the family at Brentwood to live a biography of love (1 Cor 13) more faithfully in at least two respects:

Seeking the best in the other
(1 Cor 13:4–6; Phil 2:3f; Rm 12:10ff)
Enduring and forgiving each other
(1 Cor 13:4,7; 1 Pet 4:8)

We should describe, perhaps better, the nature of being the family of God, in the above two matters. God expects us, in serving one another, to think more highly of each other, to seek the best for each other. I am not sure we are doing this. We need to hear God's love in this regard and be reminded of God's call for us to serve. In the same vein, is the need to endure and forgive. Again, I am not sure we are healthy in this regard. God knows his family at Brentwood. We each have to suppose how John might pen a letter to the angel of Brentwood today. As pastors, we must consider this.

So . . . who are we as God's people? In the family story, we remember that God called us to be a people (through the Exodus) holy to Him (Dt 7:6f; 14:2), a holy nation (Ex 19:6; Rev 1:6), as He is holy. We (should) call ourselves saints (as we are) not because we are "saintly" but because God has *dedicated* us (the meaning of being holy) for a special purpose among all the peoples and nations of His creation. We are dedicated to God, a dedicated nation . . . but dedicated to what purpose? In the family story, we remember that God delivered and protected us so that His name would be respected and proclaimed in all the earth (Ex 9:11; 18:11; Dt 4:32ff), so that all peoples would know the Lord (Jos 4:24; 1 Kgs 19:19; Ez 36:22ff), that we might be His servants, a light to the nations (Isa 42:6; 49:6). Our rebellion and disobedience brought us into exile. We waited for God to return and restore us.

God the Father, acting to respect His own name and integrity, in faithfulness to His promises, and in love, sent His unique son of Israel, a son of Judah, a son of David, His only son, to experience the life of Israel, through exodus, wilderness, exile . . . to lay down his life . . . and in the faithfulness of this son, faithful in the wilderness, suffering in exile, God the father restored us as His people, in the resurrection of the son from death, providing the son's faith and death as our own provision for salvation, as we participate in His death and life, through His Spirit holy. We are the Father's people now only because we are *in* the son, "in Christ". God is our father only because God is the father of the son, in whom we abide and live.

In rereading this document, I am struck once more of the blessing that David was to our congregation and to me personally. For a young minister learning the ropes of congregational ministry and adult education, David stood tall as a treasure trove of wisdom and insight. David was avid in leading the congregation, along with his fellow elders and ministers, to the greener pastures of a greater understanding of God's love for us and the new commandment of our love for one another. His influence on the education and worship at Brentwood Oaks cannot be missed, and so many who sat in his classes have been blessed with clearer vision of the story of God's love. A shepherd knows where he is taking the flock, and David, more than anyone whom I have ever met, led others by the grace of God with clarity and intentionality.

Language

As a teacher and pastor concerned with harmful teachings that toss the flock to and fro, David understood the importance of language as a way of shaping and renewing the thinking of a congregation. "We do as we think" was a common teaching of David. In a culture permeated with meaningless words and labels that are broadly applied as a way of avoiding the hard labor of communication, he spoke with prodigious efficiency and high precision. Words and their meanings were of the utmost importance for him, as evidenced by his unusual emphasis on certain syllables within words and strange sequencing of words within sentences. David's language resulted in what was perhaps his most endearing and frustrating quality, something Bambi encountered with the old stag on a constant basis. Returning to *Life in the Woods* once again, one story involves the capture of a wounded and sickly friend of Bambi's named Gobo by a hunter. Although Gobo's disappearance caused everyone to believe that he was dead, his return to the forest much later caused quite a stir among his friends. As Bambi told the stag about the return of his friend from the hunter, the stag said nothing except, "Poor Gobo." No commentary was added, and this phrase haunted Bambi for several days. He decided to go looking for the stag to discover the meaning of the phrase. As he inquired further, the stag remained elusive as to his meaning, but told Bambi that he would understand in due time. Bambi left the conversation frustrated, although the words of the stag proved to be prophetic, as Bambi's friend had become tame and had lost his fear of man—a trait that would eventually lead to Gobo's undoing.

David had his own version of "Poor Gobo" in the short emails he would send. From personal experience, I would mull over these one-sentence emails for days and even weeks trying to unpack the meaning. Communicating with David required stretching the mind and taking the time necessary to process and discern the meaning of words. There are many who found David's use of language to be perplexing, although the wisdom in such use of language could be seen over time. I have already mentioned his disapproval of using "good morning" in the assembly. He preferred "grace and peace" because of the theological depth embedded in such a greeting, and this was David's frequent greeting outside of the assembly. He emphasized certain syllables to draw out meaning. "Administration," for example, turned into "AD-ministry." "Woman" turned into "WO-man" in drawing out the significance of the relationship between the first couple. Even in citing the name of his grandson, "Samuel" became "Samu-EL," which highlights the rich meaning of his name. David became quite adept in changing the order of phrases. Instead of "Holy Spirit," David used the title "Spirit Holy," as this is the way the ordering appears in Greek. Perhaps no greater example of this kind of wordplay could be found than in his translation of the Lord's Prayer. With phrases like "Come your kingship," "Be done your will," and "For our bread for tomorrow, give us today," the church was given a fresh hearing of this ancient prayer. David's public prayers were almost always built around the model prayer, and this prayer maintains a special place in the life of Brentwood Oaks.

One of the phrases that he attached to the line "*lead us not into testing*" came from Jesus' words to his disciples in Matthew 26:41: "*For my spirit is willing, but my flesh is weak.*" David's language included phrases as a testimony to our need for the mercy of God. For those who sat in on David's classes or listened to his prayers, one would often hear the phrase "by God's grace" interspersed throughout his sentences. David understood that the power to be the people that God has called us to be comes not from ourselves, but from the power of God's Spirit among us. There is something incredibly powerful about a man of David's learning and presence continuing to repeat that phrase. His utterances and appeals to God's mercy were in fact words of grace in themselves to the bruised reeds and smoldering wicks of the congregation who were putting one foot in front of the other in the trials of life. One could see clearly that David's careful choosing of these phrases came not out of a distant pedagogical rhetoric, but rather a heartfelt belief. David Worley was a man who needed God every hour, as the old hymn goes, and this kind of humility embedded in his language served as a wonderful example to the flock.

As witnessed in the document above, David's vocabulary was laced with Scripture. I do not recall David using the word Saturday, but I do remember his frequent use of *Sabbath*. Of course, Sunday was always the Lord's Day in David's world. This way of speaking and writing had a way of arresting focus. Through language and sentence structure, the listener was forced to pay attention and engage in the hard labor of decoding and unpacking the meaning of words. David Worley paid attention to his words, and because of his efficiency his words carried weight. And one knows a speaker is an effective communicator whenever his listeners begin to adopt his vocabulary. The Lord's Day before this essay was written, one of the prayer leaders at Brentwood Oaks used "Spirit Holy" in his public prayer, a testament to years of sowing and tilling the soil of words in the hearts of the church. Because of David's carefully crafted language, those under his care and guidance grew to appreciate the power of words in moral and spiritual formation. David used strange language, and the church was blessed.

Pastoring the Flock

David's somewhat quirky personality and communication style might lead one to think that he did not possess the pastoral skills to effectively minister to the flock. What might be surprising to many is that David was highly pastoral in his own peculiar way. Returning to the image of the old stag, much of the second half of the book describes the interactions of Bambi, who is coming into adulthood, with the wise stag, who remains elusive and mysterious. Despite his odd behavior, the stag took great interest in walking alongside Bambi and passing on his knowledge and wisdom to his eventual successor. In one dark episode of the book, Bambi is ambushed by a hunter and shot through the shoulder. The intense pain causes Bambi to fall into a state of shock as he is ready to lie down and die. From out of nowhere, the stag, who had been watching him, comes to Bambi's aid and, through encouragement and even confrontation, leads Bambi to a place of safety where he is able to eventually recover.

David provided a similar role to the congregation. In his own unique way, he devoted himself to binding up the wounds of the weak and the broken. So many congregants who found themselves in the loneliness and sterility of hospital rooms would receive a beautiful bouquet of flowers from David and another elder. David would also send messages through his favorite form of communication: in short emails where he would express his deep concern for your particular situation. In our typical correspondence over matters of adult education and worship, David would include postscripts asking about my family. Occasionally I would receive a one-line email with the phrase, "Remembering your beloved this day." Even months after conversations about the trials of life, David would send a "Remembering . . . " email with the implicit message that he was lifting up the congregant to the Father in prayer. Although some no doubt found David's personal interactions to be odd and even awkward, he communicated genuine warmth in conversation through a series of questions. David was much more comfortable questioning others than receiving questions about himself; a characteristic that lent itself to effective pastoral work.

My wife and I had the privilege of David coming to our home twice to pray over our newly born children. During the first visit, I was anxious about the behavior of our easily excitable dog, Bucky. True to form, our dog could hardly contain himself when David walked through the door. After he leaped on and off the couch for a few minutes at a dizzying pace, I went to pick Bucky up to place him in his kennel. David sat down with the dog nestled close beside him, and he began to gently pet Bucky behind his ears. After assuring us that he was quite comfortable with Bucky, my wife and I noticed the calming effect that his touch had on our dog. Throughout the entire visit, David stroked Bucky to a state of slumber as no guest had been able to do. During our time with David, he prayed over our son, Nathan, but we discussed several other subjects, including the topic of dreams. Out of this conversation, we discovered why David said "sweet sleep" instead of "good night." David could speak intelligently on a variety of subjects, and clearly David spent some time in thought chasing down the answers to the questions of a curious mind. As unusual as David's personality could be, his gentle presence blessed many in countless pastoral interactions. On any given Sunday, one could scan across the room and find David engaged in a one-on-one conversation away from the crowds. He possessed the rare gift of being fully present in a conversation, especially one that involved pastoral counseling. David understood the relational aspect of shepherding the flock, and he did not abandon his post, as difficult as this part of being an elder may have been. Assuredly, the same pastoral gift that my wife and I experienced in David was shared by many in our congregation and beyond in hospital rooms, coffee shops, and church foyers.

David dedicated himself to the pastoral work of prayer. I witnessed his passion in prayer in a unique way during one particular elders and ministers meeting. On this occasion I had been given the task of praying over the names on our prayer list, a rotating assignment among the elders and ministers. After the group shared their requests, I started my prayer and began to read the names off of the list that was compiled during the meeting. As I prayed, I kept seeing some movement in my peripheral vision. The movement became distracting, so I adjusted my chair ever so slightly to see what was going on in the background. I quickly discovered that it was David, with his common posture of prayer—hands held just below his chest with his palms facing upward. After each name was read, David lifted up his hands as if he were sending each name to God. Those same hands that gently stroked our dog in our living room were now ever so gently lifting the names of brothers and sisters in Christ to the Father above. At David's funeral, his daughter Heatherly spent some time talking about David's hands and the different roles that these hands had played in the Worley household. As she described David's hands, this memory came back to me. When I think of David as a man of the church, I will always think back to the image of David lifting up his brothers and sisters in Christ in such a beautiful symbolic display.

Finally, we would be remiss if we did not pay tribute to David's pastoral work in mentorship. Vigen Guroian, in his helpful book *Tending the Heart of Virtue: How Classic Stories Awaken a Child's Moral Imagination*,[2] spends some time writing on the relationship between Bambi and the old stag under the theme of mentorship. In this chapter, he highlights the calculated behavior of the stag in passing on his wisdom to the next leader of the forest. Through the years, David developed the habit of mentoring future leaders in a variety of ways. He looked upon the role of deacon as "elder in training," and he spent time nurturing the leadership skills of the next generation of leaders. On occasion, he would take young men in the church to Russia to participate in seminars. He met with deacons under his charge at coffee houses and, of course, through email correspondence. He provided young

---

2. New York: Oxford University Press, 1998.

men with resources for ministry and would often challenge them to teach a class or lead a ministry.

As a recipient of David's mentorship, I could not count the number of emails I received over the last decade with instruction, encouragement, correction, resources, and prayer. Going back through my correspondence with him, I am amazed at how often he would pass on articles or videos covering topics of theology and the church. Whenever I presented overviews of upcoming sermon series, I could always expect to have my inbox inundated with helpful aids in various forms. I was not unique in receiving this kind of support, as David strove to *equip the saints for the work of ministry*. There are many things that I miss about David, this compendium of theological resources notwithstanding.

Unlike the Disney adaptation of Bambi, the classic book spends a significant amount of time detailing the interactions between the stag walking with and teaching his son who is coming of age. The relationship between the two is striking even as the stag offers correction and challenge to the maturing Bambi. A large part of mentoring the next generation involves having the courage to correct wrong thinking where needed. Confrontation is not easy, and David did not shy away from taking on this role as shepherd. On more than one occasion in the last ten years, some hard conversations with members were necessary in order for growth to take place. Sometimes some teaching needed correcting, and David would do the hard work of corresponding with the teacher. Because of the respect that David had garnered in the congregation, this correction was received more often than not in the manner it was given . . . in gentleness.

I was on the receiving end of some gentle correction from David very early in our relationship. One of my first assignments at Brentwood Oaks was to teach a class on Revelation. David recommended strongly that I place these classes on our website, to which I reluctantly agreed. As the class began, however, I grew steadily uncomfortable with having my first run at Revelation being broadcast online, so I decided not to follow through with what I said that I was going to do. It did not take long for David to see through what I was doing, and he confronted me (through email), but not with harsh words full of commentary. Rather, he simply copied and pasted my own words from our previous agreement. I was caught and realized that my yes was indeed a no. I apologized for not following through on what I said that I was going to do. At the next assembly, David sought me out to ask how I was doing. Not knowing David very well, I knew that I had disappointed him, but his gentle approach help restore any severing of the relationship. In that conversation, he talked to me about the importance of "AD-ministry" and its value in the life of the church. In later meetings between elders and ministers, David brought up a specific incident where a previous elder had offered some "gentle" correction to the group and had held their feet to the fire in following through with what they said they were going to do. I cannot say for certain if David had brought this up as a message of encouragement to me, but I took it this way. Even the elders endured correction from time to time. David maintained the rare balance of firmness and gentleness in correction that facilitated growth in members of Brentwood Oaks by the grace of God.

I end this essay returning once more to the image of David sitting on the small pew in the back of the auditorium. As a churchman, David Worley served his post at the top of the hill in the forest faithfully, warning of danger while building up the body of Christ. God blessed the church with a unique personality in David Worley, a churchman who recognized the high calling of the ministry of teaching, the importance of language, and the eternal value of walking alongside the flock. We lost a great teacher and pastor in February 2017, but his legacy by the grace of God continues to live on in the hearts of those whom God touched through David's life.

9

Living to the Praise of God's Glory
David Worley, Colleague

Jeffrey Peterson,
Austin Graduate School of Theology

I LEARNED TO TEACH the Bible as I have (whether for good or ill, only God truly knows) by following the example of outstanding teachers I was privileged to study with in postsecondary education and through conversation and interaction with teaching colleagues I have been afforded, principally at Austin Graduate School of Theology. In my most formative years on the faculty, the school was known as the Institute for Christian Studies. David Worley was the school's president and a teaching colleague who exercised considerable influence on his fellow teachers, as well as our students.

While I had heard of David for some years, we didn't meet until the morning in March 1993 when I arrived on the ICS campus to interview for an open faculty position in New Testament. The first appointment of the day was breakfast with President Worley, and in that conversation we found that we shared an appreciation for two authors who are perhaps not especially popular: the New Testament scholar Nils Dahl, who had supervised David's dissertation, and Austin Farrer, an Oxford theologian and interpreter of the Gospels and Revelation. Such a discovery tends to foster a special bond between readers, who tend to think they alone know of a hidden treasure that has escaped most others.

Over breakfast we discussed the early work on my own dissertation on Paul's christological exegesis in 1 Corinthians 15:45–49. I mentioned that my supervisor, Wayne Meeks, had encouraged me to locate a copy of the notes from Nils Dahl's lectures on Christology, which his students had circulated in typescript, and I expressed disappointment that I had been unable to track these down in New Haven. "Oh, I have those at home; I'll bring them to school tomorrow and you can copy them before you leave town," David replied, to my delight. Later that morning, I related this story to Allan McNicol, another former student of Dahl, and learned that he too had a copy of the lecture notes, which he produced from his filing cabinet. I happily copied them in the ICS library and, after a lively day of interviews and dinner with David and the faculty, spent a delightful evening giving the notes an initial reading; they have been often consulted since. Departing Austin, I began to entertain the idea that I might conceivably find a congenial home in a school where Nils Dahl was so well remembered and Austin Farrer appreciated by the school's president, and I was delighted a couple of weeks later when David called with an offer to begin teaching in the fall.

As a child was expected in August, my family's circumstances made it expedient, and well nigh imperative, to move early in the summer rather than later. To bridge the resulting gap in our family finances, David graciously offered the opportunity to work as his research assistant until I went on salary for ICS. My principal assignment was aiding in the revision of a section of his dissertation that he would contribute to a special issue of *Restoration Quarterly* in honor of his teacher (and mine) Tom Olbricht. His contribution to the issue would concern the "oath" by which God "guaranteed" his promise (Heb 6:17–18 NRSV). As usual, David had many irons in the fire that summer, and he joked that the published essay would *not* include a disclaimer absolving the research assistant of responsibility for any errors and holding only the author accountable! In fact, he offered a very gracious acknowledgement of his "colleague at ICS, Jeff Peterson, for various suggestions and recommendations."[1]

One of my tasks on that project was to read and digest the relevant information from Joseph Plescia's monograph *The Oath and Perjury in Ancient Greece*.[2] The previous year had not supplied the ideal preparation for this, as my studies had been focused on Jewish exegetical traditions that could help clarify Paul's christological exegesis of Genesis in 1 Corinthians 15. Still, I did my best to recall what I had forgotten about the Greco-Roman milieu of early Christianity since taking the comprehensive exam in that subject and determine what Plescia's argument might contribute to the exegesis of

---

1. David R. Worley, "Fleeing to Two Immutable Things—God's Oath-Taking and Oath-Witnessing: The Use of Litigant Oath in Hebrews 6:12–20" (*Restoration Quarterly* 36 [1994]), 223 n. 1

2. Tallahassee: Florida State University Press, 1970.

Hebrews. Reporting to David on progress, I indicated some uncertainty about the import of an argument Plescia made. David replied, "Have you talked with him about this?" I had not, nor had it occurred to me to seek clarification by that route, as in my understanding scholarship was an activity undertaken in the solitude of a library or study with a book or essay in hand; whatever one could not understand was one's own problem, not the author's. At David's urging, however, I found Professor Plescia's contact information and had a pleasant and informative telephone conversation with him. Thereafter I noticed how often David spoke and thought of scholarship in terms of conversation and interaction with other scholars.

One of the great debts I owe to David and other faculty colleagues in those early years at ICS is the rehabilitation of the categories "Bible," "Scripture," and "canon" as central terms in my understanding of theology, after several years of post-baccalaureate work in theological and biblical studies had done much to marginalize them. Notwithstanding the recent influence of poststructuralist literary theory, modern scholarly approaches to the study of the Bible are largely historical in orientation, often focused narrowly on such questions as how a given biblical book came to assume its present form, what circumstances called forth its production, and whether and how earlier literary sources or oral traditions were incorporated and adapted by its author(s) or editor(s). A student who has absorbed the ethos of graduate biblical studies emerges from those studies determined more than anything else not to attribute a Pauline sentiment to Matthew (e.g.) or assume that the ecclesiastical organization attested in the pastoral letters can be found in 1 Thessalonians. This concern is salutary when it helps us hear the distinctive notes struck in each of the biblical writings, so that no individual tone is lost, but it can also yield a reluctance to recognize points of harmony between different biblical books or even the chords that unite the biblical authors into a harmonious chorus.

Another of David's teachers at Yale, second only to Nils Dahl in his influence on David (so it seems to me), was Brevard Childs, who undertook to restore the concept of the biblical canon as a fundamental category in biblical and theological studies. Childs's Yale colleague Abraham Malherbe (also David's teacher and mine) once characterized him approximately thus: "If you rank him vis-à-vis other Old Testament scholars, he scores at the seventieth percentile; New Testament scholars, the fiftieth; and theologians, the thirtieth. If you compare him with everyone else who works in all three fields? Ninety-ninth percentile!"

Childs especially pressed the idea that the "canonical shape" of a biblical book is key to its interpretation, rather than the hypothetical stages of a book's composition recovered through scholarly ingenuity and industry.

He also argued that the final shape of the canon itself and the sequence of books within it ought to be accorded interpretive significance. While I had to acknowledge that taking up Childs's suggestion regarding the importance of canonical sequence led David to interesting observations that drew my attention to features of the Gospels, Acts, and Pauline letters I might have otherwise overlooked, I never fully embraced the latter perspective. Early in our association, David and I had some productive disagreement about the propriety of employing an interpretive construct such as "Luke-Acts." Among my most cherished communications from him is an email from March 27, 2014, which assessed my essay "Matthew's Ending and the Genesis of Luke-Acts: The Farrer Hypothesis and the Birth of Christian History"[3] as "quite interesting." David aptly summarized the essay as arguing "in Paul Harvey fashion" that "Acts is 'now, the rest of the story' to Matthew 28."

To Childs's contention that the final, canonical shape of a book of Scripture should be accorded interpretive primacy, though, I had already begun to be converted as a graduate student. Initially, this took the form of a reaction against the excessive confidence in source-, form-, tradition-, and redaction-criticism as methods of biblical study allowing one to trace in detail the stages by which a canonical book was composed, even in the absence of sources as clear as Mark for Matthew and Luke, on the majority hypothesis of Synoptic relationships. Conversation with David and other ICS colleagues deepened my appreciation of the biblical canon as a collection of writings disparate in origin, to be sure, but collected and preserved by the church as witnesses to an apostolic faith appropriately described as "one" (Eph 4:5).

As president and as a teaching colleague, David was admirably clear and consistent when it came to conceiving of the aim of our school's work. Scholars easily fall prey to thinking of their writing as directed toward their peers, or their teachers, or the world at large, or posterity. Teachers tend to focus on the needs and interests of the students enrolled in their classes, and understandably so. To make a long-term contribution, however, a theological school needs a strategic audience, a target to aim its varied educational efforts toward. When the question of our strategic focus would arise in faculty deliberations, David would respond simply, "The local congregation." In this way, he helped ground the work of his colleagues in a concrete reality we knew well and could envision clearly. He did not mean by this that no effort should ever be directed toward fellow scholars or to audiences other than the local congregation, and he was supportive of faculty attending and

---

3. In John C. Poirier and Jeffrey Peterson, *Marcan Priority Without Q: Explorations in the Farrer Hypothesis* (Library of New Testament Studies 455; London: Bloomsbury, 2015], 140–59.

presenting papers at conferences; I grew to look forward to his regular email following a conference asking what papers I had heard, whom I had had conversation with, and what I had learned. But he insisted that colleagues consider how our work could ultimately benefit the leaders and members of Christian congregations at home and abroad. One result of this focus was a volume co-authored by ICS faculty, *Things That Matter: A Guide to Christian Faith*,[4] which I was pleased to co-edit along with Michael Weed. This little book was adapted from a "Guidebook to the Christian Faith" that David commissioned for distribution to Russian audiences.

More than anyone else, David opened my eyes to the value for scholarship and teaching of information technology and electronic communication. When I arrived at ICS, I owned a MacPlus computer and had made some rudimentary use of email. In my first year, David saw that faculty were supplied with desktop or laptop computers—Apple, of course! I opted for the latter, and the world has never been the same. (To carry one's work station right into the library stacks and get down to business marked the dawn of a new epoch.) The school's initial electronic communications setup involved America Online accounts for external communication and a program called QuikMail for internal school business. The latter made a distinctive bell sound when a new message arrived, and faculty were heard to joke that you could tell when David was in the building because your computer sounded like a pinball machine. An early adopter in some respects, David was conservative in others; he remained the last person I knew to use an AOL email address.

When I attended my first international conference, at the University of St. Andrews, Scotland, in the summer of 1998, David served as my travel consultant. He advised flying into London a few days before the conference and traveling north by train to see England and Scotland; the gorgeous views of the countryside on that rail journey are among my happiest travel memories. To my surprise, he also advised setting aside some time to watch British television, which he judged superior to American. On returning to Austin, I enjoyed telling him about arriving in my London hotel room and, finding myself unable to sleep, following his recommendation and switching the television on—to an episode of *The Jerry Springer Show*!

David may have been the most assiduous consumer of biblical scholarship I've ever met. He frequently emailed to ask whether I had read this book or that article; and if I sent him a similar recommendation, the question in reply would often be whether I had met the author, which it never occurred

---

4. Edited by Michael R. Weed and Jeffrey Peterson (3rd ed.; Austin: Christian Studies, 2000).

to me to ask him. As the World Wide Web expanded, David amazed me with his facility for finding worthwhile lectures and symposia available to view online. The reading and viewing recommendations we exchanged were most often theological, but they were not limited to that subject; it turned out that our views and interests on cultural and political matters aligned with some frequency, and now and then we would share such material.

On March 20, 2016, I emailed David the comment with which Father Paul Scalia began the funeral service of his father, Associate Justice Antonin Scalia, which I noted struck me as "one of the most powerful I can recall":

> We are gathered here because of one man; a man known personally to many of us, known only by reputation to even more; a man loved by many, scorned by others; a man known for great controversy and for great compassion. That man, of course, is Jesus of Nazareth.
>
> It is he whom we proclaim: Jesus Christ, Son of the Father, born of the virgin Mary, crucified, buried, risen, seated at the right hand of the Father. It is because of him, because of his life, death, and resurrection, that "we do not mourn as those who have no hope," but in confidence we commend Antonin Scalia to the mercy of God.

Two days later I received an email in reply, formatted as David's emails often were; the body contained the quotation, and the subject line read simply, "Will ask to be used for my funeral." When David's son-in-law opened his service almost a year later with "grace and peace" and that passage, with David's name read in place of Scalia's, I recognized the quotation, but I had forgotten our exchange and recalled it only when I consulted my Gmail archive.

In the misdirection with which it captures the hearer's attention, the statement might be seen as better suited to a remembrance of Scalia than of David; I do not associate David with "great controversy," and as far as I know he was "scorned" by no one. In its overall force, however, the statement fits David like a glove, as in all the work of his life he did not seek to make himself the focus of attention but sought in Jesus Christ and by the power of his Spirit to live to the praise of God's glory. By word and deed he taught this lesson over and over to students and to colleagues, who benefit from his example and are blessed by his memory.

10

David Worley as Missions Promoter

Charles Whittle

A SON WAS BORN into a Christian home and educated in biblical studies at Abilene Christian College. He went on to earn PhD degree from Yale University in New Testament. Due to the death of his father, that son, David Worley, had been left with one parent in his teen years. Persevere he did; with a loving mother's care he grew. Through inheritance he became a man of substance. His father had owned several radios and television stations. Through educational and spiritual growth he became a man of extraordinary caring for the spiritual welfare of people nearby and far away. He engaged in mission activity and made many others aware of the opportunity.

When this writer was serving as chairman of World Christian Broadcasting, he heard of David's interest in our desire to enter a contract with the Soviet government to broadcast gospel messages to the Soviet people over its shortwave radio facilities. As a young man in his early forties, David joined men from World Christian Broadcasting in 1990 on a survey trip to Leningrad, Moscow, and several other cities in the Soviet Union. They not only met officials and seeking individuals but left a number with faith in Jesus Christ. That would be the first of untold trips David made to the Soviet Union and later to the Russian Republic.

With Wesley Jones and Andy Deikun of World Christian Broadcasting and Harold Baker of Tennessee, David first went to Leningrad. The purposes of their trip were: to contact Russian listeners of radio station KNLS in Anchor Point, Alaska, to contact newspapers to advertise KNLS and to offer free Bibles, to contact radio facilities in Russia to advertise free Bibles in Russian, and to seek program time on the air. They spent three weeks in May visiting Leningrad, Moscow, Novosibirsk, Khabarovsk, Irkutsk, Tashkent (Uzbekistan), and Donetsk (Ukraine). It was an act of faith in the Lord and commitment to mission that sustained and guided them on the arduous journey, using Aeroflot and trains, with totally inadequate food and rest. They had no prior contacts of radio or newspaper officials with whom to meet. They also did not know what kind of reception they would receive since electronic and print media were reputedly centrally controlled.

In Leningrad, the radio officials were very cordial and helpful. David and the team met the program director of Radio Russia–Leningrad. They were introduced to Tatiana Andreeva, who had a program, *Belief and Unbelief*, which aired occasionally. She later played on the air a tape of snippets (not intended for broadcasting but as illustrative) of several World Christian Broadcasting programs. About ten thousand people responded to that one broadcast. She suggested that they visit the *Chas Pik* newspaper. The group visited the newspaper and met an editor, Viktor, who was very welcoming. He was asked to allow them to buy an ad, but instead he volunteered to write an article about their offer of free Bibles. He wrote that when he first met the group, he thought they were spies. Early training had influenced him to think like that. Viktor expressed in the article his earlier lack of belief in God, but that in reading the Bible he was leaning more and more toward belief and was becoming a kinder person. It left a strong expectation in David's mind.

In Leningrad David and the group met Mariana Smrchek, a friend of Galina Koval of World Christian Broadcasting. Mariana, who holds a PhD in English, became an interpreter for them on this and many other occasions. She and her daughter, Melina, would become active members in the church in Leningrad.

In Moscow, the travelers went to offices for Radio Russia and met an erudite gentleman, Alexander Akhtersky. Alexander was program director for Russia's Radio 1 channel, which beamed to all the Soviet Union. They gave him tapes of World Christian Broadcasting programming. On listening to them, Alexander liked them—the format and focus. He felt that in the prior years the political system had destroyed the belief of the people and that it needed to be gently rebuilt.

The group went on from Moscow to Novosibirsk in the heart of Siberia. In Novosibirsk, as in later stops in Khabarovsk, Irkutsk, Tashkent, and Donetsk, the group visited newspapers to buy ads and radio stations to buy ads and offer programming. At almost all stops they had warm conversations, interviews, and meetings with KNLS listeners. David had compiled a list of

Soviet citizen contacts from KNLS, World Bible Translation Center, *Herald of Truth*, and *In Search* organizations. He sent a letter ahead inviting people to meet them near a hotel on a specific day and time if they wanted to receive a free Bible. Local citizens were not permitted to enter the hotels. One such person they met in Irkutsk, Julia, could not believe an offer of a *free* Bible. Julia had previously paid one ruble per hour to read a Bible. The group met in Houses of Prayer with baptized believers, was always invited to speak, and enjoyed the wonderful singing. In Donetsk approximately four hundred names of those wanting a Bible were collected. There David tried to take several young Ghanian students to breakfast. They went to three or four different restaurants and never got service. Those students returned home on completion of their studies knowing that an American brother cared for them.

In anticipation of the unforeseen, that trip around the Soviet Union brought David and the others no small amount of apprehension. After Leningrad, David was filled with expectation, not knowing how the Holy Spirit would guide and the Lord bless the group's efforts. Thankfully, only one of them, Harold, was affected with stomach problems during the three weeks. But untold blessings for the Russian people did come.

The meeting with Alexander Akhtersky in Moscow was followed in June 1990 with a visit by Bob Scott, president of World Christian Broadcasting, and Edward Bailey, director of programming. They brought more tapes and discussed with Alexander the possibility of broadcasting on Russian Radio. That was followed in August with another trip to Moscow by David, who offered to set up a corporation to sell commercial advertising on Radio Russia. He and Alexander signed a letter of intent for World Christian Broadcasting to provide programming on Radio 1 and for David to seek advertising for the network. Alexander was in Boston in September for a meeting of the International Association of Broadcasters. During his time there the contract was developed and signed. Alexander stressed that he wanted the programs to maintain a slight American flavor and for the teaching of Bible truths to be gentle. The broadcasts would begin on January 1, 1991.

Tatiana Andreeva of Leningrad was later invited to America by David and was baptized by him. Tatiana would become president of Radio Russia–St. Petersburg and a partner with David in a commercial radio venture in St. Petersburg (formerly Leningrad). David arranged for the Brentwood Oaks church in Austin, Texas, to respond to questions from listeners on which the World Christian Broadcasting staff in St. Petersburg needed help.

At the Abilene Christian University lectureship in 1991, David gave a report titled *Evangelizing the Soviet Union through Print and Electronic Media*. He was careful to identify the groups that had given names of respondees to their outreach in Moscow and Kiev: World Christian Broadcasting,

Herald of Truth, *In Search*, and World Bible Translation Center. He described their works briefly and told of the great need of funds for Bible printing and distribution. He encouraged support of their work. He also cited the preaching of Epi Stefan Bilak in Ukrainian and Yvan Kolesnikow in Russian via radio. It was a truly inspirational promotion of mission to Russia.

I met David in St. Petersburg in 1992 when he came back to follow up on his Russian radio contacts and those he had taught. He brought with him a Christian friend, Delvin Sparks, from the Brentwood Oaks congregation and several young ladies, including his daughters, Heatherly and Christiana. He shared his vision for outreach in Russia. David, Wesley Jones, and I met in my tiny flat on Fruenza Street in St. Petersburg to review the details of all who had been baptized and to plan the near-term work in St. Petersburg. David passed on to me his list on yellow sheets that had names, addresses, telephone numbers, and points of interests about each new Christian. There were about twenty-eight who had put on Christ in baptism after teaching by the various travelers to the city in 1990 and 1991. David had been very optimistic about those who had accepted the in-person Bible study and the large number who had responded to World Christian Broadcasting's messages.

The Moscow staff of Radio Russia was impressed with David's willingness to produce a daily program of Bible reading with minor commentary in Russian. That continued for more than a year in the mid-1990s and brought many responses from listeners. Many of those would become Bible correspondence students.

In St. Petersburg, David had a bit of the reputation of a ghost. He would often show up without notice and be gone before we could blink twice. On other occasions there would be time for a meeting over a double espresso in the Grand Hotel Europe or his giving a Sunday sermon at the Church of Christ on the Neva. What a good listener he was. He wanted to know about individual Christians, the church, and plans of the missionaries. He enjoyed hearing about churches in various regions of Russia and their progress. David's depth in theology and his profound commitment to the mission of telling Russians about Christ became apparent. I was always encouraged by his visits and edified by the exchange.

Before going to Russia, some of us who met annually to consider future work in the Soviet Union identified books that should be translated into Russian for the edification of the saints and church leaders. Vita International was formed in 1992 and would publish some of those books as well as others identified as their need was seen. I enjoyed interacting with David on the need and value of those books. He would later identify books that would be helpful to the Russian church. David led the staff at the Institute of Christian Studies (now the Austin Graduate School of Theology) in preparing a booklet, *Things That Matter*, for use in introducing people to faith in Jesus Christ. The booklet was translated into Russian and used widely.

In the meantime, David became acquainted with missionaries in New Zealand and Nepal, and perhaps many other areas not known to this writer. He was impressed by the work being done by the South Pacific Bible Collegeand a Christian brother in Nepal. He visited them and encouraged others to contribute to their work.

There was substantial early growth of the church in St. Petersburg. Almost ninety people attended Sunday worship services in late 1992. David, the mission promoter, often visited St. Petersburg, looked up Christians, and spoke in the assembly of the Church of Christ on the Neva. He was highly respected as a teacher. On his very short visits to the city, he would also meet with members of our missionary team to discern the needs of Christians and the church. In the early 1990s there were substantial poverty and medical needs. David worked with individuals and organizations to send aid, which would be distributed by the mission team and the church. He encouraged Delvin Sparks and Hugh Morgan of the Brentwood Oaks congregation to take suitcases full of medicines for distribution to orphanages, doctors, and individuals. The medicines and money for benevolence were substantial helps to those in need.

David worked lock-step with the mission team as the work expanded from St. Petersburg into its suburbs—Gatchina, Lomonosov, and Siverskii. Russian graduates of the Barnaul School of Preaching, Vyacheslav Yefimov and Andrei Greshnyakov, were added to the mission team to work in Siverskii and Gatchina, and they were supported financially by David.

Various mission workers came to St. Petersburg to teach. Consequently, three additional small congregations were formed. These were all eventually merged into the Church of Christ on the Neva. David and the Brentwood Oaks church facilitated that with support for preachers Igor Kravchenko, Slava Zakharchenko, and Oleg Yakimenko.

David expressed a deep concern for the mission team, and for the growth of the church and its leaders. A Saturday school was organized bringing in male and female leaders from all the congregations in the St. Petersburg region. The mission team planned the curriculum with consultation from David. That effort was quite helpful to the St. Petersburg area but did not address the needs of the church at large in Russia. With David we discussed that greater need for several years. Finally, we all agreed that we must organize a school for biblical study in St. Petersburg. What would be its focus and method? How would it operate? Where would it be located? Who would staff the school? Members of the mission team consulted with other schools in Russia and Europe and returned with recommendations.

The Institute of Theology and Christian Ministry (ITCM) was registered with the government in 2004 as a partnership of David Worley, Charles Whittle, and Joel Petty. It was our desire to offer a program of study at a master's degree level. Bible knowledge and systematic theology would be its primary offerings, with practical experiences in Christian ministry preparing the students for service.

David, Joel, and I considered long and hard a conceptual operation of the institute. The details of the operation were left to Joel Petty, Slava Zakharchenko, Oleg Yakimenko, Alexander Kaladze (preachers in St. Petersburg and Gatchina), and me. David would develop the curriculum and arrange for visiting scholars to do the teaching. Joel was appointed as president and visited churches in Russia and Ukraine to invite student applications. He also arranged the temporary facilities in the apartment of the church in Lomonosov and located apartments for students there for the first trimester.

Even as the partnership was formed, we sought the Lord for adequate facilities for the institute. An acquaintance of David read in a magazine that St. Petersburg State University, the premier university in Russia, sought partnership in the modernization of some of their buildings. Quickly, a meeting of David and a dean of the university, Dr. Bogdanov, was arranged in January 2005. Soon it was agreed that, in exchange for financing the modernization of one floor and one room on another floor of a building on Fifth Line, Vassilyevsky Island, the institute could use the area for classrooms, offices, and a dormitory. David generously provided those funds.

Knowing that much financial support would be needed, we initiated a not-for-profit corporation in Texas and began the process of applying for 501(c)3 status with the IRS. Before approval was received, the Cole Mill Road Church of Christ offered its Foundation for Biblical Study (already a US 501(c)3 corporation) for the use of receiving funds and supporting the work of the institute. David arranged for a transition of board members, and that foundation became the vehicle through which funds are sent to Russia for the work of the institute. David was elected chairman and president of the board.

Since the Institute of Theology and Christian Ministry was operational so soon after being organized, in January 2005, no fundraising had been done. David liberally provided the needed resources to finance the staff and the student stipends. That burden for David was very heavy for four years.

David and all of us involved were proud of the education of church leaders from across Russia, Ukraine, and Belarus. The teaching was done by professors from virtually all Christian universities and colleges in the United States. Classes were conducted in English and simultaneously interpreted into Russian. The English and Russian soundtracks were simultaneously recorded digitally. When the first class was graduated in 2007, the university dean, David, Tom Olbricht (then a new director of the foundation), Joel Petty, and I gave brief speeches, and Dr. Bogdanov gave citations/certificates from the university to each graduating student.

Some professors going to Russia needed travel funds. David funded a special foundation for that purpose. The Church of Christ on the Neva had always met in rented facilities and had to move far too many times. David encouraged finding adequate facilities for the church that could meet the needs of the institute. The third floor of a building was found on Sixth Line, Vassilyevsky Island, behind the university facility used by the institute. That was purchased by David and the entire floor was renovated for worship, offices, and a library. The cost of purchase and renovation was substantial. The institute and the Church of Christ on the Neva pay the utilities and for any repair of the facilities. David's generosity has continually promoted missionary-mindedness to the Christians in St. Petersburg.

It was interesting to see David's selection of professors to teach in the institute. It was never a matter of just finding someone to fill a time or course slot. He sought the person renowned for his knowledge of a Bible book—a man of wisdom. It is believed that the institute had a faculty superior to that of any graduate Bible program in Christian universities in the USA. David was similarly discriminating in selecting supporting materials for student reading. It was especially rewarding to this missionary to discuss with David passages from books like Luke Timothy Johnson's *Reading Romans* and William D. Dumbrell's *The Faith of Israel*, parts of which were translated into Russian.

The institute continued its residential teaching program in the university into 2008. Then a new university president decided that all non-university groups using the university's facilities must vacate them. The boards of ITCM and the Foundation for Biblical Study decided to discontinue the residential teaching program in St. Petersburg and to initiate a distant learning program in 2009. That was simultaneous with a growing perspective that the institute needed to be administered by Russians. Igor Egirev, a graduate of the institute, was elected to succeed Joel Petty as its president.

New members were added to the board of the foundation gradually. The agenda of board meetings were carefully planned by David, focusing upon the mission of ITCM (later the Christian Resource Center, a legally necessary name change) in St. Petersburg. That mission was to teach leaders, strengthen churches, and assist churches in improving their singing. All directors were encouraged to participate in the review and discussion of activities, goals, and direction.

Very gradually over time, several churches and individuals began assisting with support for the institute. David never gave up. By the time of his death, the foundation no longer required his underwriting.

This writer had many, many conversations and shared many email messages with David between 1992 and 2017. Those were about theology, business opportunities, Russian politics, Russian Christians, the church in Russia, the institute, the foundation, and fundraising. As a missionary I knew I had a dependable partner in David. Insights and knowledge were shared and mutual commitments made. Only the Lord knows the full extent of David Worley's promoting of mission activity to the praise of the Lord's name.

11

David Worley and the Mission of God

Joel Petty

> ...a riddle wrapped in a mystery inside an enigma.
> —Winston Churchill

IN THIS WELL-KNOWN QUOTE from a 1939 radio broadcast, the British prime minister expresses his view of Soviet foreign policy during World War II. Obviously Russia was perplexing and somewhat frustrating to him. In the last years of his life, David Worley Jr. was closely connected with Russia and her people. It should perhaps not be surprising then that Churchill's famous words offer a glimpse into what it is like to try to write about David Worley. To many people, and in a myriad of ways, David was an enigma, a mystery, and sometimes a riddle even to those who knew him well. I count myself in that number.

What was not a riddle or mystery to David, however, was the gospel and the mission of God in the world. It is this aspect of his life that I will look at it in some detail. We may be able to answer the question, "In what ways did David Worley encourage the mission of God?" A hope of mine is that, as we look at what God did through David, we will be encouraged in our efforts to participate in God's mission today.

We will first set forth David's theology of mission and evangelism which informed his participation in mission, then relate how he spoke about it, and what he taught others. We will also look at how he encouraged his own family and the family of God at the Brentwood Oaks Church of Christ. Lastly, we will consider how he encouraged the mission of God in Russia and other places in the world.

When discussing David, a man of few spoken words but a great listener, one must rely on his own written words. Thankfully we do have a few relevant sources, one being an article he wrote in 1988 and presented at the Institute for Christian Studies Sermon Seminar in 1989. It is titled "Rethinking Church Growth and Media Evangelism." In this discourse we attain a clear picture of his theology of mission. This "position lecture" informed his own understanding and expressed how he taught his own family, the churches he served as teacher and shepherd, and the new converts he met in Russia and other places. A summary follows.

David observed that Paul issued no direct appeals for the Christians in his churches to evangelize. He alleges that we "look in vain for the kind of super effort we often make in our churches to identify each Christian as an evangelist." This doesn't mean that Paul doesn't want them to be willing to speak, but Paul, instead of taking a direct approach, takes an indirect approach. David cites Roland Allen in his 1912 book *Missionary Methods: St. Paul's or Ours?*[1]: "It seems strange to us that there should be no exhortations to missionary zeal in the Epistles of St. Paul." David continues: "There are a few passages in Paul that may sound at first reading as encouraging evangelism but they are not direct." He then puts forward examples in 1 Thessalonians 1:8 and especially Philemon 1:6. "As Carl Holladay observes in his fine essay on 'Church Growth in the New Testament' (*Restoration Quarterly* 26 [1983] 100), 'the historian has little explicit evidence that Paul's churches became small hives of missionary activity.' In short, Paul nowhere tells his churches directly to go out and evangelize." David then summarizes his own view here:

> Let us be clear on what is being said. It is not that the church did not expand. It had marvelous growth in the first century and it grew in the second and third centuries. But how did it grow? What prompted its growth? From the records we have, it wasn't through a direct appeal to get out there and be evangelistic. It was rather a more indirect appeal, that the church be faithful in her life before the Father, that the members exhibit purity of conduct, and that she be a light in the world. And, for Paul, that the church be constant in prayer—In the marketplace, in their households, in their travels. Christians did proclaim the gospel,

---

1. London: R. Scott, 1912.

but their motivation for doing such was not inflamed through direct exhortations to evangelize but rather through exhortations to faithful, holy lives.

David rather sees in Paul indirect exhortations to evangelism. The indirect approach had three primary aspects. First is the call to be *"Children of Light."* David continues:

> What Paul does stress is that the church must be a light in the world (Ephesians 4–6). The light shines not only before neighbors and business associates but it also shines in our treatment of each other at home, in the husband/wife relationship, and the father with the child. You let your light shine in those relationships as well.

As we shine the light by our ethical, God pleasing behavior; as we grow in Christ, then there will be opportunities to speak the gospel, to "give a reason for the hope that we have," as Peter writes in 1 Peter 3:15. Jesus seems to connect these comments on speaking and growing in Matthew 5. David continues by quoting Henry Chadwick's *The Early Church*, in which he states that it was the lifestyle, the charity, the good will of the early Christians that attracted unbelievers to the faith.[2] "See how these Christians love one another" was the pagan comment reported by Tertullian. The love exhibited by the Christians eventually involved words, but it was first of all their lives. David was deeply concerned about the "cart going before the horse." And indeed we have all seen how zeal to share the gospel with others, if not preceded by signs of maturity in Christ, can have a negative impact. I know that was true in my own early life in Christ. I have also seen examples in Russia. We knew a brother in St. Petersburg who was quite evangelistic and eager to preach to others but whose life was so inconsistent with the gospel message that it was confusing at best and blasphemous at worst. In fact David counseled me to avoid this danger during my formative years of spiritual growth. I have often reflected on his wise words.

David sees the second feature of Paul's indirect approach as the enlisting of prayer for the evangelists. David considered it amazing, as do I, that Paul should write, "pray for me" as I share the gospel, as I open my mouth, or as I am chains. David correctly notes that Paul never pleads that the believers "pray for themselves" as they go out to evangelize, but rather, "pray for me," a missionary evangelist, as one who shares the mystery of the faith. A good example is Ephesians 6:19: "Pray also for me, that whenever I speak,

---

2. Pp. 56 (London: Penguin, 1967).

words may be given me so that I will fearlessly make known the mystery of the gospel" (see also Col 4:3–4; 2 Thess 3:1). David continues:

> I think we all have an elevated conception of Paul as the great missionary, and rightly so! Yet here he is, one called by God in a way that we were not called, on a road with an experience we have not had, and yet he really needs the prayers of others? It's hard to take that seriously. Yet, Paul was serious. He felt that in God's economy, within God's will, the prayer life of his churches would have an effect, not only in his own life, in his own efforts, but an effect within their own thinking about their own lives and their own identity in Christ.

David continues as he connects what Paul says with the teaching of Jesus, "What do we find in Jesus' words? 'The fields are white unto harvest; pray the Lord of the harvest sends forth reapers' (Matt 9). It does not say, 'See the harvest; go out.' No, it says pray to the Lord that he will assign those who go out into the harvest. There is indeed a continuity between what we have found in Paul and what we now find in Jesus." David concludes by saying that

> Scripture is a reminder that there is too little prayer for evangelism; too little prayer for evangelists. It is first and last of God's work, and we but his willing servants. If Paul could say truthfully and mean it that he was in need of intercessory prayer how much more those that we send out, and how much more those in our own churches that we feel in a special way are evangelists in communities in which we live and work.

I agree with his conclusion. At times I have been dismayed by the prayers when visiting churches in the United States. Perhaps it was the lack of time dedicated to prayer publicly in the assembly, in homes, or at Bible studies. I think it was more the lack of emphasis on prayer for the evangelists, the missionaries, the ministers—for those on the front lines. It was also the lack of informed prayer. Perhaps it was the contrast with the often deep, meaningful (and long!) prayers in assemblies in Russia and the former Soviet Union. It is a rare Sunday in Russia when prayers for the lost and those sharing the gospel are not offered. In the mystery of his will God uses prayer. As David emphasized in his work and in his own life, Paul calls us to pray for those we send out. Many congregations in the United States can do better. May the reminder from David call us to renewed emphasis on prayer!

The last aspect of the indirect approach is the example of the home. To quote David's article again:

> If you look at scripture you do sense in the second and third century that the expansion of the early church was basically by the conduct of life of the Christians, you have to say that it was the home that was the base of operation. A reverse of what I'm saying is that I think there has been an underutilization of our homes in the matter of evangelism. We know that Paul after leaving the synagogue attached himself to homes. Moral philosophers in the ancient world often attached themselves to a patron of a house and that patron would invite friends to listen to the person speaking in their home. What did Cornelius do? He had a household ready to hear when Peter came (Acts 10:24).

While home invitations may not be very widespread in the church in the United States, I think that is changing. David and his family were a shining example of how the home can be and was used to further the mission of God. The church in Russia, in general—and generalizations are misleading—unhappily has not universally learned nor applied this lesson. In Russia, however, it is not for the lack of a desire to share, though that is true in some cases. A lingering suspicion of neighbors still persists, left over from the Soviet experience. More often, however, it is a lack of opportunity. Apartments in Russia are often small—one or two rooms—and there is no possibility of hosting anyone, much less a small group.

A thoughtful and not uncommon response to David's views in this lecture was offered by Ken L. Berry, who was a student of David's at Abilene Christian University and later wrote a dissertation at Yale on Philippians. Ken observed:

> In Philippians I see Paul's concern about the proclamation of the gospel and the Philippians' participation in it. Two passages might be seen as urging them to evangelize, 1:27—"... striving together for the faith of the gospel" (cf. 4:3), and 2:16—"... holding forth the word of life." In both cases, however, as you emphasize, conduct is the primary focus: "Live worthy lives of the gospel" (1.27), and—"... be blameless and innocent ... shine as lights in the world" (2:15). Paul does tell of the preaching of the word in his location (1:14) and rejoices in that Christ is proclaimed, whatever the motive (1:18). This might indirectly encourage evangelism on the part of the Philippians. He thanks God for the Philippians' koinonia in the gospel (1:5), probably having in mind I think also their prayers for him (1:19) and their own efforts in speaking the word. He also commends Timothy (2:22), Epaphroditus (2:25, 20), Euodia, and Syntyche et al (4:2–3) for their involvement in the work of evangelism. In

these ways also he would be indirectly encouraging the Philippians to be involved in communicating the gospel. At the same time, it seems clear that not all will be involved in the same way or to the same degree. Some were intimately involved with Paul in the work of preaching, teaching, and evangelism. My reading of Philippians confirms your observations about Paul in general. You could also point to Col 4:5–6 with its exhortation to wise conduct toward outsiders and gracious, thoughtful speech in response to their inevitable questions or challenges. Faithful Christian conduct will prompt inquiry and all need to be attentive to and ready for such opportunities to speak. I think a passage like this is useful in keeping us mindful of outsiders and opportunities to communicate the gospel to them. Certainly those who teach or imply that every Christian has a certain quota of souls which he or she must personally win each year are way off base. On the other hand, it is also possible to become almost exclusively inward in focus and unconcerned about nonbelievers. This danger of course must also be avoided. In reaction to the former extreme some may fall prey to the latter danger. I agree with your suggestion that we make better use of our homes in evangelism. I have heard of people in some churches who have shied away from home meetings ... because they don't want to be confused with the (International church of Christ) "discipling" movement.

Berry's response is excellent and pinpoints the wrong conclusion that some make from David's lecture and of course the other spurious declaration, first advocated by William Carey (as a good corrective to the extreme Calvinism of his time) in a tract in 1792 that the great commission is the responsibility of every believer, not just a few chosen. I am of the opinion, along with Roland Allen and others, that we see neither in Paul nor in the church leaders of the subsequent centuries a more direct appeal to evangelism because many in the churches had already taken the great commission given by Jesus in Matthew 28 seriously. The Twelve, albeit with some delay, appropriated the commission and likely taught it to their hearers as part of the life of faith in addition to living a holy, faithful life. Each may have, as David deftly points out regarding Matthew as a "religious journalist," applied it uniquely according to their own gifts and situations. Such nuance is desperately needed today. Perhaps Paul or others did not directly emphasize that the churches add a word of testimony to the light they were shining because they were already incorporating these characteristics into their daily walk with the Lord. It would make the most sense of why we have only occasional and indirect mention of sharing the gospel by Paul and the early church leaders. David lived by what he understood and preached to others in word and deed.

David's lecture also addressed his concern about the use of media for evangelism, as well as dangerous "Miracle Gro" genetic engineering of the seed of the Word to make it more appealing.

We have assessed David's views on evangelism and mission and now turn to examples of how David furthered the mission of God. As anyone knew who knew David well, he was a man of integrity. He strove to be faithful to God and to his fellow man. As such, he exemplified all of what he wrote about in the above discourse. In his way of life, however, he was a paradox—David was both direct and indirect in his approach to evangelism. His daughter Christiana reported how he sometimes embarrassed his daughters by engaging an unsuspecting salesman in conversation about the gospel. But she also says he did not feel compelled to share the gospel in every situation. In fact, most of the time he was more subtle in approach. Secondly, David was regularly in prayer for the ministers and missionaries who heralded the gospel. Countless vocational ministers among us received emails from David. The emails were the classic Worley phrases—concise if not always clear. But he always declared that he was remembering us before the Father in prayer. In the worship assemblies he planned, David made prayer for those in the mission field a priority.

Lastly, David used his home to further the Kingdom. My family was a guest in his home many times over the ten years that we worked closely together. Melinda shared that hosting, and providing for missionaries was one of the ways that David intentionally sought to advance the mission of God. It was something that David, Melinda, and their three daughters could do together as a family. David was an example to his family and to everyone he met in each of the items mentioned above. We shall now consider a few specific examples.

I am indebted to David's family and especially his wife, Melinda, and daughter Christiana, who shared their perspective on this aspect of his life. His co-workers in the Brentwood Oaks church of Christ in Austin and fellow believers in Russia also provided very helpful insight into a very private man.

ENCOURAGING THE MISSION OF GOD IN HIS FAMILY

According to his family, David emphasized and encouraged participation in the mission of God, but, not surprisingly, indirectly. Christiana states:

> Much of what I learned from my dad came through watching him and not through what he said. While dad did insist that we

go on mission trips to Mexico with the youth group in junior high and high school I think he answered my questions more with his life. Dad shared the gospel not with short-term mission work but by investing—with his whole life—in the lives of many people across the globe.

During the research phase of this project I learned about even more people and places in whom David had invested, both spiritually and financially, and about whom I had been unaware.

An interesting aspect of David's approach to encouraging mission in his family was sharing with his daughters an infectious love of travel—seeing new places but especially meeting new people. Christiana mentioned this specifically as something that he did that helped to expose her to what God is doing in the world. Christiana continues by noting another trait of David's: he would not impose himself or insist. I saw this trait in him on multiple occasions during our shared work in ministry.

> My dad never pushed me to do missions as much as he encouraged my interest in travel. We shared a love of travel, of eating new foods, seeing new places, meeting unique people. I wonder if that was a way for him to open my mind to the various ways of doing things in the world, to see and love people who were different than I was. I think he saw all good vocations as places where sharing the gospel could occur, whether it be through art, business, or the mundane tasks of parenthood.

David, Melinda, and the girls also made trips to visit missionaries a part of their family traditions. Melinda recalled:

> In the mid-1980s we took our two oldest girls to Belize to see a missionary/ pharmacist that Brentwood was supporting. When Elena was about 5 our whole family, including Fred and Iva Lea, went to visit Mladen and Dragica Jovanovich in Croatia. I know that David went to Ghana to visit the Institute for Christian Studies graduate Y.B. Nkansa who was supported for a time by Brentwood Oaks. David always contributed financially to members at Brentwood who asked us and others to support them on short-term mission trips. David and I went to New Zealand and visited with ICS graduate Chris Pierce and his wife Didi. After that visit David became a financial supporter of South Pacific Bible College. Each of the girls went to St. Petersburg once with him, as did I.

The trip that Christiana took to St. Petersburg with her dad when she was just thirteen had a significant impact on her spiritual formation. The following quote is from her blog post entitled, What My Dad Didn't Teach Me."[3]

> My father had been traveling to Russia since the Soviet Union fell. He wanted his daughters to see where he'd been traveling, to meet the people who had moved him so much. Through a translator, Olga, told us about her life. How her father had been stolen away in the night when she was a girl, then her husband too had disappeared, then her son was killed in war. I don't remember my dad talking much to us afterwards about the high rises or Russian children's hospital we visited. At Olga's home and in the other places we visited, I learned that suffering was a common experience that didn't deplete one's ability to offer the best of what they had. My dad visited Russia several months out of the year, becoming more and more comfortable blending into the culture he'd fallen in love with, befriending and learning from the people he met. But he never offered us an "us and them narrative," or told us how blessed we were compared to them and weren't we wonderful for helping them? I could tell that his Russian friends didn't need him because he was wealthy; they loved him because he spent time with them, and wanted to share his faith with them. Even though we missed him when he left, I also knew from an early age that it was our father who needed to be with the Russian people. In Russia, I learned that we all need each other.

Melinda was able to accompany him on one trip. David also brought all three of his sons-in-laws to St. Petersburg to see God's work. He delighted to share his love of Russia and Russians, which I am confident he believed was a compulsion from God (2 Cor 5:14), with his family.

David's love of travel and visiting mission sites, including but not limited to St. Petersburg, was a witness to his family. His financial involvement with church members on short-term trips as well as his insistence—a strong word when discussing David—that his teen girls go along, were all examples for children indirectly to be participants in the mission of God. Although none of the daughters ended up as missionaries in a traditional sense, all were influenced greatly by his understanding and incarnation of the mission of God.

---

3. February 7, 2017, http://christiananpeterson.com/blog/.

DAVID AND THE MISSION OF GOD IN THE LOCAL CHURCH

David inspired, encouraged, and supported full-time and part-time missionaries in the Brentwood Oaks Church of Christ. When David discerned the call of God on my life to serve in Russia, he came alongside to walk with me. We sat together drinking cherry limeades at a Sonic drive-in and discussed Scripture. David put me in contact with Chuck Whittle in 1992. It was not long after I had been baptized into Christ, but I had already begun to sense a stirring to serve in Russia. In the fall of 1993 we met for coffee. David adored strong coffee. It was before my second mission trip to Russia but my first to St. Petersburg. At the meeting David said, "Believers in Russia come from a thousand-year tradition of faith. Many of the Christians in St. Petersburg have been in Christ longer than you, and they know more Scripture, and have more experience than you do." The answer to this dilemma and an important step for me was enrolling in Austin Graduate School of Theology (then called the Institute for Christian Studies). David served as the president of ICS. Perhaps at his home or at a Sonic somewhere, David made an invaluable suggestion. He suggested that instead of studying and then tacking on a ministry internship at the end before graduation, I should take a different approach. It was one that he himself had tried and that proved beneficial. I should study a semester or two and then undertake an internship in Russia. After that I would study another semester or two and then go back for another internship. Of course this extended the time needed to complete a Master of Arts in theological studies. However, the push and pull of theological study and mission internship during my education, instead of after it, proved warranted. The onsite ministry experience informed and refined my studies in a way I could not have imitated without that experience. It was such an excellent practice—it deeply formed and affected my thinking and practice of mission. We included mandatory internships in evangelism and in ministry during the course of study as an essential component of the program in the Institute for Theology and Christian Ministry, which we worked together to found ten years later. David encouraged my participation in the mission of God. I know of other situations where David advanced the mission of God through specific people. Space limits telling all of these stories.

From Jesus, Paul, and the early church fathers, it is clear that David heard a direct call to evangelism and active participation in God's mission. At Brentwood Oaks, even before he served as an elder David was actively involved in mission and evangelism. David made trips to meet missionaries, survey fields, and see the advances being made in St. Petersburg, Russia, Croatia, Nepal, Trinidad, New Zealand, Ghana, Belize, as well as India, and likely other places unknown to me. Sometimes David took a group with him when he was a member at Brentwood Oaks and perhaps from other churches before he moved to Austin. A frequent result of the groups he led or organized was discernment of additional needs and inspiration of others to join the mission of God. Among those traveling with David to various sites were Delvin Sparks, Hugh Morgan, Kurt Holman, Donovan Davis, Brigitte Casey, Kara Capps (nee Stokes), Connie Shay (nee Elrod), Mark Mathews, Dan Bonner, and others. Recently Woody Woodrow, a friend of David's in Austin, told of how David would smile and approvingly nod as he went on his way to Africa. It gave a Woody a sense of God's blessing on the African ministry in which he was involved.

Often, as Melinda noted, a visit to a location, such as South Pacific Bible College in New Zealand, resulted in David feeling the nudge of the Holy Spirit (as he liked to say) to help financially support a ministry or a missionary. David gave liberally of the funds he inherited and also from what he earned in his businesses. We may never know, on this side of the new creation, the full extent of what David did, whom he encouraged, and where. It would seem that he took to heart the admonition of Jesus' instructions related by Matthew in what we call chapter 6, verse 3, to "not let the left hand know what the right hand is doing." While not insisting and never imposing, David did himself prayerfully and, when convinced that it was God's work, fully invest in the part of the mission that he discerned needed his assistance at that moment.

We witnessed several bright examples of this. One of the brightest was the first ever children's Bible, called the *Beginner's Bible*, which was printed for the children of Russia. David came up with the idea of a "Bible bank" into which the children of Brentwood Oaks Church of Christ could put their donations. Perhaps over $500 was raised by the children for the printing of the Bibles. Early editions of the *Beginner's Bible* featured a blurb on the inside cover: "Paid for by donations by the children of Brentwood Oaks Church of Christ." It was David's idea. The execution of the idea followed a common pattern. David would provide an idea or perhaps even seed money, which would then develop, within God's will, beyond what he initially planned, imagined, or himself managed.

DAVID AND GOD'S MISSION ON THE FIELD

In 2002 I was serving with the church in Lomonosov, a suburb of St. Petersburg. The church was meeting in, but had outgrown, a small apartment. David was moved by the need and provided the seed money for the purchase of a larger apartment for the church to call home. With God's blessing others contributed and a facility was purchased and remodeled. The church continues to meet in that building. When David heard about a need he was quick, though never impulsive, in response. As needs were made known to him, David was used by God to provide assistance to many in St. Petersburg. Several ministers received significant assistance with the high cost of private theological education. Loans were made to several for the purchase of apartments. As far as I know, three of the individuals were able to pay David back the full or partial amount of the loans. While he was reluctant to receive funds back from those who he had helped, David gladly passed on what had been returned to care for the needs of others. David paid for the college education of more than one person. For those who could not help themselves but were in great need, apartments were bought outright. Unhappily, some took advantage of David's generosity. But David, like the Lord whom he so loved and served, forgave debts and kept no record of wrongs.

My co-worker in St. Petersburg Chuck Whittle, in his chapter in this volume on David as "missions promoter," described in detail David's active participation in the mission of God as it played out (nearly exactly following God's "script" in Psalm 2) in Russia in general and St. Petersburg in particular. I will not duplicate his good work here except to tell one story. As both Chuck and our editor, Tom Olbricht, mention in their chapters, David contributed a significant amount to remodel classroom, dorm, and office facilities at St. Petersburg State University (SPSU). The agreement was for the Institute of Theology and Christian Ministry (ITCM) to be able to use the facilities rent free as long as the joint ITCM-SPSU master's degree program was in existence. Through a professor named Ulrich Luz and Dr. Allan McNicol at Austin Graduate School of Theology, David learned that the Society for New Testament Studies (SNTS) had donated a theological library to the Biblical Languages Department of the Liberal Arts College of SPSU. During one of his trips to St. Pete, David met Anatoly Alekseev, a scholar of Greek and the theological librarian. The dean of liberal arts at SPSU, Sergei Bogdanov, offered ITCM office and classroom space in an academic building, but there was a problem. The space was not large enough for both ITCM offices and classrooms and the SNTS library. We were at an impasse. After a few days Dean Bogdanov called back to say that an appropriately sized facility had been found but that it was in a dormitory building. In what we both considered providential, the dormitory building was right across the street from the recently purchased building of the Church of Christ on the Neva in the center of St. Petersburg. The dean of liberal arts agreed with the dean of housing, and the facility was provided to us. ITCM would occupy the second floor, with the SPSU/SNTS library on the first floor. The ITCM students would live in the dorms right down the corridor on the same floor. All went well for about three years. To use a biblical allusion, one day a "Pharaoh who did not know Joel" came to power. SPSU appointed a new president. The new president decided to stop non-dorm-related use of dormitory space, which had become a problem on campus. As a result, the campus dean was fired and the agreement between SPSU and ITCM for joint use of their facilities ended, seemingly as soon as it began. Significant consequences resulted. One of these was that David lost money that he had invested. Upon further analysis, it seems that if we had accepted the initial offer from the liberal arts dean for space in the academic building, ITCM, now called CRCR, might still have the joint master's degree arrangement and use of the facilities. One issue was that David wanted to be a blessing to the SNTS library and Anatoly the librarian in particular, so we opted for the larger space in the dormitory. David was perhaps overzealous in his desire to do good. I was partner to this arrangement. Since I had worked in Russia for ten years at this point, I could have anticipated this potential problem, warned David, and recommended that we opt for the academic building. The past is the past, but it still comes to mind. It is a small illustration about how liberal generosity can sometimes have negative consequences for self and others, especially on mission fields.

THE INDIRECT APPROACH—HOLINESS

Igor Egirev is president of CRCR and my co-worker at the Church of Christ on the Neva. Igor notes that many people both here and in Russia say that David was odd, strange, or unusual. As Russians say, he was a "non-standard" person. Igor succinctly states my premise in this section:

> His devotion to God and love for His Word made him different. The more devoted we are about following the way of Jesus the more different we become.

After speaking with David, with all his awareness and attention focused on you, listening to you, seeking to know you and understand, one came away with a sense of the holy. It was if in those moments you experienced a small sense of the presence of God. David was pious in a good way. David was totally dedicated to doing God's will. It is even reflected in the name of his business, Thelese ("Lord willing"). David was sensitive to the moving of the Spirit Holy in his and others' lives. Our mutual friend Lynn Nored, former ITCM board member, notes how this sensitivity and experience impacted David's approach to missions. Lynn said, "David was reluctant to set policies and procedures in stone since (as he repeated to me several times) 'We must always be open to God and what he may do next.'" David lived and breathed Scripture and especially the Psalms. Christiana said that in one area her dad did insist on something—he insisted that each daughter memorize a psalm or two every summer. He even taped psalms to their bathroom mirrors to help them get started. David was creative in his approach to the baptism of his daughters. Heatherly and the other girls can tell stories about how he communicated the holy meaning of that event.

I experienced David's ire twice—I saw righteous anger in him. It was not when I did wrong by him, which happened on occasions, but rather when he witnessed me treating others unlovingly. The holiness of God overshadowed the surroundings through David. Stories of how David served others are legend and will be retold in other chapters. David taught me from Acts 6 and following that only as the seven grew in holiness, wisdom, and service were they given opportunity by God to speak. We see Luke describe this specifically as it relates to Stephen and Phillip in Acts 6–8. David, by virtue of his holy life, had earned the right to speak the gospel into the lives of others. He did speak the life-giving gospel of the holy-yet-loving God to many people around the globe. As Igor said, "I hope that I have become a little more unusual than I was before I met David."

THE INDIRECT APPROACH—PRAYER

David of course translated, taught, prayed, and lived the Lord's Prayer. But he abhorred pretense of any kind. Working together with David in the institute could be frustrating. When fundraising, in particular, a little self-promotion (of the ministry) is sometimes helpful. He would refuse that with his very being. I recall vividly his description of "praying like the hypocrites" (Matt 6:5ff.) as opposed to praying in private. As his daughter Christiana recalled, "dad never flaunted his prayer life to his kids, I have no doubt he was often deep in prayer, probably praying The Lord's Prayer over and over." David would ask churches in worship assemblies and bulletins to pray as Jesus charged his disciples: "Ask the Lord of the harvest, therefore, to send out workers into his harvest field." (Matt 9:38). David certainly exemplified this in his own life. He would frequently contact us, and many others who were in the fields, with brief emails that communicated, in essence, "I am praying for you," sometimes without even saying that much. I don't have proof but I think that one reason why the prayers at the Church of Christ on the Neva in St. Petersburg always include requests for those preaching the gospel, those gifted as evangelists, and for the lost is due to David's early influence. David prayed for the Kingdom to continue to come.

THE INDIRECT APPROACH—HOSPITALITY

Our God, it would seem to me, is hospitable. Peter J. Leithart in "Hospitable God" states, "Yahweh brings Israel to Sinai and shows Moses the pattern for the tabernacle. For the first time, Yahweh moves into Israel's neighborhood. And Jesus is the tabernacle of the church, God's tent and house. In Jesus, the Lord has opened *Himself*, become our dwelling place; welcomed us in."[4] Home played a central role in the gospels, Acts, and the early church. It is without question that many of the most significant moments (too many to list here) in the gospels occur at the table in a home. Regarding the church, in Acts 2, 5, 8–10. 16, 28 homes are specifically mentioned. Of course Lydia in Acts 16 compelled Paul and his companions to come to her home. About hospitality, David himself wrote, "If we really want to be a people who are light in the world, we need to better utilize our homes in this effort. We as Christians need to seriously think about the how to use our homes . . . for conversation and discourse in which we invite others to talk about life, bringing friends together to listen to a speaker. What did Cornelius do? He had a household ready to hear when Peter came" (Acts 10:24).

David and his family's home was open. About the practice of hospitality, their daughter Christiana relates the following:

> I think the biggest thing my husband Matthew and I do in our family life is try to show hospitality to others in our home. That's a huge thing that I remember about my childhood: having a lot of guests, many of them Russian or from various other countries, in our home for long or shorter periods of time. I remember having church groups for meals and having singles from the church live with us for a time. My parents had an open home and shared readily from their wealth. That's something Matthew and I feel is very important to the functioning of our family life and to our wish to show the love of Jesus to others.

In the 1990s several Russian Christians stayed for extended periods of time with the Worleys. One of these was a new Christian named Anya. Anya was an artist. Anya relates how blessed she was to spend time with Melinda and the girls and of course with David. Over the years Anya had lost touch with the church in St. Petersburg. After his death David's family granted the church on the Neva in St. Petersburg permission to hold a memorial service in addition to the one held in Austin. We were able to use it to teach the church about lament and praise and about honoring our leaders.

---

4. *First Things*, May 22, 2014, https://www.firstthings.com/blogs/leithart/2014/05/hospitable-god.

The goal was to honor David and glorify God. At the memorial service a spontaneous thing happened. Anya returned to the Neva church for the memorial. We hadn't expected her. Melinda remarked afterward that the thing we least plan is often where God is at work. David's memory probably was honored most not by what we had planned but rather by that spontaneous, unplanned moment of Anya's sudden reappearance at the Neva church.

David hosted Russian Christians from St. Petersburg at his home in Austin several times over the years. It was usually during the AGST Sermon Seminar. One of the couples he hosted was Sergei Yanovets and his wife, Lida. Sergei shares the following story about the Worleys' hospitality.

> We once visited America. David arranged that marvelous adventure! He is a servant—he served us by driving, providing for all our needs, and by planning everything. We stayed with David's family and saw how they lived. Melinda and the girls' kind, pure, and sincere relations with each other is evidence of their faith. David's family says more about him than he himself says. People were very valuable to David. I also saw people's attitude toward him. Every morning David talked with the waiter at the café and you could see the care in the relationship. Anytime that he was with people he tried to communicate something meaningful. All of his relationships were guided by his faith in the Lord Jesus.

A PERSONAL REFLECTION

David was a scholar and described himself as a "servant of the Word" (by this he meant, I think, a minister and teacher). David was also a venture capitalist and a successful businessman. As a follower of Jesus, he was a faithful steward and generous about sharing the blessings with which he was entrusted. We worked together on various ministry projects over the years. A bright memory was the founding of ITCM. In a meeting with Chuck Whittle in 2003 we discussed the need to research successes and failures of other institutes and ministry training programs. David said to me, "Go and find out what works. Don't worry about what it will cost. Tell us what works." It was a sign of his commitment to the mission of God as he discerned it in the moment. It was so empowering. As a result of God's grace, through David's generosity a unique plan was developed. Part of the plan was using synchronous translation, like that at summit meetings or at the United Nations. I discovered that practice in Zagreb, Croatia, where David had sent me to conduct research. Synchronous translation was expensive in both equipment and personnel. The freedom provided us by David's commitment of seed money allowed us to discover and implement that unique-at-the-time technology. It allowed professors from the US to teach an entire semester of material in two weeks. The other unique aspect of the program, which David funded entirely at the beginning, was the vocational component. Each graduate left ITCM with a high-quality theological education from Bible professors from the US, ministry skills taught by Russian ministers, and a marketable job skill. The job skill training allowed them to find gainful employment upon graduation. In that way a graduate could work if and until such time as God bore fruit in his or her life. If there was need and desire for full-time support then the local church—not American supporters—could arrange that with the graduate within God's will. The generosity and faithfulness of David Worley to God's mission enabled those unique aspects of ITCM to take place. It was a blessing to work with and for David.

I heard the news of his death when I was here in Russia teaching in a church. I suppose that was appropriate. It was David's deep love for the Russian people that first inspired me to consider moving to Russia as a missionary evangelist to learn from and serve the people. David was a teacher, a friend, a brother, and a co-worker in the Kingdom. As he did for so very many, David also did for us: he taught, encouraged, mentored, and blessed. He humbly showed us the way to a deeper faith, a greater love, and a tangible hope. God graced David with many gifts. I think one of the most meaningful to my family, and others as well, was that of "faithful presence"—like a shepherd with his large flock. Over the years we witnessed some of how he was used by God to be faithfully present in the lives of so many—fellow ministers, co-workers, friends, students, and of course his own family. David was present. He pledged both Yana and me to Christ in baptism and us to each other in marriage. At our wedding he stood in for Yana's father, who couldn't attend, and by so doing gave me her hand in marriage. He prayed with us for years for a child and rejoiced with us at the arrival of our firstborn. He was faithfully present in the sorrows as well—the severe illness of a child, funerals of parents, health problems, and crises in our churches and ministries. David was present. Often he was present with few or even no words at all. But his presence communicated the presence and the love of God. Ken Berry shared a sentiment not uncommon to many. "David was my only former professor who would initiate contacts with me over the years just to touch base or catch up with how my family and I were doing and offer encouraging words, even as late as last Thanksgiving." We will miss him. In this we are not alone.

I will end with a story told by our mutual friend Daniel Napier. Daniel was a student at Austin Graduate School of Theology. After graduating he served with a congregation in Santa Barbara, California, where this story took place. When Daniel was fundraising in preparation for a move to Croatia, he tried to approach David with a request for funding. They weren't able to meet but rather exchanged voicemails. David called back and said, "Glad to help with a one-time donation." A month went by and then suddenly a check from David arrived. It was an odd amount—down to even a very specific dollar and cent. When Daniel looked at the check he was stunned that David's check exactly, to the cent, met their remaining need. Daniel concludes by saying, "Even more than the money itself, about which David never knew, the amount became a sign in our life of God's presence and care." Daniel's story could be repeated over and over by many people on the mission fields David visited and in the ministries in which he was involved.

Our fellow missionary evangelist David Worley Jr. was often a sign of grace, peace, and the presence of God. Perhaps by means of this essay David's perception and practice of mission has become less of a mystery, even as the man himself remains an enigma to many, except of course the Lord he so loved. We will pay the greatest tribute to this uncommon man if we dedicate ourselves to holiness, to prayer for workers and the harvest, to mission, and to being hospitable. We thank the Lord Jesus for David's life. Now, having looked with the author of Hebrews (13:7) at the outcome of his life, we will do well to imitate his faith.

12

David Worley as Lecture and Teaching Planner

Thomas H. Olbricht

David Worley was an unusual person. One of his best skills was adding to his wealth then interjecting it into projects and operations dear to his heart. But though I communicated with David, especially via email, I heard absolutely nothing about his investments from him and not much from his associates. I mostly knew of a few people he mentioned who might help support the Russian work and with whom he expanded his holdings in joint venture-capital acquisitions. With me, anyway, we dialogued about how to effectively design programs that advance the growth of the Kingdom of God. In the middle 1990s I received a call from David. He said he was going to be in Los Angeles and wanted to get together with me for a late breakfast. We agreed to eat at his hotel, a Marriott near the Los Angeles airport. I have no idea what business engagements brought him to Los Angeles. He didn't mention the reason he was there and I didn't ask. He wanted to talk about teaching in such a way as to maintain the commitment of our students to basic Christian doctrines.

David Worley sometimes declared that the proper appellation for his persona was "shepherd." If being an organizer is the same as being a shepherd, then David was a shepherd. In my experience, David organized effectively whatever entity in which he was involved. The designated structure was never perfunctory. David always put as much energy into the why of any specific approach as he did the details of the arrangement. If he thought the focus of a meeting should be on the spiritual aspects, then these were built into the agenda and given priority.

I have been around people who regularly touted organization. When I taught at the University of Dubuque, there was a history professor/registrar who spent much of his time with students testifying to the value of organizing. That is what students mostly remembered about him. He was, however, also a knowledgeable historian so they also prized what they learned from him.

David Worley was organized in his own way, but I never heard him expound on the glowing merit of orderliness. I also generally admired the fact that he didn't insist that a group stick adamantly to the agenda if something else seemed more pressing. A few times this open discussion was a bit disarming, but for the most part, much of the digression seemed warranted. I admired David for his constant educational, evangelistic, and exhortatory planning.

In 2003 I was in Europe for various reasons and went to St. Petersburg in order to teach whoever among the church members could assemble during the daytime, normally twenty to thirty people. David Worley had written a short email in his normal laconic style telling me he was going to be in St. Petersburg and he wanted to talk with me. He said he would inform me of the meeting time once we were there. I'm not sure all the reasons he was in St. Petersburg, but I know it had to do with the Russian Bible school that had sent tracts to radio listeners since the early 1990s. David had at one time in the 90s owned a religious broadcasting station in Russia. He informed me in his email what day he was to leave St. Petersburg. The time drew near and I hadn't heard from him. I was not surprised. I thought that probably we would not get the chance to talk. Then he called the morning he was leaving and informed me that he planned to go to the airport by taxi. He would have his taxi drop by to pick me up and we would talk on the way to the airport. Then the taxi would take me back to the flat.

David and the church leaders in St. Petersburg—mostly Chuck Whittle, Joel Petty, and D'Anne Blume—were at that time in conversation about starting a school. He wanted to talk to me about what should be taught. I told him that I thought the courses should be those of the standard graduate program, including biblical studies (Old and New Testament), church history (ancient, medieval, Reformation, modern, and Restoration history), theology (biblical theology and Christian doctrine), and ministry studies (preaching, counseling, and church planting). In most instances in which we conversed, from the mid-1980s to the time of his death, David focused upon teaching or lectureship programs. Though we occasionally discussed fundraising, most of that happened in email exchange.

EARLY YEARS

I'm not certain when I first met David, but no doubt it was when he was an undergraduate student at Abilene Christian. We didn't converse much then. I became an elder at Minter Lane during that time and we sometimes said hello at church, but we didn't carry on extended conversations. I knew him to be a very good student and committed to church activities. He was involved in various phases of the congregation, from outreach to teaching, but not in such a way that he was especially noticed. Some of the first longer conversations I had with David were about Hebrews. He wrote his doctoral dissertation on Hebrews at Yale University under Nils Dahl. I had been working on Hebrews, especially its structure, and I shared with him some of my ideas about it.

Sometime in the early 1980s arrangements were made with David to teach an introduction to the New Testament at Abilene Christian. He drove from Austin once a week to offer New Testament introduction as an undergraduate/graduate course. Brevard Childs was also teaching at Yale and I knew his views of graduate pedagogy. David and I talked it over. Childs held that an important component in interpreting the New Testament is its message as ensconced in the centuries-long publications of the top scholars of the church. In other words, understanding Hebrews necessitates an insight into the history of its interpretation. Childs spent little time with conventional introduction entailing author, date, arrangement, style, and intended readers. David decided the Childs's approach was how he would teach the course. I told David I could see the importance of knowing the basic message of the New Testament books and something of the history of interpretation, but I thought the students too should confront the conventional detailed introductory matters. It might be possible and adequate for them to master these details through required reading. David had them read conventional text books but didn't test them over the normal introductory details. Most of the students were pleased with Worley's approach. I feared they would suffer when they entered more advanced New Testament studies requiring a familiarity with these details, and in deed they came to recognize the value of the standard pedagogy.

After we moved to Pepperdine I arranged for David to teach New Testament courses there. He came out once or twice a week and stayed with us. We had long discussions about fundamental courses for a graduate program and subjects for important lectures at various gatherings, such as lectureships, the Christian Scholars Conference, and Sermon Seminars.

STRATEGIES FOR RUSSIA

I now turn to program planning for the Institute of Theology and Christian Ministry, over which David had a major supervisory role. After more specific talks of over a year, the latter period in which I was involved, we gathered a class and started the official teaching of the institute in January 2005. As I told various people, we were creating a religious graduate school from scratch. We had to think through and arrange for various aspects of the program as we came to them.

David had some definite ideas about our teaching and we had to improvise as we moved along. We were launching what we considered a graduate program, not a run-of-the-mill preacher school offering, and David wanted our efforts to be a cut above. He had contacted various academics and presumed that our teachers would be established professors at our current graduate schools. He hoped that their schools would pay the expenses to and from St. Petersburg or that the teachers themselves would provide the amount needed. Some of both happened. David worked hard to recruit acclaimed teachers who stood firm in our Restorationist heritage. The newly appointed management was already at work in St. Petersburg. Joel Petty would serve as president and Oksana Boiko as dean.

David wanted the whole program to have an on-the-job component, as well as an intellectual and a spiritual dimension. David as well as others believed it was important for the future of our graduates to develop job skills. David emphasized and the rest of the board concurred that we opposed encouraging the students to seek funds from the United States for their future sustenance. At the same time, we doubted that Russian congregations would be capable of supplying more than the most basic needs, which meant that the students needed employment when they graduated that would enable them to attain a suitable income. The staff at the school was committed to help them locate such training so that they could obtain employment after they graduated. Two or three had expertise in computers and further training was arranged for them, and in at least one case a part-time job. One woman who had been involved in public relations was able to work part-time at a firm in St. Petersburg. Another woman had some experience in interior decorating and arrangements were made for her to train additionally in that field. One man was a dentist and would return to his practice when he graduated. He would teach and preach as time permitted. We also arranged for our graduates to take four additional courses at St. Petersburg State University, which would enable them to obtain a master's degree from there. Only one student—the current president, Igor Egirev—took advantage of this opportunity.

Class time was divided between the intellectual and the spiritual. Each day began at 9:00 a.m. During the first year we used the church building in Lomonosov, about an hour out of St. Petersburg, past "Putin's Palace" and near Peterhof, Peter the Great's summer palace. The agenda for each day was worked out by David with input from others. I received a copy in advance and David asked my reaction. I told him it was certainly a busy schedule, but it incorporated the Russian propensity for starting somewhat later in the morning and eating lunch at one in the afternoon. My task was not only to lecture on content but to help students improve their speaking ability. I told David I was equipped to do all of that but, after all, I was seventy-six. Nevertheless, I would do my best to make it work.

1. TIMES FOR WORSHIP EACH DAY

I normally arrived at the church building in Lomonosov at about 9:10 a.m. Some of the students had been assigned to orchestrate a devotional. Much of the activity was singing and prayer, especially for the work of the institute. The lectures began at about 10:00 a.m. We had two lectures before lunch, then lunch, normally at 1:00 p.m., a typical time for Russians, then another lecture at 2:00 p.m. for an hour. The lectures had to be interpreted in Russian and any comments from the students translated into English for the teacher. When we moved to the building on the St. Petersburg State University campus, the management team at the institute took the necessary steps to provide simultaneous translation. Simultaneous translation saved time, but I was somewhat distracted from talking and listening at the same time.

A woman, the mother of one of the students, was employed to prepare the meal on location. It was a somewhat different menu and Dorothy wasn't too impressed with the bowl of buckwheat, which was a standard Russian fare and eaten much like Americans eat Cream of Wheat. We regularly were served soup with plenty of cabbage or beets in it and cold cuts.

The early afternoon lecture was followed by a question-and-answer session for about thirty minutes or as long as needed. By 3:00 in the afternoon students presented papers as sermons or, in the case of the women, teaching sessions. The student speeches continued for about an hour. After we listened to each speech the other students were invited to comment on what was of merit and what was weak. We ended the day in a prayer circle in which each student was invited to pray for what was on their hearts—often about the classes or the problems of people they knew in their home churches. We only admitted students who were already active in one of the Russian congregations. By 5:10 p.m., I was normally in a taxi headed back to Chuck Whittle's flat on the south side of St. Petersburg. It made for a long day since I usually needed night preparation or review for my lectures. I was involved in all phases of the days' activities, especially making suggestions about improving speech making.

2. LECTURES

I taught what were considered three-hour courses. I taught two classes that met two weeks each, with lectures three hours a day. The first course was on biblical theology, both Old and New Testament. The second was on church history. I covered the whole span from the early church until A.D. 2000 in the 2005 class. In 2007 John Mark Hicks taught medieval and Reformation church history, so I was free to teach Restoration history along with early church and modern church history. I had done enough speaking employing translators into French, Spanish, Portuguese, Russian, German, and Japanese, so I tried to be sensitive to the problems of the translator or interpreter. That meant that I couldn't totally proceed as in a comparable lecture in English, but I attempted to convey information and content of the same quality as at Abilene Christian or Pepperdine in their graduate programs. I found that most of our Russian students could cope with material at this level and in some ways were more dedicated to learning than their peers in the United States.

We were dedicated to offering a curriculum comparable to an MDiv program in the US. In order to do so, considering the faculty we hoped to recruit, we had to be creative. David had thought through much of the negotiation needed. We could not count on many teachers to stay four weeks each time as I did. Most likely we would need to create courses that met for a week and counted for one credit hour. We would also need to recruit among the professors those suitable for teaching preaching or class teaching and not assume that all the professors were competent in teaching communication. We therefore, especially with Bible courses, taught shorter sections for a week, for example, Genesis, or Deuteronomy, or Psalms, or Jeremiah, or John, or Romans and Galatians, or Hebrews, or Ephesians and Colossians, or Revelation. This worked well with the biblical courses. In church history we taught small segments, for example, Reformation, American, or modern. In theology we taught systematic theology in two parts. We also taught courses in counseling, church planting, evangelizing, and world religions. Working out all the details took constant planning on David's part, but he managed to cope well with the somewhat checkered context in which we worked.

3. QUESTION-AND-ANSWER SESSIONS

The question-and-answer sessions did not work as well as David, or I for that matter, had hoped. They came later in the afternoon and the students were tired. But we usually received a few questions. When I taught Restoration history in 2007 I received many more questions, especially from the students who had backgrounds in the International Church of Christ—perhaps three or four out of twenty. They wanted to know about various aspects of the teaching of the Campbells, Barton W. Stone, Walter Scott, David Lipscomb, and Foy E. Wallace Jr. and the evangelism of T. B. Larimore, G. K. Wallace, and N. B. Hardeman. They also wondered whether these views and methods would be productive in contemporary Russia.

4. SERMONS OR CLASS TEACHING FOR THE WOMEN

When I taught biblical theology I had the students give speeches on theological points in Scripture, such as creation, covenant, laws, the life of Christ, salvation, baptism, and the church. After each speech I scheduled a student to evaluate the effectiveness of the discourse. I gave them a form to use as a guide covering, for example, topic focus, evidence, arrangement, style, and delivery. They did a commendable job commenting on each other's sermons or the class teaching. When the class was through with the evaluations I made a few comments myself. David wanted to make sure we had an application aspect of the curriculum and this was my approach to providing it, along with essay exams.

When I taught church history I had a long list of significant persons in church history on whom they could speak. The first year we had two speeches from each student on historical figures such as Irenaeus, Clement of Alexandria, Origin, Arius, Athanasius, Augustine, Calvin, Zwingli, Luther, John Wesley, and John Knox. We had one speech focused on Restoration leaders, including those listed above. The students were also permitted to speak on leaders from the Russian Restoration Movement, such as Lord Radstock, Vasili A. Pashkov (1831–1902), and Ivan Stephanovitch Prokhanov (1869–1935). The students were especially interested in speaking on the Restoration leaders, both American and Russian. The students frequently did better with these topics than I anticipated. We had to take time to interpret the addresses into English since I did not know enough Russian to understand the content.

Most of the instructors also employed standard exams, and so did I. For the biblical theology courses I used mostly essay exams, thinking essays would best convey the course content. In church history I employed both essay questions and multiple choice questions. To follow upon David's vision of practical application, I also employed short-answer questions in an oral exam. This way I could further press the students to determine the thoroughness of their preparation. I discovered that the Russian students did better with multiple choice questions and short-answer questions, which was the approach of most of their prior Russian testing. They prepared far better for these kinds of exams than did comparable American students.

5. A PRAYER CIRCLE LATE AFTERNOON

The students especially came alive at the close of the day and with the prayer circle. These daily prayer sessions certainly fulfilled David's hope that they would be involved spiritually and that we could give them some guidance. It meant, however, constant oversight on the part of the professor. The students always were ready with multiple prayer concerns.

David's planning by the second year we taught in the Institute of Theology and Christian Ministry was considerably improved. In the first place, David and others in St. Petersburg made arrangements with the appropriate dean at St. Petersburg State University to use some of their facilities. David gave the university a sizable check to refurbish a building on campus that included classrooms, offices, dorm rooms, and a university library that was of merit in the classical languages and linguistics. All of these facilities were more than adequate and had been reconstructed suitably on Russian standards. We employed the one classroom for all of our larger group activities. The dorm rooms were also refurbished, but required additional monthly payment. They could be used for singles and even for families. They were in the same building as the classroom and adjourning offices and very convenient in the cold, humid St. Petersburg winter.

6. LIBRARY

Another welcome feature was space for books along the walls and the use of the St. Petersburg State University library. The library was adequate for our use and growing. Books were given to the SPSU library by such academic entities as the International Society for New Testament Studies. The preachers for the Church of Christ on the Neva started looking for standard American books and reference works that were translated into Russian. Those that were inexpensive were purchased in large amounts and given to the students. Other reference series were added to the ITCM collection.

LOCATION CHANGE

The dean of SPSU agreed to a forty-nine-year contract for facility use for the money David provided in the initial contract. Some of us expressed concern as to whether this agreement would hold. The time came when the St. Petersburg State rector was replaced. The new rector decided that honor students should receive room and board and live on the campus. The word came from the university in the third year of our Institute of Theology and Christian Ministry that we would have to leave the university facilities within a week. I don't think David specifically planned for this development. It was fortunate that the building where the church met could be used for the institute but it wasn't purchased so as to provide a backup. David and the others involved decided that everything would have to be moved to that building. The old dean thought that perhaps some of the money given to the university could be recovered, but some of us had reservations. In the end about one-eighth of the funds were returned. So much for the non-viobility of Russian contracts! We who had worked for some years in Russia were not surprised. The dean who had arranged our facilities at St. Petersburg State had told us that a St. Petersburg saying was, "Everything is illegal, but everything is permissible." The latter included taking over the ITCM facilities. David was disappointed, but he was not inclined to bemoan past setbacks. We actually had already decided that we needed to move away from residential learning to distant learning.

David and his mother, Iva Lea Worley Barton, over a year earlier had bought the third floor of a large warehouse-type building, which, with the refurbishing, cost in the thousands. It was refurbished especially for the Church on the Neva to meet, to provide offices for the preachers, and for a wing in the back for the Russian Bible school. The people who studied in the Russian Bible school responded to several letters that they returned as the result of radio programs, newspaper ads, and other means of surfacing people interested in God and the Bible. In addition, a large one-bedroom flat had been cut out on the third floor for the visiting professor. All these were nice and convenient to the university campus. There was, however, no elevator in the building and the floors were about twenty feet above each other. But the whole floor could be suitably employed by the institute and the church despite the disappointment of having to move.

LATER DISTANT LEARNING USING SKYPE

David was never wed to prior decisions. Now it was more difficult to house students in St. Petersburg. We wanted to avoid moving people to a new location they would like so well they wouldn't return home. That had always been involved in training Africans, Brazilians, and Koreans in the United States. Now we discovered that several of the people we brought to St. Petersburg didn't want to return home after their years there. So we started to consider non-location online education, or in other words what has received the official designation "distant learning."

David and I started corresponding as to how we would orchestrate such a program. I had taught a distant learning graduate course for Abilene Christian. We wanted to use our previous lectures that had been recorded in translated form. We decided to commence employing Skype. We would put these on the Web or send them out digitized and the students could listen to them when they had the time available. Igor Egirev, who was now president of the institute, was to announce a time for people to Skype, present the course, set out deadlines, and answer any questions forthcoming. The appointment of Igor as president involved heads-up planning on David's part. It was clear that should the Russians close down schools in which foreigners were involved, our institute would be in a more favorable position if the officers were Russians. Other problems also seemed endemic, but this planning was at the heart of the decision to appoint Russians to the leadership positions. I taught biblical theology as the first distant learning course. The students also received a copy of my two books, printed as one and translated into Russian. The two volumes in one covered the theology of both the Old Testament and the New Testament.

How was I to be involved? We decided that we would have four one-hour, every-other-week sessions on Skype to which every student was to listen. The hour would mostly involve questions and answers. For each chapter in my books translated into Russian there were sets of questions. The proposal was that the students look over these questions and ask one from this set or any other relevant question. The technical problem was that there are eight time zones in Russia and my time zone also had to be accounted for. David worked with Igor and they finally created a suitable plan. I would open up Skype at 7:00 a.m. The student questions had to be interpreted for me and when I replied the answer had to be interpreted into Russian for them. Lena, one of the earlier Russian students, worked in the office. She was capable in English and knew the material, so the interpreting went as well as might be expected. Several courses have been taught this way since, but improved technical means of communication have emerged.

David designed many programs in his lifetime, all of which created additional problems. But he was always sensitive to flexibility and worked on whatever conundrums arose so that an acceptable solution was forthcoming. Whatever he did by way of stabilizing lectures and teaching, he made up for it in seeing that untried ideas got off the ground. While a diversity of techniques may have transpired at the Institute of Theology and Christian ministry in Russia, they only exhibited the quality and spiritual dimension projected because of David's leadership.

BROTHERHOOD FORUMS

David was a committed schoolman and churchman. He became concerned that our brotherhood forums did not seem to pass the baton of our early theological and biblical findings to the next generation. We talked, or more likely were in contact by email, regularly about these inadequacies. I normally taught a three-session class at the Pepperdine Lectures. I decided in the early 2000s to at least address the sorts of questions David raised. I was not as convinced as he that lectures would change the direction of many of those in the so-called thirteenth generation.

I gave the overall title to the three lectures, "Do We Need to Begin Again?" The three individual lectures were: (1) "The Scriptures as a Foundation," (2) "The Ancient Gospel," and (3) "The Church as the Body of Christ." I received several commendations after each lecture from the baby boomer generation, but not many from the thirteenth generation—if they were even present. David obtained the tapes of the lectures and was generally aware of what they contained. He thought they were of merit and arranged for me to present them at the Sermon Seminar at the Austin Graduate School of Theology the following year, in May 2004.

LECTURES AT DIFFERENT FORUMS

David continued to bring up the need to present topics like these as he anticipated the various forums. I told him he should design a program and line up the speakers he thought would reflect his outlook. I paved the way for him to develop a session at the Pepperdine Bible Lectures with Jerry Rushford, the Abilene Christian College Summit with Brady Bryce, and the Christian Scholars Conference with David Fleer. For some reason none of these sessions ever came to fruition. But David continued making proposals with the conviction that a younger generation needed to take seriously the earlier positions taken by the forefathers.

TOPICS FOR FORUMS

David and I discussed various topics that affirmed the basics of the Restoration Movement. He agreed that the three topics I developed in the early twenty-first century were fundamental. He was pleased with my approach of quoting statements from our forebears. The positioning of these doctrinal propositions by the forefathers and their wording varied from generation to generation, helping convey a commitment to past beliefs in a new form and vocabulary. One of the values of a non-credal approach to the faith is that proclaimers are free to open up the Scriptures anew to assess them rather than exhausting the hours explicating the creeds.

THE SCRIPTURES AS A FOUNDATION

I will here set out a shorter version of my first lecture on "Do We Need to Start Over Again in Respect to the Scripture?" as an example of the sort of message the thirteenth generation needs to hear. I basically developed the topic chronologically in order to call attention to the fact that commitment to the Scriptures was reaffirmed from generation to generation.

I commenced with the declaration of Walter Scott, one of four first-generation thought leaders. He pointed out that the forefathers of the Restoration affirmed three basic doctrines.

> The present century, then, is characterized by these three successive steps, which the lovers of our Lord Jesus have been enabled to make, in their return to the original institution. First the Bible was adopted as sole authority in our assemblies, to the exclusion of all other books. Next the Apostolic Order was proposed. The True Gospel was restored.[1]

The Apostolic Order was the contribution of Alexander Campbell in respect to congregation independence, elders and deacons as officers, weekly Communion, etc. The True Gospel was Scott's declaration that humans believed, repented, and were baptized and received from God redemption, the Holy Spirit, and eternal life.

---

1. *The Gospel Restored* (Cincinnati: O. H. Donogh, 1836).

Barton Warren Stone and his cohorts, in *The Last Will and Testament of Springfield Presbytery* (1808), declared the hegemony of Scripture over loyalty to creeds or any other religious writings.

> We will that the people henceforth take the Bible as the only sure guide to heaven; and as many as are offended with other books, which stand in competition with it, may cast them into the fire if they choose; for it is better to enter into life having one book, than having many to be cast into hell.

Thomas Campbell in his "Declaration and Address" considered proper interpretation of Scripture the basis for religious unity and the means through which one obeyed God. Affirming propositions of the Scripture resulted in salvation.

> ... nothing ought to be inculcated upon Christians as articles of faith; nor required of them as terms of communion, but what is expressly taught and enjoined upon them in the Word of God. Nor ought anything be admitted, as of Divine obligation, in their Church constitution and managements, but what is expressly enjoined by the authority of our Lord Jesus Christ and his apostles upon the New Testament church; either in express terms or by approved precedent.

Alexander Campbell, son of Thomas, likewise proclaimed the critical role of Scripture for the believer in what might be designated his "systematic theology" in *The Christian System* (1839).

> The Bible alone is the Bible only, in word and deed, in profession and practice: and this alone can reform the world and save the church. Judging others as we once judged ourselves, there are not a few who are advocating the Bible alone, and preaching their own opinions. Before we applied the Bible alone to our views, or brought our views and religious practices to the Bible, we plead the old theme,—"The Bible alone is the religion of the Protestants." But we found it an arduous task, and one of twenty years labor, to correct our diction and purify our speech according to the Bible alone; and even as yet we have not practically repudiated the language of Ashdod. We only profess to work and walk by the rules which will inevitably issue in a pure speech, and in right concretions of that pure, and holy, and celestial thing called Christianity,—in faith, in sentiment, and in practice.

In 1906 David Lipscomb received a letter from a Washington official, S. N. D. North, who was in charge of a mandated federal religious census. North surmised that a rift had developed in the Disciples of Christ movement and he wanted to report the data as depicting two different groups rather than one. At first David Lipscomb did not wish to lend his support to an alleged split in the Restoration Movement, but finally it became clear to him that such a division was going to be reported in the census whether or not he was involved in collecting the data. He therefore secured helpers, for example, J. W. Shepherd, and they proceeded to poll the more traditional members, who took the name Churches of Christ for congregations and membership totals. About the Churches of Christ, Lipscomb wrote,

> There is a distinct people taking the Word of God as their only sufficient rule of faith, calling the churches 'churches of Christ' or 'churches of God,' distinct and separate in name, work, and rule of faith, from all other bodies or peoples . . .
>
> Their aim is to unite all professed Christians in the sole purpose of promoting simple, evangelical Christianity as God revealed in the Scriptures, free from all human opinions and inventions of men.[2]

These convictions continued among the Churches of Christ down through the decades even though they were expressed in different images and vocabulary. In 1966 the Abilene Christian University lectureship was the major forum for the Churches of Christ. A foremost spokesperson was Ray Chester, who had preached for the large and influential Sixteenth and Decatur congregation in Washington, DC, and at that time was the minister of the College Church of Christ in Searcy, attended by many Harding University personnel and students. In 1967 Chester became minister of the Brentwood Oaks congregation in Austin, later the longtime home congregation of David Worley.

Chester embraced the authority of the Bible but declared that the Bible must be viewed from a proper perspective. He was still committed to the Scriptures as a fundamental authoritative foundation.

> To properly understand the authority of the Bible we must get some other thing clearly in mind. One thing is that ultimate authority resides in God and in His revelation of Himself in Jesus Christ. Our religion is not of a book. It is a religion that centers in a person. We begin then, in both evangelism and apologetics, not with proof for a book, but with the proclamation of a person. Recently in a certain area a television program was started.

---

2. In *Gospel Advocate*, July 18, 1907, pp. 457.

> The first program dealt with the infallible book. The effort was made to establish our source of authority in this book by rather elaborate arguments from fulfilled prophecy, miracles, and its excellence in various ways. Then on the basis of the infallible book, knowledge of God arrived.

Everett Ferguson, professor of church history at Abilene Christian University, confirmed the importance of Scripture from a developmental or diachronic (that is, through time) foundation. Ferguson held a PhD from Harvard University and became a respected voice regarding ecclesiology because of his courses and books on the church. He too approached the authority of Scripture from a different perspective than the forefathers, but still embraced its weightiness in much the same manner as Walter Scott or Thomas Campbell. We quote Professor Ferguson from his 1996 book *Church of Christ: A Biblical Ecclesiology for Today*:

> Although the church was historically prior to the Bible as a given collection of books, the word contained in the Bible was theologically prior to the church. The recognition of a canon of scripture was an acknowledgement by the church that it was not its own authority and was an act of submission to the authority of apostolic preaching inscripturated in the apostolic writings. Hence, the standpoint of this study is the normativeness of the apostolic word (the teaching of apostles and other apostolic persons) contained in the scriptures accepted by the church. Later historical developments may throw light on that word (and such is another story) but are not themselves normative and must be judged by that word. This is so because the witness of the first generation of Christians about what was authoritative for them is an irreversible decision and remains determinative of what the essence of Christianity is.[3]

Somewhat earlier, Rubel Shelly and Randy Harris also professed the import of Scripture for the believer and the church. Shelly was the well-known minister of a large congregation in Nashville. He later served as president of Rochester College and a professor at Lipscomb, and Randy Harris was renowned as a preacher at the large Donelson congregation in Nashville and a Bible teacher at Lipscomb University, then later as an especially beloved professor at Abilene Christian.

> We believe the Scripture to be the Word of God, the God who created us and who is unchanging in his nature. Given God's eternal faithfulness to his own identity, his Word is eternally

---

3. P. xviii (Grand Rapids: Eerdmans, 1996).

binding and always relevant. Scripture can never be ignored, nor can we outgrow it. It is the primary source of our knowledge of God today. Thus we affirm without hesitation such classic texts as 2 Timothy 3:16–17 ("All Scripture God-breathed") and 2 Peter 1:21 (For prophecy never had its origin in the will of man, but men spoke from God as they were carried along by the Holy Spirit").[4]

DAVID WORLEY AND FUNDAMENTAL CHRISTIAN DOGMA

David Worley may have expressed what he understood to be the basic doctrines of Christianity in a still different manner. He affirmed the power of fresh language and metaphors. He was of the conviction that these fundamentals needed to be showcased before the post baby boomer crowd so that such commitments would continue sacrosanct and indelibly fixed in the minds of future churchgoers.

I too prized the consequences of good planning. But I tended to wait until faced with a course or lecture before entering into the planning stage. I tended to worry more about the discourses and documents in which I was involved at the moment, which were often several. David, however, lifted his eyes in hopes that he could visualize what was over the horizon, trying before hand to conceive what sort of arrangements were necessary to inculcate basic faith and spirituality. David Worley was an inveterate planner and, we might add, a par excellence planner, should one agree with his objectives. The salient features of his planning were (1) an emphasis on the spiritual, (2) special attention to changed circumstances, (3) flexibility in face of new challenges, (4) a willingness to employ his own resources, (5) the enlisting of especially qualified people to carry out the tasks involved, and (6) personal concern for the recipients of his planning.

---

4. Shelly and Harris, *The Second Incarnation: A Theology for the 21st Century Church* (West Monroe, LA : Howard, 1992).

13

David Worley as Worship Planner

R. Mark Shipp

It is my honor and privilege to offer this tribute to David Worley. I have known David and Melinda since 1992, when I began working at the Institute for Christian Studies (now Austin Graduate School of Theology), where David served as president from 1993 to 2001. David was also an elder and served on the worship committee at Brentwood Oaks Church of Christ in Austin, Texas, for much of that time. It was my privilege to worship with many David Worley–planned services at Brentwood Oaks and Austin Grad, to work with him on a metrical Psalter review committee, and to confer with him about my metrical Psalter project, *Timeless*. I will proceed with this tribute along these lines: David Worley as worship planner, David Worley's passion for the recovery of psalm singing in the church, and David Worley and the Lord's Prayer as a model for Christian worship.

DAVID WORLEY AS WORSHIP PLANNER

At Brentwood Oaks Church of Christ

From the early to mid-1990s until shortly before his death, David was instrumental in the planning of worship at the Brentwood Oaks Church of Christ. This was evident in at least two ways: first, the theological sensitivity of the weekly Brentwood Oaks Order of Worship, and second, in his minute attention to detail in the organization of that order. David firmly believed in "Christian worship as a sacrifice of praise, rather than as experience," according to minster Charlie Johanson.

Worship inevitably began with a Pauline quote: "Grace and peace from God our Father and the Lord Jesus Christ." David felt that it was critically important to speak these words each Lord's Day as a means of calling the gathered people of God to worship. Unlike the practice at some churches, I was struck in those years by the lack of "announcements" at the beginning of worship, or other introductory matter tangential or distracting to worship. We began with the "grace and peace" to provide the theological introduction, then went right into worship in song.

Worship was always highly organized, usually around a topic of concern for the Sunday. The song service was organized this way. The songs were selected for their coherence under a particular subtopic. After two to three songs, an elder would read a foundational text, such as the Beatitudes in Matthew 5, with the congregation standing, and then lead the congregation in prayer.

Prayer was central to a David Worley–planned worship service. The entire congregation was to be silent and reverent during any prayer, but especially the "Shepherd's Prayer," given by an elder each Sunday, and movement of any kind during the prayer was discouraged, according to former minister Roger McCown. In the course of time, one Sunday a month was set aside for focus on prayer for specific groups. One Sunday it might be on caregivers, such as mothers, fathers, teachers, and hospital or nursing home workers. Another Sunday might focus upon various ministries of the church, local and international. Usually, three members would go to the front and lead specific prayers during this special prayer time. Sometimes the last in the sequence would be a prayer of intercession for the sick, disoriented, or oppressed, followed by prayer for the offering, which was always carefully separated from the Lord's Supper.

In the course of time, one Sunday per month was set aside for an "extended meditation" at the Lord's Supper (which David referred to as the "Lord's Meal"). This meant longer than usual and, hopefully, well-thought-out comments by the one officiating at the table. Sometimes David would provide the text for the meditation; other times the reader would select his own text. One feature of the Lord's Supper continuing to the present was the quoting of the "words of institution of the Supper," now always from Matthew 26:26–29; verse 26 was read after the prayer for the bread and verses 27–29 were read after the prayer for the cup.

Each sermon would have a text that was read either by a congregational member or by the preaching minister himself before the sermon. David was instrumental in the separation of the invitation for response from the sermon itself; many worship services would have an invitation, for example, near the beginning of worship, then several songs, the Lord's Supper, and the sermon much later in the service.

Finally, each service would conclude with a benediction, usually taken directly from Scripture, to which the congregation would respond, "Amen." Nothing says it, however, like an actual order of worship! The following is the Order of Worship for May 4, 2014, for the Brentwood Oaks Church of Christ:

Brentwood Oaks Church of Christ
May 4, 2014

CALL TO WORSHIP

The Steadfast Love of the Lord
We Bring the Sacrifice of Praise
God is the Fountain Whence

Grace and Peace

Jesus Is Lord

Shepherd's Scripture and Prayer   Philippians 2:1–11

Servant Song
None of Self and All of Thee

As we sing this hymn, we invite you to take your children
ages 2 1/2 to 5 (pre-Kindergarten) to our children's worship in the chapel
(Name tags provided in the pew rack.)
Children with special needs are invited to a time of worship in Room A-108.

SINGING THE PSALMS

Worthy Lord, I Give Praise to You!   Psalm 18

PRAYER OF INTERCESSION AND THANKSGIVING

This is My Father's World

MINISTRY OF THE WORD

Sermon *Walking Out of Step*
Revelation 2:18–29

THE TABLE

'Tis Midnight, and on Olive's Brow

All who profess Christ as Lord
are invited to share in the Bread and Cup.

Bread

Cup

Praying the Prayer that the Lord Taught His Disciples

THE INVITATION

There Is a Place of Quiet Rest

As we sing this hymn God may stir your heart to respond to his grace in your life.

Perhaps you would benefit from having people pray with you. If you have never confessed publicly your faith in Jesus and been baptized, this would be the right time to do this. We welcome for membership believers who have been immersed. If we may help you, come now to the front pew and speak with a minister or elder.

GATHERED AND SENT

Family Matters
Be Thou My Vision

David Worley's Influence on Austin Graduate School of Theology's Chapel Services

David was president of the Institute for Christian Studies/Austin Graduate School of Theology from 1993 to 2001, then chancellor until 2017. He left his mark on all aspects of the school, not least of which was weekly chapel.

As with worship at Brentwood Oaks Church of Christ, chapel worship at AGST began with, "Grace and Peace from God our Father and the Lord Jesus Christ." In keeping with David's emphasis on recovery of the Psalms in public reading and singing in Christian worship, a psalm was read after the "grace and peace" at every chapel service. Also in keeping with David's emphasis upon the entire canon of Scripture being addressed by the church, the Psalms were read aloud sequentially, one psalm per week, until the entire Psalter was read. Then the process was repeated. This practice continues to the present. According to Charlie Johanson in a conversation on June 7, 2017, David also initiated the four-year cycle of Bible study at Brentwood Oaks, where in the church's adult education program all books of the Bible were covered in the course of a four-year period. Also, learned in conversation with Joel Petty, a contributor to this volume, on June 8, 2017, David also was extremely influential in the content and ordering of worship in churches in St. Petersburg, Russia. Also, the text for chapel homilies would rotate through the Old and New Testaments, with a book or series of biblical books being the lectionary text each semester. There would be a final prayer and then usually a benediction.

DAVID WORLEY AND THE RECOVERY OF PSALM-SINGING IN THE CHURCH

David Worley and the Psalter Review Committee

David firmly believed that the church should sing psalms in its corporate worship, in keeping with the commands of Paul in Ephesians and Colossians. Around 2003, Dr. David Worley assembled a group of people to discuss how to get Churches of Christ to recover psalm singing in worship. The group included Mel Witcher, Dan Merrell, myself, Philip Camp, David Worley, and Bruce Evans. The decision was made to evaluate metrical Psalters that had been published in the past decade or two in various communions in order to cull out the best songs, which would be appropriate to sing in the a cappella tradition of the Churches of Christ.

A committee of several Brentwood Oaks members was formed to review a number of metrical Psalters over a period of two years, meeting on Wednesday nights. The members of this committee were: Mel Witcher, chair, Judy Witcher, Dan Merrell, Libby Weed, Becky Stewart, Melinda Worley, Michele Broadway, and myself. Several metrical Psalters were considered, but the following were the main resources for review:

> *The Book of Psalms for Singing* (Reformed Presbyterian Church, 1998)
> *Cantus Christi* (Christ Church Idaho, 2002)
> *Psalter Hymnal* (Christian Reformed Church, 1988)
> *Trinity Psalter* (Crown and Covenant Publications, Reformed Presbyterian Church and Presbyterian Church in America, 2000)

In addition, the wonderful lyrics of Michael Morgan in *Psalter for Christian Worship* were evaluated for use in a cappella worship, utilizing a variety of traditional musical settings.

Meeting once a week, at the end of two years we were able to complete only book 1 of the Psalms (Psalms 1–41) in the books listed above. The consensus was that many of the songs in all of the books considered, with the exception of Michael Morgan's, were either inelegant or awkward lyrically, often had a poor choice of musical settings for congregational use, or a poor marriage of text and tune. The only songs from this period that ever got sung at Brentwood Oaks were a few from Michael Morgan's *Psalter*.

Regardless of the uneven application of psalm singing based upon recovery of metrical psalms from the recent (and more distant) past in the review committee, a permanent aspect of this two-year review was the practice of singing a psalm in almost every worship service at the Brentwood Oaks church, continuing to the present. This may not have happened without the guidance, influence, and patronage of David Worley.

The Timeless Psalter/Commentary Project

I remember asking the committee assembled by David in 2003 if there was any possibility of composing our own metrical psalms. No one on the committee, with the exception of myself and Mel Witcher, had ever composed. This was not really the direction the committee wanted to go, but I mentioned I would pursue it.

In July or August 2005 I was invited to go to St. Petersburg to teach Isaiah, Exodus, and Joshua in the Institute of Theology and Christian Ministry over a three-week period. I taught in the mornings, but was free in the afternoons and evenings every day. Due to the American missionary Joel Petty being gone during most of my time there, I was asked to stay in the faculty apartment and not wander around the city. I had previously heard

Konstantin Zhigulin's wonderful hymn "My God and King" in student worship, and mentioned I would like to translate it into English. During the three-week sequester in the apartment, Konstantin came by almost every day and we translated about twenty of his hymns into English, many of them psalms. I also composed my first metrical psalm while in Russia, "How Blest Is the Man," a setting of Psalm 1, and played it for the Russians. I decided at that time, with Konstantin's help, to begin working on a new metrical Psalter with all new compositions. This eventuated in the three-volume "Psalter/Commentary," *Timeless: Ancient Psalms for the Church Today*,[1] an ongoing publication of new compositions of metrical psalms, new commentaries, and new translations of all the Psalms.

David Worley was very interested in this project and followed it with keen interest over the past twelve years. Periodically, the two of us would meet and discuss the Timeless project at his favorite coffee shops, first Texpresso and then Whole Foods' coffee bar. David was very interested in recordings of all the (eventually) over 350 new musical settings of psalms. We had at least three false starts in this endeavor: electronic MIDI files, then amateur "learning CDs," then a small professional group of singers. David "nixed" all of these. Finally, in about 2013, a professional group of singers out of Orlando, Florida, named Vocal Tapestry, agreed to record *Timeless* songs at Lone Pine Studios, produced by Joseph Martin of Shawnee Press and directed by Tony De Rosa. That began a relationship in the studio that has continued to the present, eventuating in three professionally recorded CDs with a fourth in planning stages. David pronounced these "just right."

Another idea David had was to find someone to write an application to run on a mobile device that would play these psalm settings, especially as a morning-by-morning "wake-up call" or alarm on a smartphone. We are in the process currently of contracting for a new website with music downloads, learning/rehearsal music files, and apps to run on mobile devices, as David had dreamed.

A final dream that David had relative to psalm appropriation was to take our project and put it in the hands of youth ministers and campus ministers throughout the US. David felt that a "sea change" was needed in church culture in order to bring about the reading and singing of the Psalms in worship and daily devotions. This cultural change, he felt, was only possible by influencing the youth of the church, something that could be facilitated through ministers involved with young people. This has not been implemented yet, but discussions continue to go on about the best way to bring this about.

---

1. Edited by Mark Shipp (Abilene, TX : Abilene Christian University Press, 2011–).

The Psalm Fest at Brentwood Oaks Church of Christ

I mention earlier in this article David's love for singing the Psalms in corporate worship. This connected with the Timeless project in the 2012 Psalm Fest at the Brentwood Oaks Church of Christ in Austin. The Psalm Fest was a festival of singing (mostly metrical psalms written for Timeless) and reading the Psalms, with some plenary speakers on Psalms topics as well. David was the first of these plenary speakers on the program. His topic was "Singing the Psalms: The Culture of Praise." After rehearsing the history of metrical psalmody, especially in the French Reformation, David said that book 1 of the Psalter reminds us that the book of Psalms is the hymnal of God's people, that it reminds us of God's ordering of chaos, and that we have a king in the line of David. David believed that the book of Psalms ultimately speaks about and summarizes Jesus, the true Son of David.

As opposed to the way the early church and the Reformers appropriated the Psalms in the life of faith, most of us did not grow up reading or singing the Psalms. David thought this was odd, considering that we have direct commands in Ephesians and Colossians to sing them. Not only this command, however, is apparent in Paul's writings; David also believed that

> As we read and compare Paul's words in Ephesians 4–5 with the Psalms we can detect that Paul's thoughts and words have been shaped in a more comprehensive way by Paul's own chanting of the Psalms, . . . both from the introduction in Psalms 1–2 as well as the Psalms which follow (Ps. 4:1, Ps. 6:1) . . . Paul's orientation toward God was imprinted by his chanting the Psalms.[2]

"How can we recover a daily reading or chanting or singing of the Psalms?" David asks. He suggests the following disciplines: (1) listening to psalms as we drive, to stimulate reading, chanting, and singing; (2) developing our own habits of "reading daily, serially, and listening to what the Spirit says in the very ordering of the Psalms"; (3) finding opportunities to "encourage the brethren to take on the Psalms in our assemblies . . . that they may entrust them over time to the next generation"; (4) "May the Psalms even form the background sounds for the nurseries"; and (5) for older Christians, balancing the cacophony of the culture on the radio and television with the reading of the Psalms at the breakfast table.

---

2. David Worley, "Singing the Psalms: The Culture of Praise" (in *Psalm Fest 2012: A Celebration of the Psalms in Song, Readings, and Meditations* [Brentwood Oaks Church of Christ, February 11, 2012]), p. 3.

The Appropriation of the Psalms in "Learning to Love God"

In 2016, Woody Woodrow, coordinator of the online program at Austin Graduate School of Theology, edited David's "radio spots" for Russian radio on all the books of the Bible and collected them in the volume *Learning to Love God: A Guide to Understanding the Bible*.[3] The section describing the reader's appropriation of the Psalms occurs on pages 85–102. David believed that the Psalms should be read sequentially, that they largely describe King David's life and faith, and that these point to Jesus, the latter-day Messiah and great Son of David.

> [The] 150 psalms are largely attributed to King David ... Many of the Psalms have a heading or title indicating the situation which gave rise to the Psalm.

He says that the first two psalms are the introduction to the Psalter and provide the themes of the Psalter: righteous living and honoring God as the only true king. David goes on to summarize the contents of the five books of the Psalter and writes that books 1 and 2 "have the ring of truth largely because of their composition by King David." He focuses attention on Psalms 3–4 and 22–24, reflective of David's life, faith, and challenges. These are not only, however, the words and deeds of David; they are also reflective of the words and prayers of Jesus, the Good Shepherd.

Book 3 is largely the work of faithful musicians in Israel, Asaph, Korah, and Ethan. They "felt deeply the presence of God with Israel, men who found words to express the struggles and expectations of their hearts before the Lord." David focuses upon Psalms 73, 78, and 89, the latter two because they raise the issue of God's promises and covenant with David, and the tragedy of its demise. This demise of human kingship in the line of David leads David Worley to say:

> The Psalms in book III reflect a progression of thought and emotion beyond the earlier songs in books I and II. Just as a transcript of our prayers 10 years ago put alongside our petitions today would show growth in our understanding of God's will, so the Psalms through this collection reveal a shift of emphasis *away from* hopes dependent upon an earthly king (with temple, with land) *to* hopes dependent upon God as the only true king.
>
> The final step in interpretation comes with the first followers of Jesus who understood in his resurrection that God finally kept His promise of an eternal kingdom, that Jesus as David's

---

3. Edited by Robert Woodrow (Austin: Thelese Pub., 2016).

son is the true king of Israel—and not just of Israel, but kings of all nations of the earth.[4]

In books 4–5, David draws the reader's attention to Psalm 90, with Moses as God's mediator, and then to the "Enthronement Psalms" of God's kingship, Psalms 93 and 96. Book 4 ends with Psalm 106, a psalm of Israel's rebellion and God's judgment. Book 5 "records the mature words of praise." David focuses upon Psalms 111–117, the "Hallelujah Psalms," which often begin and end with "praise the Lord," and Psalms 146–150, the five-psalm closing doxology of the Psalter, "bring the collection to a joyous conclusion. Struggles behind, cries for vengeance silent, the Psalmist can now enthrone God in unadorned adoration. Words go begging."

DAVID WORLEY, WORSHIP, AND THE LORD'S PRAYER

One of the most interesting legacies David has left us is his commitment to reading, structuring worship, and living out the implications of the Lord's Prayer. One can see the influence of the Lord's Prayer in the Brentwood Oaks Order of Worship printed above, but that extended beyond influence to involve the life lived around, and worship structured around, the Lord's Prayer. One could say without exaggeration that to David the Lord's Prayer was not just the model prayer, but the model life.

Below is the Order of Worship for December 9, 2012, which betrays David's careful, and idiosyncratic, use of language; and, most notably, the entire worship is structured around the Lord's Prayer.

Lord's Day Assembly
Second Sunday: Lord's Prayer
December 9, 2012

GRACE AND PEACE

Singing God's Grace
Saying Grace and Peace
Welcoming One Another

---

4. Worley, *Learning to Love God*, p. 95.

CONSECRATED BE YOUR NAME

On Zion's Glorious Summit

As we sing this hymn, we invite you to take your children ages 2 1/2 to 5 (pre-Kindergarten) to our children's worship in the chapel. Children with special needs are invited to a time of worship in Room A-108.

We Listen for God's Word in Deuteronomy 6:4–9
We Respond with AMEN to the Word, in Prayer

COME YOUR KINGSHIP

Glory to the Newborn King

BE DONE YOUR WILL

Prince of Peace
Bread
Cup

All who profess Christ as Lord
are invited to share in the Bread and Cup.

OUR BREAD FOR TOMORROW GIVE US TODAY

Ancient Words
Ministry of the Word   God Breathed
                                        2 Timothy 3:16–17

FORGIVE US OUR DEBTS, LEAD US NOT INTO TESTING

Hymn of Profession and Response

We encourage your response to God's grace in your life. We are ready to pray with you or hear your confession of Jesus as Lord and assist in your baptism. We welcome for membership believers who have been immersed. If we may help you, please come to a front pew and speak with a minister during this hymn.

Intercession and Collection
Encouragement to Bible Study in 2013

CLOSING EXHORTATION

Reminder of the Word Preached and for Prayer
It Came Upon the Midnight Clear

Pray the Lord's Prayer Daily

David believed that the life of faith of the believer and his or her walk with the Lord could be summarized in the Lord's Prayer. Not only did David structure worship around the Lord's Prayer; often his own public prayers were elaborations on the model prayer.

DAVID WORLEY AND THE ELLIPSIS: A LIFE WELL LIVED

Those who received emails from David are very familiar with his use of the ellipsis (. . .) in his correspondence, suggesting that "there is more to be said here," or "subject to be continued." David's earthly life is over, but his influence is . . . , an ellipsis, to be continued. His attention to worship planning, incorporation of the Psalms into worship, and structuring of prayers, worship services, and life around the Lord's Prayer will be long remembered and his influence will be . . .

14

My Own Experience as a Friend

Igor Egirev

THIS ESSAY IS NOT an attempt to create a collective image of David Worley as a friend. In some manner all this book is about David as a friend—the same topic looked at from different angles. He had many friends and because he was a multifaceted, versatile person his friends, I'm sure, have their own very specific, personal stories of their friendship with David. When I look at the list of those who contributed to this book, I realize that these people were David's friends much longer than I was. And because of that they have much better reasons to write this chapter. But on the other hand, it feels like I've known David much longer than the actual ten years. Our friendship was very intense, packed with events and bright moments, and was also significant because of the great positive influence his friendship had on me. It changed my life drastically. So I will mostly share from my own experience, hoping that what I write will resonate with the memories of those who knew him personally for a long time, and that it will help those who didn't know David to appreciate what a blessing it was to be David's friend.

I'm thankful for the opportunity to write this essay. It gives me a chance to say good words about David, which I have always wanted to state to him, but never did. This is not to say that I failed to compliment him, but I don't think I did that enough. David himself was the reason for the slight. He always left compliments dangling, ostensibly changing the subject, shifting the focus from himself to something or somebody else. In one way or the other he discouraged me from expressing my gratitude and admiration for him. There were times when I composed long letters to David, in which

I tried to express my love and respect. I did that many times, especially during the course of his fight with cancer. I wrote long emotional letters, and then started to edit them the way David taught me, as one of his students. Little by little I took out all the things I thought he would consider superfluous, until finally I had a brief, compact sentence with just information left. And then I hit the "send" button in my browser. These unspoken, deleted feelings somewhat burdened me. So in this essay I'm going to write what I always wanted to write to David.

A BROTHER AND A FRIEND

A brother may not be a friend, but a friend will always be a brother.

—Benjamin Franklin

My comments start with the assumption that we were friends. What makes people friends? They know each other, they spend time together, they care, and they are not afraid to share something personal, knowing they will find support in each other. At best, friends not only have fun together but have the same goal in life. When I look at those traits I realize David and I were good friends. He was not simply my supervisor, my teacher, my brother in Christ, but my friend. That speaks a lot to me. In this era all the roles mentioned above (teacher, supervisor, brother in Christ) don't reveal much specifically about one as a person or the level of relationship between two parties. Even when we call each other brothers or sisters in Christ it may not describe our closeness, our personal relationship—we are brothers and sisters in Christ not because we chose each other, but because we all chose to follow Jesus Christ and through him became children of the same Father. And just as in our earthly families we are brothers and sisters because we have the same parents but unfortunately are not necessarily friends; in the body of Christ brothers and sisters unfortunately are not always friends either. As we say in Russia, "We don't choose our relatives". But since we do have the freedom to choose friends, another saying comes to mind: "Tell me who are your friends and I will tell you who you are." All of that sounds right. But having said that, in all honesty, I need to admit that when I say "David Worley is my friend" I don't feel like that describes me at all. In my particular case it describes David. I look at our friendship like it was undeserved goodness—grace. We were friends not because I was good enough to be his friend, but because he valued something in me I didn't perceive, or he saw in me somebody I can become. And he trusted, he believed, he encouraged me no matter how I performed. I'm afraid I failed his expectations many times, but nevertheless he did not give up on me. It really helped me to develop, to mature. I knew that our relationship did not rest on my performance. It reminds me of the attitude God has toward us. But we should not take advantage of God's kindness.

David says "Grace to you" and blesses you with his friendship.

OUR FIRST MEETING

I met David in the spring of 2004 in Peterhof, in the suburbs of St. Petersburg. David taught a seminar on the book of Ephesians and many church leaders from different locations in Russia attended. At that time I was a minister at the Rostov Church of Christ. We came to the seminar with brother Nikolay Chertkov. As I recall, there were more than twenty brothers there from all over Russia. We immersed ourselves in the Word. David impressed us so much—for the first time we saw a teacher reading from the Nestle-Aland Greek New Testament, making his own translation on the go. Another thing that impressed me personally so much was the fact that David applied the Scriptures more literally into our lives than most of us—ministers of congregations—did. For example, we read Ephesians 5:3, "But immorality or any impurity or greed must not even be named among you, as is proper among saints." David said that we were not only not supposed to do these things, but really even to talk about them would be inappropriate. That approach was different for me, because by that time I had already learned to look at many passages in Scripture in a symbolic way and that was not always healthy.

As I watched David later I noticed that this approach was quite common for him. Often he took Scripture more literally than many of us did, and that was reflected in his lifestyle. A person who takes the Sermon on the Mount literally would look and act much differently even compared with the majority of Christians. We often create a way to escape following Scripture by taking it too symbolically. I heard many times from different people that they thought David was an unique man, not like anyone else. I believe this was true. His devotion to God and love for his Word made him different. The more serious we become about following the way of Jesus, the more unusual we are. His life was liturgy, if we take the original meaning of this word into consideration. His time, wisdom, energy, health, and resources were focused on glorifying God and strengthening his Kingdom on the earth in every possible way. It was very obvious to anyone who knew him. David was like a walking sermon to me. When he said "Peace and grace to you" he meant every word. Many times in Russia I watched David interact with secular people. Before we departed, instead of saying goodbye to them he said "Peace and grace to you." Sometimes he said it in Russian: *"Мир и благодать."* He stated this saying seriously, and almost every time you could see that the person was surprised to hear the phrase but received these words with gratitude. His "peace and grace" was not just a figure of speech—part of Christian cultural talk. He was blessing a person with these words. I noticed this from the very first time I met him, and the more I knew him, the more I appreciated his sincerity and realized that the way he interpreted Scripture was the best way.

STUDENT YEARS

I became a student at the Institute of Theology and Christian Ministry in January 2007. I knew that David would be one of our professors, and anticipated meeting him again. I was rewarded with the rest of our group.

Like many other students, at first I was surprised at David's requirements. He made a great emphasis on being very brief when we did our written assignments. He wanted us to formulate our thoughts using as few words as possible and didn't want us to quote Scripture, just put Scripture references in our papers. He could always easily determine whether a student had information and something to say or if he or she just sought to present the required number of pages. That was probably true with all our professors, but for some reason only David was remembered for this trait. Another thing I remember is that he always demanded that our assignments be submitted on time. In 2007 David taught Romans, and all the students were required to write research papers. We wrote in Russian, interpreters translated our works into English, and then they were sent to David in Austin for grading. After the course was over I went to the United States by the invitation of the Eastern European Mission to speak at one of their events. I spoke in Austin and I noticed that David was in the audience. After the evening was over David came to me, we warmly greeted each other, he probably said a couple of words about my presentation, and then he asked me why I still hadn't submitted my paper. I was surprised to hear that, because I did it on time. Later we found out that there was some kind of delay in sending my submitted paper to him and that worked out well. But David's question in Austin demonstrated to me how serious David was about being on time.

These incidents may describe David as a very strict teacher. But yet, even being his students, we noticed that in personal communication he could make you feel like you were very special. His classes were not only informative and helped us learn and understand much that was new, they were also very inspiring, because David sometimes became poetic. During my time as a student I wrote a tune and thought it could make a song. I had a melody and cords and I could hum it, but I didn't have lyrics. I struggled for lyrics a long time, until we had a class on exegesis in which David used Genesis 1 as an example. I was much inspired by the comments and on my way home from school, while on the subway, all of the sudden lyrics came to me. I could not wait until I got home and wrote them down. I emailed David about the hymn later. I didn't know how he would react, but to my surprise his reaction was very encouraging. He asked me to translate the lyrics into English. I did that and soon he sent me his own poem in return. It was a very beautiful, elegant poem, with a very sophisticated structure. I still treasure it. I never knew he liked poetry and wrote it himself. I felt like David graciously opened to me another side of his personality. These kinds of incidents bring people closer, and a friendship started growing.

WORKING SIDE BY SIDE WITH DAVID

In January of 2009, while I still was a student at ITCM and at the same time studying in the MA program at the St. Petersburg State University, David taught a course at ITCM. One day he invited me to talk. He asked me if I would consider becoming president of ITCM. That was a big surprise to me. It would have been a lesser surprise had I been offered a staff position, but an offer to become president was completely unexpected. I felt I was not ready for such a prestigious and demanding position—was not qualified to become president. But David had faith in me and he said that it was the ITCM board of trustees' plan from the beginning for a Russian to become president of ITCM. It was not obvious who would be appointed, but generally the board was in favor of indigenous leadership, and was prayerfully requesting guidance. We decided that I needed time to think and pray over it. I told my wife, Natasha, about the offer and we decided we would stay in St. Petersburg and I would accept the presidency. Needless to say, it was a great honor for me to become president of the school in which I was a student. I had a wonderful example—Joel Petty, who was ITCM president from the beginning and did an outstanding job. I'm so blessed to have him as my friend and co-worker in Christ.

When we discussed our family's move to St. Petersburg I explained to David that we didn't have enough funds to purchase a place to live in St. Petersburg. Property prices in St. Petersburg were some of the highest in Russia. We would not get enough money from selling our small place in Rostov-on-Don. Even with the addition of our savings, it would not be enough. David said he would help us personally to solve our living accommodation problem. So he did! About four and a half years later, in 2014, we moved into a new apartment. It became possible only with David's help. I knew of at least three other Christian families in St. Petersburg whom David previously helped buy apartments.

His generosity is also demonstrated by the fact that in 2004 David purchased with his own money a floor in a three-story building and gave the space to the Neva Church of Christ. The floor area is over 6,200 square feet. It was not only bought, but also renovated with David's personal funds. The location of that place is great. It's not far from the historical center of St. Petersburg. It's easy to get there by public transportation, which is very important in Russia, where many people don't own cars. I am going to mention this property later in this chapter.

One of the greatest benefits of being president of ITCM was being able to work side by side with David. By that time I had already developed much respect for David and was attracted by the sweetness and uniqueness of his personality. He often came to St. Petersburg and even while I was still a student at ITCM we visited, dreamed, and planned for the future. He surprised me by the way he was able to look ahead—his imagination had no limits. As brother Konstantin Zhigulin, an ITCM graduate, wrote about David, "He was a forward-looking man, looking far ahead, and, if you remember David, even when I look at his photo, I always had an impression of him of a man who never walked with his head down. His head was always up, and it expressed his character—it made you think he looked far ahead. Even when he was looking at someone he looked far ahead. He looked far ahead when he was starting his projects and when he supported other projects. I would say that David was a modest person with his head held high". This is so true. He was always looking ahead and seeing ahead. He was very creative, challenging the routine, and yet very reasonable and balanced. He stretched my mind, showing new possibilities in a rapidly changing world. It took time for me to see where he was leading. All of that was a great experience for me. I'm still learning from him.

One of the greatest conditions for nurturing friendships is communication. It is virtually impossible to remain friends if you don't communicate. Of course, the best way to foster relationship is face-to-face communication. David and I met every time we had chance, either in Russia or in the US. But since we were in different places most of the time we constantly kept in touch by email. That was another kind of emailing. I usually was pretty good at responding to emails (or at least I thought I was), but communicating with David was something different. We wrote each other every day, several times a day. David wanted me to respond to his messages immediately. If I didn't know the answer to his questions right away, or I needed time to collect information, he asked me to at least write him that I received his message, and indicate when I expected to respond. Quite often our emailing turned into chatting. Sometimes I would receive his message in the evening, around 8:00 p.m., respond to it immediately, receive his response to my message, and from there it went on and on. If you consider the eight to nine hours of time difference between the US and Russia, "chatting" may continue rather late. I became used to it and now I miss it so much. Through his emails he guided me, sometimes indirectly, by asking questions. He was a master at asking questions. In answering him I discovered something new (this is probably how he taught me). I often formulated our plans, saw something that needed to be developed, something to which we needed to pay closer attention. I wonder if he already knew the answers and asked questions only for my benefit; he wanted me to learn new things and learn how to think. It's only a guess.

Now, with David being gone, I sometimes feel an emptiness. Nobody asks me many questions any more. But since David asked me so many questions, I know pretty well what he would ask me right now. It's like the famous question WWJD? I ask myself, WWDA?—"What would David ask?" After being with him for more than ten years, I think quite often I know the answers to those questions.

ONLINE PROGRAM VERSUS ON-CAMPUS PROGRAM

It's great for a friendship when friends work together toward one goal. David saw something I didn't see, but I trusted him, following his direction, knowing that he saw something I didn't.

Immediately after I started to work as president we considered changing ITCM teaching to distance learning. That was David's idea, which was supported by the ITCM board. We needed to change over for several reasons. One reason was financial. It became very expensive to keep on-campus training in St. Petersburg. Since the beginning of ITCM in 2005, we had a joint program with St. Petersburg State University that allowed us to use their dormitory for the students and to have our auditorium, library, and offices in the university's facilities. But in 2009 the situation changed and the university decided to stop this program. We had to rapidly move out of the university facilities. Fortunately, we did not have to move far. The place that David purchased in 2004 for the Neva Church of Christ was only one block away from the university campus. ITCM students carried ITCM furniture, books, documentation, and everything else to the new facility. Since then ITCM (now Christian Resource Center–Russia) is located in the Neva Church of Christ facility. But we had lost dormitory space so it became difficult to host students from outside St. Petersburg.

Another reason was the economical recession that hit both the USA and Russia. Housing and food became more expensive in St. Petersburg and we couldn't afford to accommodate students in St. Petersburg. Also, we have to admit that one of the negative aspects of having on-campus training in St. Petersburg was the fact that many ITCM graduates, after living in St. Petersburg for two and half years of study, didn't want to go back to the places from which they had come. This despite the fact that initially, as I recall, there was a great emphasis made upon the necessity for students to return home. That was very bad for local congregations because these students were some of their most dedicated members.

There were also positive reasons for implementing online training, such as Internet development in Russia, opportunities for the students to use online materials in their local congregations, and overcoming great distances in Russia. The distance learning program also connected Christians all over Russia. And of course the financial outlay for the online program was much lower.

After we started to discuss the shift to online training I remember that something in me was still in favor of good old auditorium study. That was until we tried online program. The first course offered online, "Introduction to Biblical Theology," was taught by Dr. Tom Olbricht from materials available in St. Petersburg in 2007. The course proceeded extremely well and we all were much encouraged. From that time on we had no doubt that we would move to distance learning. By 2009 we had all the courses that were taught at ITCM recorded on video and translated into Russian. By the way, the idea to make video of all the courses taught at ITCM also came from David Worley. Because of all the videos, we can now teach Russian leaders at a graduate level, because our teachers in St. Petersburg were David Worley, Tom Olbricht, Everett Ferguson, James Thompson, Mark Hamilton, Curt Niccum, Ken Cukrowski, Paul Watson, and many others great professors from US Christian universities.[1]

I need to mention that even though I was president, David as my supervisor never acted officiously. His gentleness and consideration turned our working relationship into a partnership (a word he liked to use). He treated me as a partner in the gospel—as a friend. I especially treasured his demeanor. Being his friend, I had much freedom to dream; he supported

---

1. See http://crcrussia.com/en/teachen/itcm4.

my ideas and helped me to think through the details to bring those ideas into life. He created a friendly working atmosphere in which it was easy to dream—all ideas were taken into consideration. For example, for many years, since probably 1996, we had a dream to start a newspaper in Russia that would unite the Churches of Christ in Russian-speaking countries. The idea was born in 1996 after the Christian Writers Seminar that was taught in St. Petersburg by Jack Welch, a professor at ACU and a co-editor of the *Christian Chronicle*. The seminar was organized by Chuck Whittle, who at that time was president of the Vita International Foundation. The idea began to take shape in 1996 in St. Petersburg, after two issues of the newspaper *Christian Life* was published. But for various reasons that periodical didn't continue. In 2010 I shared with David and the rest of the board the idea of resuming the newspaper in electronic format (PDF files) rather than in paper. I didn't know how that idea would be received since publishing a newspaper was different from what ITCM had been turning out. But as I discovered it was received very well. David and Chuck Whittle, who was also an ITCM board of trustees member, advised us on ways to make the newspaper more interesting and helpful, and they encouraged me to translate the newspaper into English. The first issue of the newspaper *In Christ* was sent out by email in February 2011. It is still being published monthly.

Here I also would like to comment on the meetings of the board of trustees. The trustees met twice a year in the United States: in the spring (usually April) and in the fall (either September or October). David did a lot of preliminary work. Almost as soon as I was back to Russia from my trip to the States, we started to get ready for my next trip and David asked me to prepare a set of questions for the next board meeting agenda. After that he sent an email to all board members inquiring about a date and place that would suit everyone. David, as a chairman of the board, invited various friends to our meetings—people who had experience and a heart for mission work. Some of the visitors eventually became board members. Meetings lasted six to seven hours and I made presentations about mission work in Russia and answered multiple questions. I was a bit anxious about these meetings, knowing that I was to be the center of attention, and do most of the talking in a foreign language (in English). But as soon as I entered our meeting room and saw smiling David, experienced his embrace, and heard his "Peace and grace, welcome"—to which he then added in Russian, "Добро пожаловат"—I relaxed and knew that everything was going to be alright: I'm among friends who are getting together to think about Russian missions, to pray for Russia; who are going to engage all their knowledge, experience, and love for God and his people, for the sake of spreading the good news in Russia. I'm always thankful to David for creating such an atmosphere. I think he understood my feelings and was very sensitive to them.

Talking about sweetness of relations, to keep balance I need to add something. There is one Russian saying that probably will not work in the USA. It goes like this: "Real friendship is like good tea. It should be hot, strong, and not too sweet." Our friendship was a friendship of two adults, not a friendship between father and child. His goals for me were high—sometimes I felt like they were a little too lofty—but I think they were realistic and I needed to work harder to meet his expectations. But that allowed me to grow. So our friendship was a good growing experience for me.

DAVID WORLEY AS A FRIEND OF THE RUSSIAN PEOPLE

I asked David once, "How did you get involved in Russian mission work? How did it start?" I asked this question because I wondered why, many years earlier, David had become interested in other mission fields. And also I wondered, "How can we involve more people in mission work in Russia? How can we get them interested? Maybe there is some kind of secret." But his answer was very simple: "My friend invited me to Russia initially. I came and met Russian people." David became their friend. They invited him home, shared their food, told him what brought them joy and what worried them. Knowing David, I am confident that he was interested in all of that. He asked them questions, listened to their answers, and remembered them. Many times when David came to Russia he took me to visit with somebody who had been his friend for a long time. During one of his visits to St. Petersburg his schedule was very busy, as usual, but he told me that he wanted to visit one lady who was in the hospital with her daughter. I didn't know the young woman. He had met her long ago and heard that her daughter was ill. David asked me to help him find the lady and so we did. David had toys for the girl, which he brought from the US. David usually did not like to bring a lot of things with him; he travelled with a small briefcase that looked like a computer bag. The fact that he brought those toys tells me that he was thinking about that girl, and that he was willing to change his normal routine for her.

David rented a room in St. Petersburg near the Chernaya Rechka metro station. This was where he kept the personal items he needed in St. Petersburg. That allowed him to travel only with a briefcase. I always knew that such a place existed, but had never been there with David. During his last trip to St. Petersburg David asked me to go with him to visit his room and meet the owners of the apartment. He wanted to take his suitcase from the room and have me keep it. I guess he realized that it would be his last trip to St. Petersburg. I was not aware of the seriousness of his illness. On the way to the room he told me much about the owners of the place, exhibiting considerable insight into their lives. That alerted me to the fact that when David asked questions it wasn't just for the sake of conversation. He really cared about what was going on in your life. He was interested in people. We came to the house and the owners, husband and wife, met David like he was their best friend. They put their best china tea set on the table and served hot Russian tea with cookies and candies. They didn't speak English, but the lady spoke German and so she and David communicated in German (that was the first time I heard David speak German). Sometimes I translated for all of us from Russian into English and vice versa. I saw how the owners and David looked at each other and knew that they really appreciated each other. David pointed to waffles on the table and told me that was his favorite treat. They were very simple waffles. You can purchase them in every store in Russia. The other treats on the table were very simple too, but David genuinely enjoyed everything. The tea was great, like real friendship. We had such a wonderful time—lively conversation in three languages—and by the time we finished visiting I felt like I had known these people for a long time, and I liked them almost as much as David did. That was also one of David's traits—the love he had for other people was contagious.

I'd also like to mention that the people I have just described, including the lady with a girl in the hospital, were not church members. David introduced me to many other people in St. Petersburg—his old friends—who were not Christians. But they were his dear friends. I did not notice that he liked them less because they were not Christians. I learnt a lesson from that. It's another godly quality that we need to inherit from our Heavenly Father. Jesus in the Sermon on the Mount teaches us to be like our Father, who loves and treats people on earth equally, regardless of their performances. David had always been a Christian among secular people, but his Christianity was not puffed up. His faith was loving, embracing, and inviting persons to a new a relationship with the Father. He said "peace and grace" to every one.

PERSONAL DAVID

I can only guess how busy David was. He wore so many hats. By the intensity of our email communication I got some indication of all he was doing. But I knew as a fact that he was involved in many different roles and activities. He was a husband, father, grandfather, church minister, theologian, and entrepreneur. And yet he managed to be personal, to find quality time with people. When we were together it seemed like no one else and nothing else existed for him. His focus was just on you. The time spent with him was yours only. Although people say he was a private person—and maybe that is true in some ways—in a personal setting he became very open, like friends usually do.

I remember once when we were driving from one city to another for two hours, just he and I. Maybe that was a good opportunity to talk about Christian Resource Center–Russia, but instead we talked about things unrelated to business. We talked about very personal things. I felt comfortable telling him the story of my family—how we ended up in the Magadan region because my grandfather, with his wife and two young daughters, was exiled there by Stalin. One of his daughters was my mother. I related how she met my father there and they stayed in the Magadan region even after my grandfather's exile was over. He and my grandmother returned to the Rostov region. I made a sad joke saying that probably I should be thankful to Stalin for exiling my grandfather, because otherwise my mother would not have met my father and I would not be born. I regretted that my father passed away without becoming a Christian. David started to tell me very personal things, which I am not going to share in detail here. I will mention only that he told me about his father and how he felt when he passed away. We shared one story after another. I wish our conversation had been more than two hours. But there were several other occasions like that. Each one of them I will remember for the rest of my life.

David was very much interested in what was going on with the Neva Church of Christ. He was glad to get any news from St. Petersburg. He rejoiced with us about new converts, new projects, and new classes. He also grieved with us when we went through sad times. He asked me to write him in detail about the Annual Festival of Evangelical Culture "Epiphany Night," in which the Neva Church of Christ choir participated. Being a big supporter of a cappella singing, David rejoiced when coordinators of the festival offered our congregation the privilege of coordinating an opening evening of the festival, which has always been a concert of choral singing. Eight or nine choruses from different churches sang their opening hymns of about three songs and then all choruses together sang five hymns. We sang in the old Lutheran cathedral in St. Petersburg center, near Nevsky Prospect. The cathedral was big enough to hold about eight hundred people, but the altar platform was not big enough for all the choruses. When we sang hymns together part of choruses stood on the platform and the rest were placed on balconies. That has always been a magnificent event not only for the Christian community of the city, but also for all who live in St.

Petersburg as well as guests of the city. David shared our joy of participating in this event as if he participated in it himself.

He was a personal friend to many church members of the Neva Church of Christ. I would like to share with you part of a letter that was written by the Neva Church of Christ conductor, Luka Bolshakova. David and Luka were long-time friends and she wrote her letter in memory of David. She used such wonderful words to describe him as a friend. Luka graciously allowed me to use what she wrote:

> I recently read all my correspondence with David since 2005 when we met. It took me several hours. As I read the letters, all the events of those years revived in my memory. I remembered how caring he was and how God revealed himself through David. I felt as if I experienced the love of our Heavenly Father through this man's love once again. What a big heart David had. David's messages could be just one line long, but that line got exactly "to the point." For example, one time when my husband was sick with high blood pressure suddenly a message from David appeared: "I'm thinking about you" or "We'll meet on the Lord's Day." David was always very interested in what was going on with our church with its ministries and especially with the choir. He kept abreast of everything. I shared all our news with him. He always encouraged me to persevere in this ministry of glorifying God, writing, "It is a sacrifice of praise that is offered to God by our lips" and "We ought to offer this sacrifice of praise." David always saw deeply into what was going on with my family. He was interested in what we were singing.
>
> I'm amazed when I think about who I was in his life—how he was able to find all this time for me? From this all I came to the conclusion that David was, indeed, a man who contributed his time for the people who surrounded him. He himself though always preferred to stay in the background. In him God's light was constantly present and anyone who happened to be alongside of him was warmed by this light—it was that strong! Melinda wrote to me in one of her letters that David loved our church tenderly, and that everything that was happening here always interested him very much. He never stuck out in a crowd and never showed himself. And his family is amazing too! God once gave me the possibility to be a guest in their house—a very big group of different people gathered. I met David's mother. She welcomed me as if I were a member of the family—and we talked almost all night. From my conversation with his mother I understood better why David was so loving. It was his family that

had reared him and handed down this love to him. Somehow I ended up in the wonderful "orbit" of their love—David's mother Iva Lea, Melinda, Heatherly, Christiana and Elena—they all became an example of God's family. I now wish everybody could have this kind of relationship in their family—a relationship of grace and peace. In different complicated situations in my life I asked David for advice. He always understood the situation and helped me. I don't know where I would be now but for his help. He always listened to me very attentively. My own father passed away in 2001. In David I found fatherly love and compassion. He prayed for me. I received unbelievable support through it! Alexey and I invited him to our wedding. David wrote us, "I wish so much I could be with you!" His responses were always so informal, so keen. Even when his health was already in a bad state, he received our choir news in November. I wrote to him, "David, we pray for you! How are you?" In his turn he forwarded our news to twelve people. It would seem, why should he care about this news, being so ill and in such a grave condition? I was just astounded with his response! For me, David is a man of light. He is a man through whom God showed and continues to show his love.

Luka Bolshyakova

OUR LAST MEETING

Our last board of trustees gathering was in April 2016. Prior to this meeting we missed the previous one due to David's health. And now he was with us again. And he was the same David. He had lost weight, but he looked good and he was active as usual. It gave me hope that he was going to overcome his illness. We had many guests at that meeting. It was as great as usual. And then I saw him once again during the same trip. It was in Austin, at the Austin Graduate School of Theology library, which was named for David Worley. I came to Austin from Belton, Texas, with my friend Joe Richie, an elder at Belton Church of Christ. He is also a member of the board of trustees at AGST. He was going to Austin for the board meeting and he invited me to go there because it would give me chance to see David again. I was sitting in David Worley's library by myself, reading, waiting for the board meeting to finish. After the meeting was over, David came to the library to see me. There were just two of us again. We spent half an hour together. We did not talk about work. I didn't ask him about his health. There were just two of us. We walked down the aisles, between book shelves. He showed me articles written by Church of Christ professors, many of whom had taught at Christian Resource Center–Russia. We talked about the Churches of Christ Scripture teaching and legacy. It was a sunny day. I talked with him and could not believe my blessing—I was with David again and he was sharing with me his time, just with me. I will keep his image in my heart for the rest of my life and offer thanksgiving to God for allowing me to know him, making him a part of my life. I hope I became a little more unique in a good way because I had such a friend as David Worley.

15

David Worley as Teacher

M. Todd Hall

In 1974, Pope Paul VI argued that "[m]odern man listens more willingly to witnesses than to teachers, and if he does listen to teachers, it is because they are witnesses."[1] This is ironic, insofar as pedagogy in modern times (especially in higher education) is largely conducted along the lines of what Paulo Freire termed the "banking model," that is, education is generally seen as transference of *information* (knowledge) from the teacher to the students.[2] Real education, though, as Paul VI suggests, is conducted incarnationally— it is an invitation into the life of that which is studied. Education is thus meant to be at least as *transformative* as it is informative.

Transformative teaching is especially true, of course, with the gospel. If the gospel is to truly be learned, teachers must both practice it and mentor students into it. As Jesus' invitation makes clear, students can only truly grasp the gospel through practicing it. As Freire expresses,

> [The incarnate Word] could never be learned if, at the same time, its meaning were not also grasped, and its meaning could not be grasped if it were not, also, incarnate in us. This is the basic invitation that Christ made, and continues to make to us, that we come to know the truth of this message through practicing it, down to the most minute detail . . .[3]

---

1. Apostolic exhortation *Evangelii Nuntiandi*, December 8, 1975.
2. *Pedagogy of the Oppressed*, trans. Myra Bergman Ramos (New York: Contiuum, 1970).
3. Ibid.

In addition, Freire suggests,

> I cannot know the Gospels if I take them simply as words that come to rest in me or if, seeing myself as empty, I try to fill myself with these words. This would be the way to bureaucratize the Word, to empty it, to deny it, to rob it of its eternal *coming to be* in order to turn it into a formal rite. On the contrary, I understand the Gospels, well or badly, to the degree that, well or badly, I live them.[4]

The best teachers, then, both express and embody truth, especially the truth of the gospel. Insofar as we are here reflecting on the various ways we have known David Worley, it is fitting to reflect upon David as *teacher*. David embodied his faith in ways that have molded and shaped generations of students, from courses he taught as adjunct faculty at Abilene Christian University in the 1970s and Pepperdine University in the 1980s, to the various radio broadcasts in Russia for which he was responsible, to the many students he invited into his home and life during his tenure at Austin Graduate School of Theology. And this is to say nothing of the various day-to-day interactions David had with Christians around the world, gently correcting and directing through word and deed. In this essay I will reflect on David as teacher (1) in the classroom, (2) in his public devotion, and (3) in personal pastoral relationships. In each of these David Worley was a teacher *precisely* because he was, in word and deed, a living witness.

DAVID AS TEACHER IN THE CLASSROOM

Ironically, but perhaps fittingly, the classroom is where I knew David as teacher the least. My wife, Jennifer, and I began taking classes at Austin Grad, then the Institute for Christian Studies (ICS), in the fall of 1998. My first interaction with David was at his house, where he hosted an annual gathering of students and faculty prior to the beginning of the fall semester. It was a year, I think, before I had class with him, but those early interactions with him were my first introduction to things that mattered to David as a teacher, especially the importance of words. I'm sure others in this volume will comment on this aspect of David's life, but I wish to emphasize the way in which David's care for words was central to his teaching in the classroom.

The first course I had with David was a study of the media and its impact on faithful living. The major project for the course consisted of listening

---

4. *The Politics of Education: Culture, Power, and Liberation*, trans. Donaldo Macedor (South Hadley, MA: Bergin & Garvey, 1985).

to four hours (!) of pop radio from one of several genres (I listened to the oldies station) and noting the unfolding narratives in each song. We then came together as a class and discussed themes that emerged in the songs. Ultimately David guided us into reflecting on the "meta-themes" found in music in general.

Though the exercise was straightforward, it invited the students into a new discernment that was central to David's intention to teach Christians to interact faithfully with media. The procedure continued in additional exercises, especially our analysis of television advertisements and ultimately of full-length feature films. David saw the classroom as something of a laboratory in which he could guide students toward his own careful attention to words and the stories they tell.

David did not demand that students come to his conclusions regarding the various media under study. I remember disagreeing about the theme of a particular movie we had watched for the course, and David recognized my disagreement in my facial expression. He invited me to disagree and this led to a deeper discussion of the careful attention required for this kind of critical analysis. I don't know that David changed his mind, but he certainly allowed room for my disagreement. His careful attention to detail and willingness to engage in dialogue entailed more than a mere passing on of information to us, his students. They invited us to enter into a life of careful study, attention to detail, critical analysis, and dialogue. I remain a critic of media today because David *mentored* me into it.

The second course I had with David was, perhaps, the most important course I have ever taken. David regularly taught a course on the Lord's Prayer at Austin Grad. It was clear to his students, immediately, that the prayer was formative for David—not just theologically, but morally, spiritually, and devotionally. The prayer for David was not a collection of theological concepts. Rather it was, in its brevity, the most complete picture of Christian thought and life. For David, the prayer's structure and language is indispensable; it provides a model not only for prayer but for life.

With each petition of the prayer, David developed a series of reflections and requirements designed with the goal of his students *implementing* the prayer. In one exercise that remains with me to this day, David reflected on the petition, "forgive us our debts, as we forgive our debtors." Consistent with his dedication to the importance of words, David focused in on the words "debts" and "debtors." The financial metaphor is important, David suggested, insofar as the metaphor acknowledges the *cost* of forgiveness—something is owed—and that it is painful to release the debt. The class spent a little over an hour discussing what possible meanings this had to living the Christian life, after which David distributed paper to each student. He then suggested that we put the petition into action. "Think of someone who owes you something, someone who has wronged you in this debt, and write them a letter forgiving that debt."

Perhaps it was the timing, but the exercise was a life-changing moment for me. As it happened, I had lost a not insignificant amount of money to a former friend's investment scheme a few years before the class. I knew the money was gone, but I held the debt firmly in my heart. As we studied the prayer, I could feel David's teaching about this petition working its way like acid into the vice that held the debt. In the end, I wrote the letter and mailed it to the friend. I've not heard from him, but the point of the exercise was met, nonetheless: the prayer is not mere reflection on God's forgiveness and on the forgiving nature God requires of his people. No, the prayer, and the Christian faith in full, calls for *action*. And David's intention as a classroom teacher was to move his students toward implementation.

DAVID AS TEACHER IN HIS PUBLIC DEVOTION

David's concern for the proper use of words was evident in his public devotion, as well. Perhaps it was partly due to his grounding in the tradition of Churches of Christ, who call "Bible things by Bible words." David was absolutely devoted to using biblical language in his interactions, especially in public devotion. I think that David believed that the words of Scripture have a special providence that helps keep believers from the subtleties of worldly thought. Sitting around the faculty lunch table at Austin Grad, one can regularly hear stories of times we have each been rebuked for saying, for instance, "fortunately . . . " Any time someone said "fortunately" in David's presence, he would say, "We don't believe in the goddess fortuna" or something similar. David employed, rather, the word "happily" in matters of circumstance, always recognizing the coming of God's kingship into everyday life.

Constant reflection upon words was evident in all David did; as I have said, David was devoted to words. But David was not so much a wordsmith as a word conservationist. I once suggested the book *Caring for Words in a Culture of Lies*[5] to David, though I'm not sure he got around to reading it. He would have found in McEntyre, who suggests that language be viewed as an ecosystem, a kindred spirit. He believed that words *are* power; that they are tangible objective things rather than merely signs. I was with David one day at a coffee shop when a person he was talking to took Jesus' name in vain. The moment the word left his mouth, David looked to the heavens and said, "Blessed be he." This was his common practice, to speak blessing in the face

---

5. By Marilyn Chandler McEntyre (Grand Rapids: Eerdmans, 2009).

of curse. This was in keeping with his practice of saying "grace and peace" to people, because David believed that words spoken are *things*.

Thus, in his personal devotion, David used peculiar phrases that very often surprised people who heard him. They were like his personal idiosyncrasies: "the Spirit Holy," "grace," "Come your Kingdom," and many other sayings. But for David these were not evidence of his eccentricity. They were in keeping with Jesus' exhortation, "I tell you, on the day of judgment people will give account for every careless word they speak, for by your words you will be justified, and by your words you will be condemned" (Matt 12:36–37, ESV). In his public devotion, David took care to teach those around him the importance and power of using true (and right) words.

In addition to this focus on words in public devotion, David also made it his effort to infuse the church with the sense of the "everydayness" of Christian faith. For instance, David has an extensive reflection on "Radio Listening" in *The Complete Book of Everyday Christianity*.[6] Perhaps the most complete picture of David's development of the everydayness of Christian faith can be seen in a series of classes he developed. These classes, which he called "24 Hours in Christ," were designed for reflecting on almost *every* activity of the day in light of Christ. He offered these reflections at his home congregation (Brentwood Oaks) and elsewhere (including the Pepperdine lectures). Each of these lectures was intended to assist others in developing habits of personal devotion designed to draw them deeper into their faith and separate them further from an idolatrous world.

I include here a few outlines from these lectures in order to offer a view into the extensive thoughtfulness encompassing them. In some ways, these lectures capture the theological pedagogy of David Worley more than anything else; he was a holistic teacher, seeking to connect his students (whether church members, conference attendees, or classroom students) with the notion that the power of the teachings of the church can actually transform life.

We begin with David's reflection on "Awakening":

24 HOURS IN CHRIST #2: AWAKENING

Review and Introduction

    A. Life in Christ is more than certain religious acts. Kingdom life is not just prophesying, exorcism, mighty works (Matt 7:22f) (apparently some disciples of Jesus were given to this conception), it is testing and doing the will of God in and through the ordinary and routine.

---

6. Edited by Robert Banks and R. Paul Stevens (Downers Grove, IL: InterVarsity, 1997).

B. In Christ, 24 hours a day

Our aim: to alert us to the ordinary moments of our lives and how to re-view

e.g. awakening: Did anyone think about your manner and mood in awakening?

C. Our approach in the Spirit

1) Wherein we are conformed to the world/unmask of the principalities, powers; suggestion: read *Screwtape Letters*/ Buechner's *Alphabet of Grace*
2) WISDOM: whose aim is right time, place, extent of activity (Eccl 3:1ff) so recognition of limitation on our energies
3) Our purpose: to live to the praise of His glory; seek ways to ease distractions and be attentive to the Father's ways

FOCUS: In awakening from night's sleep what can we do (be alert to) which will better dispose us to live the day to the praise of God's glory and remind us that his mercies are new every morning (Lam 3:22ff.)? (assumption: morning disposition is important for the rest of the day, Ps 90:14)

4) Does WHAT arouses us from sleep make a difference in our inclinations?

a. Phone startling/Early alarms
b. The what now: 35% alarm/ 27% bio/ 20% radio/ 6% family, 6% nature
c. The what then: 2% alarm/ 2% bio/ 2% sounds/ 82% family, 6% nature
d. Grandparents: 9% clock/ 21% bio/ 4% family/ 48% nature

EFFECTS

Need for alarm or radio vs. bio or nature . . . suggestive of rest
Disposition from nature (light/birds/smells)
From family or friends (cf. 1 Sam 9:26; Matt 8:25; Mark 4:38; Luke 8:24)
Kind of alarm/push button
Kind of music/news program/TV ? . . . entering into story line (Isa 29:8)
YES . . . what arouses us makes a difference

RECOMMENDATION . . . awakened with tapes of Psalms . . . (Awake my soul)

5) What else effects our disposition at awakening?

    a. day and night before
   anger/worries . . . Sun of my Soul #2 . . . Ps 30:5; Mic 2:1

    b. sleep
   late bedtime/poor rest . . . dreams Gen 41:8

    c. health
   feeling ill/headache . . . weather

    d. day ahead
   Jesus up

    e. one's character
   Prov 6:22; Ps 3:5; 17:15. . . . Sun of my Soul #4

RECOMMENDATION . . .

6) WHEN we should be awakened
Prov 6:9 ad Ps 127:2

7) What should follow our getting up?

Though there are gaps between this outline from which David taught and the spoken content, it is clear from reading through the outline that David intended his hearers to think deeply about the way habits form "thick practices" in our lives. The way we awaken to begin a new day will impact the way we conduct ourselves that day, and so David paid special attention to the various habits surrounding the moment of awakening.

Next, David moved into ways in which the gospel might shape the very mundane things of life, and the way that these mundane activities offered opportunity to reflect on the meaning of the gospel for everyday life. Ordinarily we do not expect to find theological exposition on things like bathing, exercising, and grooming, but these were all, for David, brought under God's kingship as well. Thus David offered the following suggestions for how Christians might further bring themselves under God's reign.

24 HOURS IN CHRIST #3: EXERCISE/BATH/DRESSING

REVIEW

"Be not conformed to this world"
Recommendation: tape for alarm clock

INTRO: considering the mortal body in view of exercise, bathing, clothing

> Rom 6:12, After baptism we are mortal bodies able to say no to sin
>
> 1 Cor 9:27, I pommel my body and subdue it
>
> Rom 12:2, cf. Heb 10:10, In saying no, we present our bodies living sacrifices
>
> 1 Cor 6:19, the Spirit within the body
>
> 1 Cor 6:20, So we glorify God in the body (redeemed from slavery to slavery)
>
> Rom 8:22ff., We groan with creation for redemption of our bodies
>
> Phil 3:21, He will change our lowly body to be like his glorious body

EXERCISE

> Difficult to overestimate our culture's exercise binge
>
> 75% exercise (half over, half under 30 minutes/ half morning, half evening)
>
> Of 25% who didn't, 2/3 said they should!
>
> "soothes my conscience"/ "sense of well being"
>
> proliferation of exercise places/ advertisements/ Olympics now
>
> Also in 1st century, Seneca *Ep.* 61:1–2 (though for Romans more with baths)
>
> What do we as Christians say as to our reasons?
>
> 50% preventative health
>
> 25% curative health
>
> Other: marriage/meditation/temple of God

Scripture

> 1 Tim 4:7–8 warning about ascetic (cf. Seneca *Ep.* 15:1–3)
>
> Paul's body ... 1 Cor 9:24–29
>
> Did the "temple of the Spirit" argument constrain Paul's decisions?
>
> Rather Spirit intensifies our alertness to our washing away
>
> We each have to determine how intense our quest for body health
>
> Healing in Gospels ... feeding of the thousands
>
> Can exercise be an occasion for something beyond its result for body?
>
> e.g. thanksgiving to the Father ...

BATH

Heb 6:2!

Judaism: purifications/John the Baptist/ Matt 15

Romans: building of public baths

In the afternoon . . . social occasions . . . process and rooms

38% sing in showers . . . why?

Our washings and the one baptism

"I love the clean, refreshing feeling"

Constant reminder of "cleansing" . . . 1 Cor 6:11; Acts 22:16

Difference: 1 Pet 3:21

John 13

Give thanks in all circumstances

Do we overlook this time for prayer?

24 HOURS IN CHRIST #4: DRESSING AND GROOMING/CLOTHES AND HAIR

REVIEW

Our theme: The Christian walk includes the ordinary and routine

(cf. Thomas Howard's *Hallowed Be This House/ Splendor in the Ordinary*)

Last week: exercise and bathing

Our confession Jesus is Lord has meaning for exercise of the body

It is that ordinary experience of cleansing through bathing which prepares us for the significance of baptism which, unlike the frequent Jewish/pagan bathings, washed away our sins

CLOTHES AND DRESSING

To dress is to acknowledge that we have eaten of the tree of good and evil

Gen 2:25; 3:7–21 . . . Mark 14:51; 16:5

Mark 5:15//Luke 8:35

To dress is also to acknowledge that we desire to be further clothed

Already we are putting off and putting on . . . Col 3:5ff (cf. Lev)

But we yearn for greater clothing—2 Cor 5:4 . . . ("clean clothing"?)

We have seen the transfiguration—Matt 17:2

> We shall receive white garments—Rev 3:5, 18; 4:4, cf. 7:9; 15:6; 19:14
>
> Dressing for church
>
>> 1 Tim 2:9 . . . expensive clothing (and gold, pearls)
>> Clothes can express priorities and values Luke 16:19; Jas 2:2ff
>> Both for those who wear and those who observe, cf. 1 Sam 16:7
>> Clothes can reflect not only status but function Mark 1:6; Matt 11:8
>> Quality not excluded per se . . . Prov 31:22; Luke 22:15
>> 1 Tim 2:8ff . . . modesty . . .
>> Dressing for husband
>> 1 Pet 3:3 . . . jewels (gold)
>> Isa 3:16—4:1
>> Perictyone, *Duties of a Woman*
>> For whom and what do I dress . . . other women, husband, other men??
>> In dressing how does a wife "respect her husband" Eph 5:33
>
> GROOMING AND THE HAIR
>
>> 1 Cor 11:14-15 . . . cf. Acts 18:18 (cf. Luke 8:38; John 12:3)
>> The appearance of male and female . . . preoccupation with hair
>> 1 Tim 2:9; 1 Pet 3:3 . . . Juv VI 487ff.; Epict I 16:9

As one might expect, there are several more reflections from David on each routine activity, from media consumption to commuting and ultimately to sleeping. In each of these, David sought to help his students appreciate the penetration of the gospel into the life of the Christian. Simply put, *every aspect of the believer's life is meant to serve as a reflection on God's transformative grace in the gospel, and is thus in turn to be transformed*. What then seemed to many of us the quirks of an eccentric—even oddball—were in fact his acts of personal and public devotion, as he sought to bring himself more deeply under the Father's reign.

DAVID AS TEACHER IN HIS PASTORAL INTERACTIONS

It may well be that David most effectively taught as a pastor. Many others will testify, I am certain, of ways in which David witnessed to the gospel in such a manner that demonstrated that he cared, pastorally, for others. I will reflect here on a few of our interactions that were particularly groundbreaking for me. I do so in order that others may see David's example and follow.

I got to more fully know David in the year 2000. The year had been something of a "whiplash" for me. My daughter, Madison, was born April 21, and my wife, Jennifer, died June 16, leaving me a single dad in seminary. David came to the hospital when Jennifer was sick, and he never left. He stood with my family and prayed with us, and through his silence, presence, and love taught us how to grieve and how to care for those who grieve. I will never forget his kindness in those early days of grief. It was a terrible storm, and I was a vessel traveling through rocks and shoals, and David was the light during that time. As I have tried to minister to those around me who grieve, I have drawn deeply from David's pastoral care. I perhaps learned more about life from David's teaching as he stood by our side than most anywhere else.

A second interaction with David reveals that he was capable of exercising great wisdom and firmness in pastoral care. I had worked for David for a few years in the early 2000s, and we had regular meetings at his favorite coffee shop. We sat and talked for hours, almost never about things having to do with work. David began our sessions with the words, "So, tell me about your life this month. How are things, and what's happening?" He would then sit and listen for those hours, sometimes exploring lines of thought and sometimes saying nearly nothing. His openness, his willingness to focus solely on the person to whom he was speaking, and his obvious and expressive care and concern served as a witness, as a teacher to the gospel of Christ, and to the manner in which pastoral care should be done. At one of these sessions, he exercised a bit of discipline on me. I had been involved in some conflict at my congregation for some time, and I was complaining bitterly about it. David listened for about an hour, and when I had finally finished emptying myself (for probably the third meeting we had had together) he leaned forward and spoke. "Can you suffer more than God?" I sat for a moment, and finally stammered out, "Well . . . no." And David said, gently, almost under his breath, "Then shut up." Later when I sent him an email complaining about something else, he emailed back simply, "Slaves to the church." Through a life formed to the gospel, David was able to see inside the heart of the person to whom he was minister and offer the appropriate word.

DAVID WORLEY, TEACHER

David Worley was a complicated man, as all men are. As a teacher, David was concerned with making disciples rather than scholars. He understood and believed that the gospel of God's "Kingdom come" is the central organizing tenet of Christian life, and he called others to recognize this truth. At times this focus on the coming Kingdom was manifest in ways that many of us found eccentric. Perhaps, though, the fact that we found him eccentric says more about us and our progress in submitting to God's reign than it does about David. He was utterly committed to this principle.

Several times in the last months of his life I wrote to inquire as to his health and progress. In November I posted an email to David saying, "I have been praying for you, much, lately. But today I am feeling a special burden for you. Please know that I am praying, right this moment, for you for peace, for healing, for deliverance from pain." David's response was his final teaching to me, and perfectly sums up the content of David's teaching: "Come His healing Kingship over all of us . . . " May it be so! Rest, David—witness and teacher—until that day.

16

David Worley as Fundraiser

Royce Money

DAVID WORLEY WAS MY friend, the type of friend who was in a category of his own. I mean that in the nicest way. He had this uncanny way of getting me involved in doing things that he thought were important. And in the process, of course, he would convince me that they should be important to me as well. Most of the time, David's interests were closely aligned with those of the church, both in its dimensions of congregational worship and global outreach. David, more than any other of my friends and acquaintances, was extremely passionate about the spread of the gospel throughout the world. His special focus was Russia, but his vision was worldwide. This scholar/businessman/missionary left his quiet mark on countless lives. Most of the time these thankful recipients never knew the identity of their gracious benefactor.

I knew David more as a significant donor to Christian education than I did in any other way. During my presidency at Abilene Christian University, I had the privilege of working with his wife, Melinda, as she served on the board of trustees. They were quite a talented and unusual pair—educated, refined, humble, gracious, generous, accepting, innovative, and deeply dedicated to the lordship of Christ in their lives. Others in this tribute volume will ably elaborate on these characteristics. But, truth be known, I may be in an unusual position to give a few impressions about David as a fundraiser.

Let me state it clearly: David Worley did not like being a fundraiser. He would much rather quietly write a check from his own funds and cover the needs than ask others to give. He was a modest man, a private man.

Yet, in the words of his faithful disciple, Igor Egirev, current president of Christian Resource Center–Russia, "David's input in Russian mission is very hard to overestimate." That is the thesis of this essay, but there are a few more interesting details about his fundraising experiences. (In 2015, at the "encouragement" of the Russian Ministry of Justice, the name of the Institute of Theology and Christian Ministry was changed to Christian Resource Center–Russia, in order to avoid confusion that ITCM might be perceived as a degree-granting institution.)

If you knew David Worley at all, you knew that he was vitally interested in mission work in Russia. David was a successful entrepreneur who had international interests. Those countless trips nearly always blended mission and evangelism with whatever business interests he had. One time a few years ago, I asked David how many trips to Russia he had made. He was unable to tell me—perhaps the only time I recall that David could not come up with an answer to one of my questions. Once when David learned that Dr. Brent Isbell and I were going to St. Petersburg to conduct a weeklong workshop for Russian preachers, he immediately began to tell me the preferred airlines and routes to and from the city. It soon became obvious to me that David must have had them all memorized!

In David's mission activities in Russia in the 1990s, there is not much evidence that he relied on any fundraising efforts to advance the body of Christ beyond those of his own. He used his business connections to get a World Christian Broadcasting program on Russian Radio One, the most popular FM station in the nation, where it remains to this day. In fact, the response to that program provided the basis for the Russian Bible School, which evolved into a series of correspondence courses still in use. Those in turn created quite a number of contacts.

David Worley, Chuck Whittle, and Joel Petty had discussions in the early years of Russian mission about beginning some sort of school of theology or Bible training, especially designed for Russian preachers. According to Whittle, David was initially a bit reluctant to establish any sort of school, but by 2003 he became convinced it was the best way to ensure that Russian ministers were adequately prepared. Thus, in 2004 the Institute of Theology and Christian Ministry (ITCM) began to be transformed from a dream to a reality. Predictably, David paid for all the start-up fees and expenses, including those of the initial class of students. Joel Petty was its first president. The goal was to provide master's-level work for ministers, and the first class graduated in April 2007.

Also in 2004, David purchased a floor of a three-story building for the Neva church (more than 6,200 square feet) in his own name, but he gave it to the church to use free of charge. At first he helped to pay all utility bills, property tax, and building manager's salary, estimated to be about $15,000 a year; later the congregation gradually took over payment of these expenses. In addition to the purchase, David paid for extensive renovations, spending a sizable sum, according to Egirev. He could have later sold the floor for a nice profit but instead chose to dedicate it to the Neva congregation for its use.

The future looked bright at the time because of an unusual opportunity presented by the St. Petersburg State University for a cooperative program in graduate studies in 2005. In addition, the university offered ITCM use of some living quarters for the students, as well as classroom space. It was at that juncture that David first contacted me about possible cooperative efforts with Abilene Christian University. In my correspondence with Egirev, he estimated that David spent a considerable amount of his own money on the renovation project on the university property that was now theirs to use. Four years later, the agreement was abruptly cancelled when a new president came to the university. Neither Worley nor ITCM ever received more than a fraction of repayment for the renovations after the university withdrew from its arrangement with them in 2009.

Especially during the optimistic years between 2005 and 2009, with the new facilities and the surprising arrangement with the university, David envisioned some type of cooperative agreement with ACU, although the language barrier proved to be formidable. All we were able to work out was a means whereby our ACU College of Biblical Studies faculty could teach at the institute. At least a half-dozen faculty did teach there, and their travel and lodging expenses were covered, once again in many cases, through the personal generosity of David.

The "Traveling Mercies" endowment had been set up by David at ACU in 2003 to provide travel funds for Bible faculty to teach free of charge, first in St. Petersburg, then later at any mission point throughout the world. To date, the total number of faculty who have benefitted from the Worleys' generosity is twenty-two, with several going on multiple international trips to teach. They have taught in seven international schools of higher education affiliated with the Churches of Christ. To my knowledge, David did no fundraising to accomplish this wonderful opportunity; he simply and quietly gave to a generous endowment from his personal funds.

There is some evidence at ACU that David would occasionally partner with his mother, Iva Lea Worley Barton, in funding various projects, but the transactions were so private that it is difficult to trace them with any accuracy. At any rate, by 2005 David realized that he could not personally continue to fund the steadily expanding Russian ministry alone. He then began to turn his thoughts to the very thing he did not like to do—fundraising.

The ITCM board was chartered in 2004 in North Carolina to provide a US-based non-profit with oversight of the institute in St. Petersburg. The founders had some difficulty with obtaining non-profit status, perhaps because of their disclosure that the money raised would go to Russia, or perhaps because of bureaucratic entanglements. According to Dr. Tom Olbricht, "We took up the offer to appropriate the Foundation for Biblical Studies from the church where Paul Watson preached" (Cole Mill Road Church of Christ in Durham, North Carolina). There is apparently some sort of Russian board that also existed, primarily for Russian legal purposes, but there is little mention of it. On the American board, original trustees of what later became known as the Foundation for Biblical Studies (FBS) were Worley, Joel Petty, and Chuck Whittle. Olbricht was added the next year, followed by others such as Dr. Bob Jones, a cardiac surgeon and member at the Cole Mill Road congregation; Dr. Harold Hazelip; and Lynn Nored. No doubt David, from its inception, expressed a desire for the board members to participate annually in the financial ongoing of the ministry. Joel Petty, the first president of ITCM, also had fundraising responsibilities but had little experience and training for that responsibility. Also, perhaps it was a human tendency for people interested in ITCM to simply assume that David would provide whatever was needed. In any case, the annual expenses were mounting.

By the December 20, 2007 meeting, there is ample evidence from the FBS minutes that David's fundraising initiatives were well underway. A "Pay-for-a-Day" program was in place, a technique he also used in his leadership role at the Austin Graduate School of Theology. The minutes of the FBS meeting indicate that David had sent these solicitations to twenty-five people. At the meeting he also asked that each board member contact three other people to get them interested in supporting ITCM. Petty had previously written to a number of churches whose members had expressed an interest in the work, but the effort was not very successful. David then asked that even more churches who had expressed any interest in financially supporting the Russian work in the past be contacted, this time personally. Tom Olbricht made an extensive report on foundations and trusts that he had contacted. There also was preliminary talk of a possible Nashville-area fundraising event.

Obviously, by 2007 David had his attention focused on forming a broad base of financial support for ITCM. He was in full fundraising mode. At the same time, however, there was also no doubt that the bulk of the operational funds were still coming from David himself.

In 2009, David invited me to attend one of the foundation board meetings at Dallas-Fort Worth Airport (David's favorite meeting place). On

March 23, Dr. Bruce Evans and Dr. Mark Hamilton flew with me to the DFW airport for my first meeting with the board. Gradually I realized that this "board" was loosely organized, and I suspected I was being quickly assimilated into it. It was shortly after my initial meeting with the board that David approached me with an important question: "Royce, can you help me find churches who can help the foundation bear the financial load of an ever-increasing operation in St. Petersburg?" He explained in brief terms that he could not personally continue at the pace of his personal financial involvement as the primary means of support for the ministry.

Two things come to my mind now as I reflect on David's initial request of me. First, I had no idea until later of the enormous amount of money David had given to the Russian mission effort in St. Petersburg. The money had been given quietly and privately—David's favorite stewardship method. Second, I wonder if he was preparing for a new phase of existence of the ministry beyond himself. He was broadening the base of support and involvement. Perhaps yet a third thing was happening: David was in a sense preparing for the St. Petersburg ministry to be self-sustaining, particularly if the time ever came when funding from the US would be prohibited by the Russian government.

As I had suspected, shortly after attending my first board meeting of the foundation, I realized more fully that David assumed I would be a regular part of the group thereafter. Soon the frequent emails and the occasional phone calls began coming my way. They had a common theme: "Can you help us find churches who are interested in supporting the ITCM ministry in St. Petersburg?" At first I did not come up with any viable possibilities. Then several things began to take place that proved over time to be quite successful in providing adequate funds for the St. Petersburg ministry.

One day in April 2012, I got a call from David asking me a somewhat strange question: "Do you know any congregations in Alabama whose members might be interested in supporting the Russian ministry?" (Upon reflection, apparently David found out I once preached in Montgomery, Alabama, in the 1970s.) I replied that the only person I had really kept up with through the years who was in a congregational leadership role was Jerry Atkinson. Pam and I had become friends with Jerry and Roberta shortly after moving there, and we kept in occasional contact with them. David persuaded me to contact Jerry and see if he would be interested in hosting Igor Egirev for a visit to Alabama in his upcoming trip to the US. Gratefully, Jerry was not only interested; he was enthusiastic about it.

The rest is history, as they say. Jerry and Roberta warmly embraced Igor and treated him almost as a son. Jerry was an elder at the Grace Point Church of Christ and well-respected in the central Alabama area. He and

Igor drove to various places across the state of Alabama, with Jerry utilizing his extensive contacts with congregations and individuals who might have an interest in the Russian ministry. One by one their successes began to build, and the result was the beginning of a broad base of support for ITCM all across the Southern states. Ironically, a typical first response they encountered was something like, "We did not even know there was still a Russian ministry with Churches of Christ after all the American missionaries were required to leave Russia." After they met Igor, they were convinced beyond a doubt that Church of Christ missionary activity in Russia was alive and well. Jerry also saw that his own congregation supported Igor and the ministry.

In addition, Jerry contacted one of his sons, Douglas Atkinson, who was a businessman living in the Little Rock, Arkansas, area and attended the Pleasant Valley Church of Christ. Not only did Douglas convince the leadership there to be involved in Igor's work, but he made additional contacts with individuals on behalf of the Russian ministry and became a donor himself. Douglas and Jerry now serve on the board of the Foundation for Biblical Study.

About the same time as Igor was being introduced to Alabama, Tim Bruner, a former missionary and current fundraiser for York College in Nebraska, volunteered to spend a few days traveling with Igor throughout the South, contacting churches about the Russian work. Dr. Steve Eckman, president of York College, graciously gave Tim paid release time to travel with Igor a few days when he made his semi-annual trips to the US.

Meanwhile, in Abilene at the University Church of Christ, where Pam and I worshipped, an unusual opportunity presented itself in late 2012. One of the members, who chose to remain anonymous, had given $400,000 to the church in an estate gift with the following stipulations: the entire amount must be spent on mission, and it must be spent within the following five years. As soon as I heard of the good news, I contacted one of the elders and encouraged them to consider a part of the funds to support the mission work in St. Petersburg. The result was that the elders and mission committee decided to designate $30,000 a year for five years toward support of the Institute of Theology and Christian Ministry. At once we became the largest contributor among the growing number of churches who supported ITCM. This second major opening from the Lord came from an unlikely source and the University Church still supports this ministry in Russia.

The third blessing came from central Texas, where my roots are, and specifically from the Church of Christ in Belton. Since my childhood I had known Dr. Joe and Ann Ritchie, who were members of my home congregation in Temple. Joe was a soil scientist who spent most of his professional career on the faculty of Michigan State and had been a leader in every congregation where they had lived. I also knew Joe as one of the trustees at Abilene Christian University during my presidency. I called Joe and asked if perhaps the Belton church would be interested in supporting the Russian ministry. Once again, Igor was the one who convinced Joe and the Belton elders to join the growing number of supporters. Currently, Joe is on the board of the foundation, and the Belton Church of Christ is one of the leading congregations advocating support of the Christian ministry all across Russia.

Two other congregations in particular need to be added to the "donor" list. First is the Brentwood Oaks Church of Christ in Austin, where David and Melinda have worshipped for a number of years, and where David faithfully served as one of its shepherds. Throughout all the personal interviews I conducted and the books on the Russian mission work I read, the Brentwood church is repeatedly mentioned in some supportive role. They, of all people, knew the love David had for the Russian people and the extent to which he went to share the gospel with them. The second is the West End congregation in Nashville, Tennessee. Chuck Whittle, a veteran businessman-turned-missionary to Russia in the 1990s, persuaded his home congregation, the West End Church of Christ, to be a sustaining supporter of the Russian mission work in St. Petersburg. Whittle now serves as chairman of the Foundation for Biblical Studies, succeeding David Worley in that leadership role.

There are other stories of David as a fundraiser that I do not know, and it has been difficult to find information. He was the towering figure behind organization and development of the Austin Graduate School of Theology, without a doubt. Fundraising was a constant challenge in that environment. Once again, David would have rather contributed himself than to ask, but he was responsible for making sure that an adequate fundraising program existed for its continuance. David and Melinda were also pivotal in the early years of Brentwood Christian School in Austin. Today it stands as one of the premier Christian K-12 schools founded by Churches of Christ.

One goal of David's was never to be realized during his lifetime. Soon after I began to work with David to secure congregational funds, he asked me on several occasions if I could help him find a group of elders at a strong, established church who would be willing to take sponsorship of the Russian ministry in St. Petersburg. He envisioned that somehow the Foundation for Biblical Studies board would remain intact, but that a local congregation would oversee the ministry. I never quite understood how all that would work, but David had come to some conclusion that it would and that it would be the best arrangement possible. I do not know if he arrived at that conviction for theological reasons or whether he was simply seeking some relief from carrying so much of the financial burden himself. He never gave me a clue. Nonetheless, it never happened; it was a hard sell. The independent Foundation for Biblical Studies board to this day oversees solicitation, collection, and distribution of ministry funds and oversees the work of CRC-Russia.

In the midst of all the fundraising stories about David are some other stories that he surely meant never to be told, at least in his lifetime. Repeatedly, I ran across accounts where David privately helped Russian ministers and missionaries financially. On one occasion, he wanted to assist one of them and did not want the source of the gift to be traced. He gave a rather substantial amount to a mutual trusted friend, who in turn gave it to the astonished recipient. David had "giving in secret" down to an art form. I am convinced that he took great joy in using his own resources to be a blessing to countless people. He certainly was a blessing to me.

"Blessed are the dead who die in the Lord from now on. 'Yes,' says the Spirit, 'they will rest from their labor, for their deeds will follow them'" (Rev 14:13). May he rest in peace—rather, make that *grace* and peace.

17

David Worley as Philanthropist

Judy Siburt

Those who have material possessions and sees a brother and sister in need . . . show by their actions that their love is from God.

—1 John 4:8 NLT

This essay is written with love and appreciation for my friends David and Melinda Worley, and in honor and memory of David as philanthropist. My hope is that as we learn of the many ways that David gave of himself to develop, nurture, and bless others and to the projects he generously supported, we will be inspired to become wise, thoughtful, and generous givers—philanthropists ourselves, giving of ourselves freely for the good of all.

David was a quiet, thoughtful, and cheerful philanthropist who often gave in secret, so it would be impossible to list all of the many ways he benefitted others with his gifts. David's own words in the Order of Service from his memorial give us insight to his approach to philanthropy: "*David learned to express 'Grace' to all whom he met.*"

David shared his dollars, but also so much more. "Good giving" is not just the giving of dollars, but also prompting wellness, empowering, nourishing, developing, and helping others to thrive. He did not seek recognition but gave to promote the welfare and wholeness of others. David chose to care for others not only through financial support, but also through the gift of himself, his presence, and his strategic and intelligent approach to solving problems. And he did so even when the commitment to the benefactors or projects became difficult. He gave with kindness and the wise investment of his love in action so that others could know God and the things of God and so the communities where they lived and served could flourish.

David and Melinda shared their gracious friendship with Charles and me while we were students at Abilene Christian University. We were newlyweds and sojourners living in adjacent apartments. The Worleys and the Siburts were among scores of graduate students who enjoyed the living arrangements of these compact and efficient Witt Apartments, which were owned by the kind and respected ACU chemistry professor, Dr. Paul Witt. We shared a washer and dryer, and cooked burgers on the hibachi on our small back porch. There we rehearsed the new and challenging thoughts and truths learned as we all studied and grew up together across the street from the university. We were rich with relationships as we shared our time together. These fifty years later our friendship remains intact.

David was a man of few words, quiet, reserved, pensive, and even sometimes eccentric. He was a man of uncommon piety, which may be seen as eccentric because it is a rare quality. He was different because he was a man of God with an intention to honor God in all things. He continued to mature into the *love of Christ and fullness of Christ* his whole life. At his memorial, his daughters spoke lovingly of their daddy: *"His heart was full of love, his eyes reflected joy, and in his strong hands were kindness and gentleness."*

After a private graveside service for David, family and friends gathered at the lovely home of his oldest daughter, Heatherly, and her husband, Les McDaniel. Knowing that David was a quiet, reserved only child who lost his father at a young age, I imagined how happy David would be to witness this group of loving family and friends all together. Every corner of every room had folks sharing memories, visiting and comforting one another. It was anything but a quiet, somber gathering. A gaggle of grandchildren were playing, running, laughing, and enjoying each other, and I envisioned David saying, "My cup runneth over."

David grew up in a giving family. His mother, Iva Lea Worley Barton, modeled strong business acumen, and successfully maintained and grew the businesses left to her at the death of David's father. She impressed on David, "To whom much is given much is required," and "much" is what David invested and gave to others his whole life and even unto his death. Learning to trust God, to work hard, and to give wisely to others became his goals. He was a man of wealth but he was not a "foolish rich man" storing up his goods. He understood that possessions are not the source of strength or meaning in life.

This childhood fable of the nightingale that traded its feathers for worms illustrates David's philanthropy.

> Just one feather from its wings was all the peddler asked, and it was a painless kind of daily transaction. But, of course, in time the nightingale had traded so many feathers that it could no longer fly. Then one day as the peddler made his rounds he found the nightingale standing by the road. It had worked through the night to dig enough worms to reverse the trade. But the peddler only laughed and said. "What do you think I'm in this for? My business is worms for feathers, not feathers for worms."

David understood that the world is in an eternal skin game and will trade with us at any time. David never took the trade. His success in business never changed his heart for God.

Richard Gundermann's book *We Make a Life by What We Give* (Indiana University Press, 2009) advises a wise philanthropist to develop himself; to learn more about God, Christ, and the Holy Spirit; and to come to know himself so that out of true integrity he may generously and wisely give. David and Melinda's time at ACU and then Yale for more study and preparation were wise investments. Those years helped them both to understand the things of God more deeply as they prepared themselves to teach, to serve, and to give. David was a dedicated, lifelong learner. He was a gifted and beloved teacher and professor. His deep love of Scripture and his commitment to be a child of God formed and shaped him with wisdom that informed his philanthropy.

Matthew 6:1–4 (NLT) gives insight into David's heart and his desire to become like Christ:

> "Watch out! Don't do your good deeds publicly, to be admired by others, for you will lose the reward from your Father in heaven. When you give to someone in need, don't do as the hypocrites do—blowing trumpets in the synagogues and streets to call attention to their acts of charity! I tell you the truth, they have received all the reward they will ever get. But when you give to someone in need, don't let your left hand know what your right hand is doing. Give your gifts in private, and your Father, who sees everything, will reward you."

Because of his commitment to giving quietly and without fanfare, many of David's works are known and *seen* only by God.

David possessed an uncanny ability to see needs and then see how to help, to subsidize, to finance, to underwrite, and even to create, so that the good of all was served. The following testimonies of some of those that he blessed so richly with his philanthropy give us a glimpse of his impact. The education of God's people was one of David's passions and he believed strongly in Christian education.

AUSTIN GRADUATE SCHOOL OF THEOLOGY

AGST was one of the many places David assisted for good, serving as president from 1992 to 2000 and remaining as chancellor until his death. Stan Reid, current president, described the many ways David shared generously with Austin Grad, though all of his gifts were given anonymously.

> You might find it ironic that the library at Austin Grad is named in David's honor. David was initially resistant to the idea. However, when he learned that a large donation to our Building the Dream capital campaign was contingent on this idea, David acquiesced. He said, "You've got me between a rock and a hard place." He then smiled sheepishly and closed the conversation.

David was a leader, investor, and friend to AGST, and also teacher, professor, and mentor to staff and students. He gave of his expertise as he shared from his distinguished training and his life of study of God's Word. As a revered and beloved professor he challenged and encouraged countless numbers of students as they prepared themselves to serve in the Kingdom of God.

BRENTWOOD CHRISTIAN SCHOOL

Brentwood Christian School in Austin was served and supported by David's investments of resources and his leadership. President Emeritus Marquita Moss has said that of his many contributions to the school three stand out: his leadership of the school board, his fundraising, and his nurturing of the faculty. He served on the board from 1981 to 1998 and as chair from 1984 to 1987 and 1991 to 1992, which were key years in growth of the school to include high school. Later he served on the development advisory board. Moss said,

> David believed that every aspect of the school should lead students to love God and should help them to understand every dimension of God's creation. He believed that the school should enable students to approach all of life with a biblical perspective . . . everything from the selection of a husband or wife to such activities as voting or going to work. His most valuable gift

was his support for keeping the school faithful to this mission when others would have been content with just Bible classes, a rigorous academic record and a strong athletic program. Generations of children will be in debt to a man they may never have known for making such an education possible.

THE PSALMS PROJECT

The project for setting the Old Testament Psalms to music was close to David's heart. He had special concerns about how believers listened to radio and experienced entertainment, and that believers should learn to sing the Psalms. He was working with Mel Witcher and Mark Shipp on this project to develop scripturally based and musically well-developed hymns based upon the Psalms. The music David chose for his memorial service highlighted his desire that hymns and choral presentations were of theological substance and musical quality.

David believed in and supported the work of musician and composer Mike Showalter. Mike's piece "Be My God," written and composed in David's honor and in his memory, was sung at his memorial service.

HOUSING FOR THOSE IN NEED

Housing for the needy was one of David's "in secret" projects. He anonymously supported an untold number of brothers and sisters in the US and beyond, enabling them to buy homes and apartments. Tom Olbricht tells of a time that he was on his way to Russia when David gave him several thousand dollars in cash to take to Russia to help a preacher's family there buy a home.

David invested in many other ways, including to Eternal Threads and Eastern European Missions, and supporting many trustworthy friends to start and to sustain businesses, whether in healthcare, energy, media, transportation, education, or the arts. He gave to the South Pacific Bible College and encouraged friends such as Tom and Dorothy Olbricht to teach there. He was a faithful supporter to specific interests at Abilene Christian University, including various scholarships programs honoring LeMoine Lewis and Abraham Malherbe. He gave to the Thomas H. Olbricht Christian Scholars Conference, and he supported various book publications, however, he did not usually donate to scholarly publications, as observed by Dr. Tom Olbricht.

David was a successful financial investor. He was president of Thelese Management, which encompasses a family of companies, investments, and projects in diverse geographic and economic areas. The name Thelese is taken from a passage in the book of James that highlighted his belief that all businesses are the work of the Lord—only possible through his grace. David knew that all that we have and receive is from the Lord, and we are to become the stewards of those gifts. He realized the impossibility of giving to every project. Many voices came asking, requesting, and wanting some of his wealth for their projects. David was prayerful, passionate, and intentional about where he chose to give himself and his dollars. His giving was strategic and pastoral. He believed, "First do no harm," and understood that some methods of giving could diminish others. He gave so that others would also learn to give, knowing how much joy giving brings to the giver.

David was committed to treating all respectfully. He gave in ways that would be enriching and empowering to the recipients and, with the grace of God, would serve the Kingdom over the long haul. He was a positive influence to all those leading businesses. He understood the old adage, "Give a man a fish and you feed him for a day; teach a man to fish and you feed him for a lifetime." Creating jobs for others lessens their dependency. David understood that philanthropy should make recipients more productive and help them learn, in turn, the importance of the sharing their own resources. He was insistent that others of ability make their own contribution to the enterprises in which they and he were involved. The board members for the Russian work paid their own expenses when the board met. The professors who taught at the Institute of Theology and Christian Ministry either paid their own way or the university at which they taught helped them. David only subsidized those who were unable to make the trip without help.

David was a philanthropic missionary. As an evangelist, preacher, teacher, and missionary he promoted and shared the gospel everywhere he went. He shared his wealth and himself as he went about sharing the gospel. He was called to invest in God's Kingdom and it was this call that he answered his whole life.

As his friend, I was aware of David's involvement in Russia. I had no idea of the depth of the spiritual, personal, or financial commitment given for the church and the Russian Christians until 2013 when I accompanied a mission group from University Church of Christ in Abilene, Texas, to Russia. There I began to understand the extent of his commitment to the work. It spanned years and involved extraordinary generosity. There I came to know and to appreciate Igor Egirev and Joel Petty, two strong, committed leaders of the work in St. Petersburg and beyond. Both have talked about the great love, support, and friendship that David invested in them. He was always present—if not physically, then emotionally and spiritually by phone and email. Elsewhere in this volume, Chuck Whittle and others give detailed information regarding David's time serving the Russian church. I summarize by saying David gave of his money until it hurt and he gave of his wisdom with persistence so that the brothers and sisters in Russia came to know Christ through his gift of friendship and hospitality.

Many have said David often came quietly and was present to give encouragement and hope for the future and then was gone like a ghost. Because of the seed of David's giving, the work in Russia has developed leaders such as Egirev, Petty, Luka Klimanova and many, many others. The Christian Resource Center focuses on a threefold mission:

- *Mission Learn* includes the Russian Bible School, with online teaching of hundreds across the vast country of Russia.

- *Mission Edify* reaches and serves new converts and churches across the country. CRCR provides retreats, conferences, and an online newspaper that connects and informs churches across Russia and beyond. Beautiful music, especially a cappella singing, was one of David's passions. David believed in and helped to support Luka Kilmanova and her ministry of music. Through her ministry she develops, teaches, and blesses the church by sharing the gospel through friendship and by teaching a cappella singing.

- *Mission Teach*: The Institute of Theology and Christian Ministry (ITCM) has video-taped the finest of scholars and professors from virtually all the Church of Christ–related universities to Russia to prepare and train ministers and leaders of God's Kingdom. These professors were once in St. Petersburg in person, but now their videos are shown by means of the Internet. David worked tirelessly to get the ITCM established in St. Petersburg, taking on in the early difficult days planning, negotiating, groundbreaking, and a major financial burden for the work. ITCM was registered in late 2004 and operations began in January 2005. Russian congregations were blessed by David's commitment to and investment in the growth of Bible knowledge and understanding of Scripture applied to lives today.

"We make a living by what we earn, we make a life by what we give." This old adage teaches us that what we give away we never lose because it was never ours to begin with. David created a joyful life. He understood that in giving we not only bring joy to others but that it is the only path to a joyful, meaningful life. David Worley was the grateful receiver of the gifts of the love and grace of God and he believed that everything he had was from above. God provided, blessed, and empowered him to develop and to grow the talents he was given, and as a faithful servant of God he took these talents and diligently grew them to empower others to prosper and to also become givers, to experience for themselves a joyful life.

Gundermann stated, "the liberal model of giving cultivates and celebrates the philanthropic potential of every human being."[1] As we have learned of ways that David gave of himself to develop, empower, nurture, and bless others, and the places that he generously gave of his resources to promote the wellness of others, may we be inspired to become philanthropists, in the best sense of the word—wise, thoughtful, generous, and joyful givers of our resources; and more importantly that we give of ourselves, our time, our hearts, and our presence as we live out the love and grace of God in our world.

1. Richard Gunderman, *We Make a Life by What We Give* (Bloomington, IN: Indiana University Press, 2009), 19.

18

The Center for Heritage and Renewal in Spirituality (CHARIS) at Abilene Christian University

JOHN B. WEAVER

> It is this backward motion toward the source,
> Against the stream, that most we see ourselves in,
> The tribute of the current to the source.
>
> —ROBERT FROST, *WEST RUNNING BROOK*

WHEN I ARRIVED AT Abilene Christian University (ACU) in 2011, a repeated question among faculty and administrators was how to maintain the Christian identity and mission of the university. There was a clear commitment among university leaders to the beliefs and practices of the religious heritage of the school among the Churches of Christ. This was reflected in the publishing of a document by the ACU board of trustees entitled "For Such a Time as This: Identity, Mission, and the Future of Abilene Christian University."[1] The document described seven core values from the university's heritage, including "the authority and inspiration of Scripture" and "a high view of the church." My conversations with the authors of this document, including senior administrators and church historians, made it clear that there was a need at ACU for concerted and consistent attention to cultivate

---

1. In *ACU Today*, Fall–Winter 2013, 24–39.

knowledge and appreciation of this heritage among the broader faculty and the student body. A shared desire was to focus on the development of faculty conversation and engagement with the religious heritage at the school, providing focused programs in spiritual formation and other theological education. These programs would invite investigation and reflection on the importance of the core values and heritage of the university, but would avoid an approach that degraded other beliefs or backgrounds, including dissenting voices and alternate points of view. In short, there was a need for intentional and inclusive conversation that created and maintained faculty awareness of the religious heritage of the university. As Dean of Library Services and Educational Technology, my responsibilities included oversight of the conventional areas of library activity, but also of the Adams Center for Teaching and Learning, which operated new faculty orientation and other faculty development programs. I also helped to steward the Center for Restoration Studies (CRS), which in partnership with the Graduate School of Theology at ACU has oversight of the development of collections documenting the Stone-Campbell Movement, and especially non-instrumental Churches of Christ. Conversations with leaders in both these areas made apparent the need for a new collaborative effort that integrated (1) the themes and practices of the school's religious heritage with (2) the mission and identity of the teaching faculty.

Based on such statements of conviction and commitment, we convened multiple meetings to develop the possibility of an initiative at ACU that would be dedicated to the promotion of the healthy understanding of the best of ACU's religious heritage. During these conversations, I was introduced to David and Melinda Worley. I discovered that the Worleys had earlier articulated a vision for the creation of an endowment at ACU that would support faculty development in relationship to Christ and the church. As I read the charter document for this endowment, I recognized sensibilities that were deeply rooted in the Restoration Movement. For example, a goal of the Worleys was to cultivate relationships that were Christ-centered, but the language used to describe this relationship was deeply biblical in orientation.

> . . . The purpose of this fund is to inspire, encourage, and train faculty members to teach "in Christ," to enable students to think "Christianly," remembering the story of God's love for His people and His creation through scripture. Teachers will be encouraged to understand and teach their subjects within the Biblical preoccupation and framework of faith, hope and love "in Christ.[2]

---

2. "The Melinda Slone Worley Faculty Development Fund: For Teaching 'In Christ,'" February 16, 2008.

Throughout the document, the phrase "in Christ" denotes the Worleys' concern for a faculty steeped in understanding of Scripture and committed to relationship with other Christians in ways that are aligned with the Stone-Campbell Movement, but that do not idolize the tradition or promote a denominational understanding of the Churches of Christ. In the charter's language, I saw a concern and commitment to supporting biblical Christianity and conscientious Christian discipleship among the faculty and students of the university, with an underlying dedication to the Christian formation of young adults through purposeful and principled teaching.

Looking back on my earliest communications with David in 2012, I can see priorities in his communications that would continue throughout the next five years of our almost daily correspondence via email: First, a deep and constant concern for the relationship of the church and the university, namely, that it should be one of Christian love. Second, expressions of interest in the Christian beliefs and practices of university faculty, especially their importance to the formation of students in the image of Christ, and particularly in undergraduate Bible courses. Third, a concern for the language used to describe Christian formation of faculty and students, namely, that the language be biblical in its origin or orientation. Fourth, a cautious, even critical approach to the cultural influences of secular society on the consciences of Christian educators and administrators. Fifth, an interest in reaffirming the university's connection to biblical teachings about Christian practices, particularly about worship, and especially singing to God from the heart with only the voice and without musical instruments.

I came to understand that David's frequent admonitions and encouragements were born of hard-won insights from his work as a Christian businessman and his experience as an elder in the church. David's responsibility as an elder often shaped our conversations, and led me to new appreciation of the value of the presbyter's perspective in advising, if only indirectly, programs of spiritual formation within the Christian university. There were certainly other experiences and backgrounds that informed the advice that he offered to leaders at ACU. Many of these roles are seen in the contributions of the present volume: his leadership of a graduate school of theology in Austin, his role as a visionary and fundraiser for global Christian mission, and, perhaps most significantly, his instincts and insights as a scholar of early Christianity. But it was his role as an elder that seemed to focus most clearly his view of a healthy relationship between the church and the university. First, David often emphasized the importance of personal example among those with leadership responsibility, especially university administrators, for supporting faculty and students' closer relationship with God. "Service leadership" can become a hackneyed phrase, but David emphasized the importance of Christian faithfulness in the lives of those who directed programs at the university. His comments to me often focused upon the need for faithful behavior and humble service among those who sought to lead, and only secondarily upon what they said needed to be done. Second, his concern was often focused on the relationship of faculty and students to the life and work of the local congregations both in and outside Abilene, particularly their work in Bible study and mission. Third, and most pervasively, his questions revolved around faithfulness to the New Testament in faculty teaching and student learning.

When I shared with David the emerging idea of a new Center for Heritage and Renewal and Spirituality (CHARIS) at ACU—an idea that was developed in coordination with leaders across the university—his first questions were about the language that was used to describe the center: How was it orientated in relationship to biblical language and teaching? How would CHARIS support lives that are lived "in Christ" with "faith, hope, and love," and how would it cultivate faculty and students' "love for the church"? How would CHARIS focus on "the four characteristics which we have inherited in our tradition as Churches of Christ: believer's immersion for forgiveness of sins, weekly participation in the Lord's meal, a plurality of elders for leadership, and a cappella singing"? He did not articulate these principles in a creedal fashion as a set of beliefs that must be believed and recited by only the faculty, but rather as a core set of biblical practices that should be reflected on and practiced broadly within the university and beyond.

As already mentioned, the Center for Restoration Studies (CRS) is an important catalyst for institutional memory at Abilene Christian University. Its distinctive and important mission is to share and to grow the documentation of the history of the Stone-Campbell Restoration Movement, and specifically the Churches of Christ. The remarkable success of CRS is seen it its ability to communicate the importance of the Stone-Campbell Movement within the broader circles of American and global Christianity. Even with these successes, the leadership of CRS acknowledged the relative lack of impact that it had had upon the academic culture and faculty development programs at ACU. CRS was recognized as a center for the study of history with a network of conversation partners around the world, but it had not significantly impacted ongoing university conversations about teaching and learning and the mission of the university. The desire was to cultivate a historical consciousness of the university's Christian heritage that effected meaningful spiritual growth among faculty, staff, and students.

Initial ideation sessions and planning documents for CHARIS were focused upon conventional forms of faculty development: small group conversation, faculty orientation, chapel services, summer retreats, and partnerships with other organized efforts of spiritual formation on campus. The challenge to such efforts was indirectly articulated by a group of external consultants who were commissioned to analyze spiritual life at ACU. One of chief findings of the group was the undefined and decentralized religious leadership at ACU. After commenting on the highly autonomous and segmented nature of the polity of Churches of Christ, the consultant observed that this church organization seemed to correspond to the absence of central or coordinating spiritual leadership on the campus. Absent a religious leader, such as a chaplain, and absent a formally appointed or broadly acknowledged leadership group charged with spiritual development of faculty or students, the university relied on tacitly assumed or informal influences and authorities to shape the values beliefs and practices of faculty and students into closer relationship to Christ and the church, as well as deeper integration of these faithful practices with the activities of teaching and learning. The pressing question was how, with such a fluid organization of spiritual leadership, could ACU cultivate the Christian lives of faculty, staff and students in a purposeful and coordinated way? The answer offered by the CHARIS planning group was to focus initially on the information provided to new faculty, as well as reflective dialogue about the Christian backgrounds of faculty, and particularly their experiences as members of churches of Christ. (All full-time faculty in the undergraduate colleges of ACU are required to be active members of a Church of Christ.) These new faculty orientation and conversation groups were facilitated by leading scholars from the Graduate School of Theology, and new faculty were asked on a voluntary basis to reflect on their past Christian commitments and communities and to discuss their importance to their teaching, research, and service within the university. Faculty were invited to confidential conversations in non-threatening environments that sought to dispel fear of open dialogue. Scholarly presentations on the history of Churches of Christ and the history of ACU provided helpful context to faculty discussion and discernment. During one particularly poignant moment, a faculty member cried out to the entire group in dismay over his own lack of understanding of the religious heritage of the university, and his need to learn more. The positive feedback from a couple years of these sessions was sufficient to convince university leadership to make these spiritual formation sessions a requirement of all new faculty during their two-year orientation to teaching at ACU.

RENEWING HERITAGE

A concern for a university center focused on religious heritage is that its efforts are not nostalgic—not a wistful recollection of past events for the emotional impact of remembering. The question of CHARIS was, from the start, how to create a vibrant and meaningful engagement of the past for the sake of loving and serving God and neighbor. This involved listening to the historical voices of our heritage, but also to the contemporary voices of our faculty and our students as they discerned God's will through interpretation of Scripture, participation in the church, and other service to God in the world. The goal of healthy appreciation of the heritage was, therefore, not recreation of the past, but renewal of faculty commitment to the Christian vision and ethos upon which the school was founded.

The emphasis on faculty conversations helped to maintain this emphasis on spiritual renewal. By prioritizing the importance of personal experience, we sought to balance the authority of ancient Scripture and church tradition, on the one hand, with present-day perspectives on what is most important to the integration of faith and learning, on the other.

It was David Worley, however, who emphasized the importance to a broader societal perspective to renewal of Christian identity and commitment at the Christian university. He emphasized the importance of expanding the conversation to like-minded or sympathetic voices within the broader Christian world. As we developed a series of CHARIS lectures and authors for the CHARIS website (www.char.is), David encouraged the CHARIS advisory board at ACU to include "outsider" voices with which we might find some unity, or at least mutual understanding. One of David's primary and persistent contributions to the work of CHARIS was his recommendation of scholars, church leaders, and public intellectuals whose voices on the ACU campus could help our faculty and students to understand better their own faith, partly by hearing guest speakers describe Christian beliefs and practices among Churches of Christ and similar groups. David was regularly invited to provide ideas for a series of CHARIS speakers, who twice a year addressed both faculty and the broader public on topics related to Christian heritage and renewal. For example, it was David who drew our attention to the work of Methodist church historian Dr. Ted Campbell, whose blog post "Why the Churches of Christ Were Right after All"[3] had drawn national attention as a sympathetic acknowledgement of the Churches of Christ, including his memorable identification of members of Churches of Christ as the "hobbits of the Christian world." With the support of David and others, we invited Dr.

---

3. Campbell, Ted. "Why the Churches of Christ Were Right After All." Spring Garden Church of Christ. http://www.churchofchristdeland.org/index.php?option=com_content&view=article&id=74 (accessed September 5, 2017). Cf. Ted Campbell, "Why a Methodist Thinks the Churches of Christ Were Right After All" (2013). Lectureship and Summit Audio Collection. 354. Available online at: http://digitalcommons.acu.edu/sumlec_audio/354.

Campbell to ACU for a series of presentations to administration, faculty, and students on the history and nature of Churches of Christ.

This was one of several CHARIS lecturers by speakers from outside Churches of Christ over the past five years. Each of these presentations, in different and valuable ways, has helped ACU faculty and students to see ourselves as others see us.

David recommended that we seek scholars outside the Stone-Campbell Movement who were sympathetic to biblical perspectives on baptism, inter alia, pointing to the work of Dr. Anthony Cross, an Oxford University theologian whose work explored the importance of a "sacramental" understanding of baptism.[4] Although different in history and terminology than the predominant understanding of baptism among Churches of Christ, Dr. Cross brought a perspective with valuable theological and historical depth to an understanding of baptism as more than symbolic in Christian salvation. His dialogue with leading scholars at ACU, including Dr. Everett Ferguson, raised new awareness of the meaning of biblical teachings on baptism, and their significance to potential unity with believers in other traditions, such as the British Baptists. The CHARIS lecture with Dr. Cross is an example of how an inclusive effort to create a healthy appreciation of the university's Christian tradition can deepen understanding and appreciation of the core principles upon which the school was founded.

CHARIS speakers often addressed challenging topics in the life of the university and the church. This was the case with Dr. Claire Smith, an Australian biblical scholar and expert on gender roles and relationships in early Christianity. When Dr. Smith visited ACU to discuss her book *God's Good Design: What the Bible Really Says About Men and Women*,[5] David advised us on how her "complementarian" viewpoint of the relationship of men and women in church and family might be helpfully discussed in both the university and the church. He suggested that we host a lunchtime roundtable with ACU faculty and local preachers representing different perspectives to discuss Dr. Smith's book. We sought to represent different viewpoints and to structure the event for intellectual growth and spiritual renewal through a collaborative and prayerful investigation of different interpretations of gendered roles in ministry and family. The roundtable session was a success, and represented David's focus upon scholarly study of the Word of God in service to the church, through faithful interpretation that is fair-minded in its consideration of different viewpoints.

---

4. See *Recovering the Evangelical Sacrament: Baptisma Semper Reformandum* (Eugene: Wipf & Stock, 2012).

5. Kingsford, NSW: Matthias, 2012.

CHRISTIAN SPIRITUALITY

The phrases "spiritual formation" and "integration of faith and learning" are often utilized to describe ideas and practices that are intended to support university faculty and students in their relationship with God. From the earliest days of seeking to cultivate faculty understanding and engagement of the Restoration Movement in their teaching and research, CHARIS utilized the language of "spirituality" to denote this Christian relationship and identity. The final word in the acronym CHARIS (Center for Heritage and Renewal in Spirituality) is an indicator of the importance of spiritual formation and renewal as outcomes of faculty exploration of university heritage. David never opposed the use of this language, but often cautioned us about misguided understandings of "spirituality" that might view it as inimical either to community practices of the church or to individual life guided by God's Word. David would return to the importance of spiritual practices of Christians gathered in community and/or individually focused on a persistent life "in Christ."

His misgivings about the language of "spirituality" notwithstanding, David's own support of CHARIS at ACU modeled a Christian spirituality that has shaped our efforts. David taught us that our use of biblical language is itself a form of spiritual discipline. His utterance of biblical phrases was a habitual practice in his communication. He maintained this discipline in a way that was both predictable and prophetic, speaking biblical words to both Christian interlocutors and to a broader world that he knew needed to hear the distinctive and transformative articulation of God's words. Second, David's life and work modeled engagement of the church's worship as spiritual discipline. Especially in his attention to singing and the Lord's Prayer, David showed us that practices of praise, thanksgiving, and petition are core to the Christian's relationship to Christ. Though he was not unique in this, David's emphasis on the Lord's Prayer as a model for Christian piety was a distinctive influence that still impacts the way we speak to God at ACU. Similarly, the significance of a cappella singing as a form of New Testament spirituality was an emphasis of David's life that served to balance against cultural influences and ecclesial trajectories that de-emphasize the wisdom of such worship. His advocacy for such ancient forms of spirituality was rejuvenating to those who worked with David, not only because of his diligence in ministry, but also because his prayer and singing were activities of personal devotion. He would prompt prayer at the end of every meeting, and was daily engaged in reading and singing the Psalms.

This authenticity extended to how David modeled spiritual guidance in helping others to see what in his first email to me he called "the biblical portrait of the Church of Christ." He habitually guided his conversation partners into a deeper relationship with God in Christ, and into a deeper love for the church of Christ. There is a biblical tradition of spiritual guides or wise mentors that is not often enough modeled in our day, but David Worley caused me to know the precious gift of a Christian guide and mentor who exemplifies a persistent concern for the faith and courage of his fellow Christians. He showed me that the most formative aspects of programs of spiritual formation within the Christian university are not the public lectures, or the administrative policies, or even the small group discussions about history. He showed us that the most impactful aspect of such programs is the spiritual direction that Christians provide to each other through processes of prayer and conversation focused on increasing awareness of God amid their teaching and other life experiences. Through his regular prayer and conversation, David gave to me and many other colleagues the gift of spiritual direction that continues to guide us "in Christ."

Images

David Worley

Worley family
Top row: Les McDaniel; 4th row: Christiana Peterson, Addie McDaniel, Cailin McDaniel, Heatherly McDaniel; 3rd row: Grace McDaniel, Jane Coggin, Owen McDaniel, Neva Peterson, Elena Coggin, David Worley, Chris Coggin; 2nd row: Matthew Peterson, Annalee Peterson, Melinda Worley, Jude Peterson, Sam Coggin (seated), Lincoln Coggin; 1st row: Iva Lea Worley Barton (David's mother)

Elena's graduation, the three Worley daughters
From left: Christiana, Melinda, Elena, David, Heatherly

IMAGES 211

Chuck Whittle and David Worley in St. Petersburg in the early 1990s

David Worley, Russian radio executive, Chuck Whittle

David Worley, Melinda Worley, Patricia McNicol, Allan McNicol

Allan McNicol, David Worley, James Thompson, Michael Weed

Mark Shipp, Gary Holloway, Allan McNicol, David Worley, Michael Weed

Jeff Peterson, David Worley

David Worley teaching Russian students at ITCM, St. Petersburg

Igor Egirev, president of ITCM, David Worley

Worley sons-in-law in St. Petersburg
David Worley, Les McDaniel, Chris Coggin, Matthew Peterson

Award to ITCM at the Pepperdine Lectureship
Luka Klimanova Boshakova, Tom Olbricht, David Worley, Konstantin Zhigulin,
Joel Petty

ITCM graduation, 2007
Tom Olbricht, Joel Petty, ChuckWhittle, David Worley.
Seated in foreground: Sergei Bogdanov, dean of St. Petersburg State University

ITCM class and staff, 2005.
David Worley is at front center

David Worley, Bill Stewart, Becky Stewart

www.ingramcontent.com/pod-product-compliance
Lightning Source LLC
Chambersburg PA
CBHW070252230426
43664CB00014B/2506